*Reducing Cost of Energy in the
Offshore Wind Energy Sector:*

A Supply Chain Innovation Perspective

Jan Stentoft . Ram Narasimhan . Chee Yew Wong
Thomas Johnsen . Kannan Govindan . Ole Stegmann Mikkelsen
Erik Skov Madsen . Christopher Rajkumar . Morten Brinch

© University Press of Southern Denmark and the authors

Copies from this book are only allowed according to agreement between Copy-dan and the Ministry of Education.

ISBN 978-87-408-3247-1

Published by
University Press of Southern Denmark
www.universitypress.dk
Layout and Print: Specialtrykkeriet Arco

Reducing Cost of Energy in the Offshore Wind Energy Sector:

A Supply Chain Innovation Perspective

University Press of Southern Denmark

Contents

Preface 9
Foreword 11

SECTION I

1. Introduction 15
   1.1 Background and purpose as stated in the project
       application in 2012 15
   1.2 Organization of the ReCoE team and work packages 17
   1.3 Relevant research 18

2. The offshore wind energy sector 21
   2.1 Wind energy is clean and pollution-free and a growth sector .. 21
   2.2 Innovation focus and industry life cycle 23
   2.3 Offshore wind farms in five phases 25
   2.4 Levelized CoE 26

3. Supply chain innovation framework 31

SECTION II

4. Supply chain management practices 37
   Reducing cost of energy (CoE) in the offshore wind
   energy industry: The promise and potential of supply
   chain management 39
   Formation of new interfirm relationships: Case studies
   of offshore wind firms 49
   Transformation to systems integration in the
   wind power industry-efficacy of supply chain integration 59

5. Innovation fostering practices ... 73

Fostering supply chain innovation in offshore
wind power (OWP) projects: Context and a framework ... 75

Supply chain innovation practices optimize market
and operational performance ... 87

Innovation-processes in green industries: The role of
governance ... 97

6. Supply network strategies ... 105

Strategies for managing complex supply networks
in the offshore wind power industry ... 107

Supplier relationship management in the light of
competitiveness and hard benefits ... 117

7. Operations and maintenance ... 131

Improving maintenance of offshore wind farms through
modularization ... 133

Operations and maintenance issues in the offshore
wind energy sector ... 141

8. Maturity ... 149

Developing a process map for CSR in supply chain
management —a maturity model ... 151

Evaluating the essential barrier to offshore wind energy
- an Indian perspective ... 161

9. Emerging issues ... 169

Value creation mechanisms of big data in supply
chain management ... 171

Framework on offshore wind energy circular economy
maturity—a circular business model approach ... 183

The need for vocational education in operations
and maintenance of offshore wind power ... 193

Industry 4.0 ... 203

SECTION III

10. The offshore wind energy sector: Past, present and future ... 219

    10.1 Main developments in the offshore wind energy during
    the past five years ... 220

10.2 Outlook: Possible developments in the offshore
wind energy sector during the next ten years................. 223
10.3 ReCoE reflections................................... 230

ReCoE publications during the project...................... 233
PhDs from the project..................................... 237
About the authors... 241

Preface

The former Vice-Chancellor of the University of Southern Denmark Jens Oddershede allocated DKK 111 million to strategic research projects among the university researchers in 2012 in an initiative named SDU2020. The amount of money came from past years' surpluses. With the SDU2020 initiative, the University of Southern Denmark wanted to support research areas that the EU and the Danish Government at that time emphasized in their research programs. Projects were funded that were perceived as pivotal for future welfare and growth.

The Executive Board received 86 applications that, after the first round of evaluations, were reduced to 24 applications that were all of a very high quality and deemed worthy of support. The number of applications was further reduced to 14; all these projects received financial support. These projects fulfilled in particular the evaluation criteria of a high professional quality, a convincing project plan, a clear plan for applying for external funds in Denmark and abroad, and a strong cross-disciplinary perspective.

The present book is a practical dissemination of one of these 14 projects from SDU2020. The project is concerned with Reducing the Cost of Energy in the offshore wind energy supply chain (ReCoE). The project has been cross-functional, with researchers drawn from the Faculty of Business and Social Sciences as well as from the Faculty of Engineering. The whole project applies a managerial approach to the offshore wind energy supply chain and, as such, is not a technical project about wind turbines.

There are several people I would like to thank for their support before and during the project. Firstly, I would like to thank the former Vice-Chancellor Jens Oddershede and the Executive Board for making this project possible by granting the project financial resources. Next, I would like to thank my foreign colleagues Professor Ram Narasimhan (Michigan State University, United States), Professor

Chee Yew Wong (Leeds University, United Kingdom), and Professor Thomas Johnsen (Audencia Business School, France). I would like to say thank you to Professor Kannan Govindan and Associate Professor Erik Skov Madsen from the Department of Technology and Innovation at the Faculty of Engineering at University of Southern Denmark. Also, thanks to my colleges Associate Professor Ole Stegmann Mikkelsen, Assistant Professor Christopher Rajkumar, Morten Brinch, Ph.D., PhD students Thorsten Krægpøth and Victoria Baagøe-Engels, and former colleagues Professor Antony Paulraj (now at Nottingham University Business School China, Ningbo in China), Jesper Kronborg Jensen, Lone Kavin, Ivan Martinez-Neri, and Lisa Thoms.

Finally, I would like to thank the wind energy associations and companies we have engaged with during the project for sharing your knowledge and practices with us.

It has been a great journey working with you, with many hours of meetings and discussions and with dissemination of the findings in practical and academic outlets.

Jan Stentoft
Professor in Supply Chain Management
Head of ReCoE

Foreword

Those of us who have been active in the wind industry since the beginning in the late 1970s have been lucky. We have been involved in an industry that is technologically challenging and fascinating and commercially exciting and that serves what is arguably the most important purpose of the 21st century—the fight against devastating climate change. We have seen turbine sizes increase by orders of magnitude, and from having turbines that could serve the needs of a farm, we now have turbines that can individually deliver the power needs of 10,000 households.

Offshore wind power is a particularly promising application of wind power. The potential of offshore wind is enormous. It could meet Europe's electric energy demand seven times over and the United States' energy demand four times over. And when offshore wind farms are located 40 km or more off the coast, they do not create opposition due to visual impact, since the turbines are below the horizon.

After the introduction of auction systems in the major offshore markets, the cost of offshore wind power has reduced dramatically. Projects scheduled for installation in the first half of the 2020s have levelled the cost of electricity to less than half its cost in 2015, and in some markets, subsidy-free offshore wind power is becoming the norm. It is no surprise, then, that the offshore wind power market is booming. Since the world's first offshore wind farm was installed in 1991 at Vindeby, Denmark, individual offshore wind farm sizes have grown from 5 MW to more than 1,000 MW, and in several countries offshore wind power is on the fast track to becoming the largest source of electricity.

Success has its own challenges, however. Whereas wind turbine manufacturing has itself been industrialized quite extensively, the infrastructure supply chain has not been industrialized to anywhere near the same extent. Furthermore, because of the sector's growth and the continued need for further reductions in energy costs, it is necessary to build out and streamline the entire supply chain, both for wind turbines and for the infrastructure.

Although this may seem straightforward, it is not so easy to put to practice, and there has been a conspicuous lack of research available to support this process. Therefore, it is with great interest and gratitude on behalf of the sector that I have followed the ReCoE project's work. The research has focused on some of the most important levers in cost reduction and supply chain buildup, including industrialization, holistic supply chain management, standardization and modularization, and process optimization. I consider the project's effort to investigate and understand these topics to be very well done, and I am certain that the findings will improve the wind industry's abilities to efficiently manage its growth.

Anyone interested in the supply chain challenges faced by a rapidly growing, young industry should read this book carefully, be inspired, and heed the recommendations. This is not ivory tower research—this is applied research at its best.

Henrik Stiesdal
Stiesdal Offshore Technologies

SECTION I

1. Introduction

This first section introduces the research program Reducing Cost of Energy through Supply Chain Innovation (ReCoE) by referring to text in the application for funding. The subsequent subsection on background and purpose thus includes text from the original 2012 application. Then follows a subsection on the project's organization and division into work packages (WPs). The final subsection is about relevant research both in terms of theoretical and practical relevance.

1.1 Background and purpose as stated in the project application in 2012

This multidisciplinary project has its focus on the offshore wind turbine (OWT) industry in Denmark. The purpose of the project is to conduct strategic research that delivers solutions to reduce cost of energy (CoE) for sustainable offshore wind power energy systems (including the wind turbine and the balance of plant [BoP]). Reduction of CoE is the main focus in The European Strategic Energy Technology Plan (SET-Plan) as well as the Danish Megavind recommendations. The SET-Plan is the principal backbone of the Horizon2020 Societal Challenge called "Secure, Clean and Efficient Energy."

The basic hypothesis in the project is that CoE can be reduced through industrialization. Reducing CoE—and thus making offshore wind energy competitive with fossil fuel–based energy production—requires a holistic supply chain management (SCM) perspective that transcends the single companies within the offshore supply chain through integration. Potential sources to reduce CoE are to be found in redesigns of the supply chain and new forms for collaboration among existing and new actors in the supply chain. The project also focuses on how small and medium-sized enterprises (SMEs) can improve competitiveness to make a positive contribution to the industry. Special emphasis will be placed on the organization of the development process for offshore wind projects that will allow these improvements to be driven by industrial demands. The project will create new knowledge on the need for redesigning the offshore wind power supply chain and will provide scenarios for different business models to reduce CoE.

The offshore wind industry is a relatively young industry in comparison with, e.g., the automotive industry. Effectively, it is still in its infancy (e.g., it is characterized by low integration between supply chain actors and a lack of demand, order, and inventory transparency and collaboration). From a societal and political perspective, the aim is for Denmark to maintain and expand its status leading the world in green energy technologies. This vision also includes offshore wind power energy. The Danish wind industry builds on strong skills throughout the supply chain. These are world-class skills, whether it comes to wind turbine manufacturers, energy utility companies, components suppliers, services providers, or consultants. The supply chain perspective on the wind energy industry has hitherto been limited in the scientific community.[1] The supply chain comprises new areas of competitive advantage through innovation[2] and relationship management.[3] Different business models exist among the main wind turbine producers (vertical integration vs. manufacturing split by using a high number of subsuppliers), which affect the supply chain performance. To obtain competitiveness against fossil fuel–based technologies of electric energy production, CoE of offshore wind power energy must be reduced.

Characteristics of industrialization include standardization of designs and modularization, standardization of production, formal and codified documentation, reuse of concepts, and continuous process optimization. The sharing of knowledge within the industry is generally low compared with other industries, and the ambition of the project is to provide a platform for knowledge sharing among the current heterogeneous actors in the offshore wind industry by learning from other industries.[4] Based on in-depth industry involvement, the overall objective of the project is to provide new knowledge on means to reduce costs of offshore wind energy through industrialization of the sector with a supply chain approach. Such an approach focuses on removing suboptimizations within the single-company silos by applying a holistic cross-company perspective. Thus, the main objectives with ReCoE are to develop

- Theory on the influence of the supply chain on industry and business models

- New knowledge on how to industrialize and create innovations in green supply chains

- New supply chain and value propositions method to reduce CoE

- Theory for increasing innovativeness and efficiency for SMEs to meet new industry demands (industrialization)

1.2 Organization of the ReCoE team and work packages

The ReCoE project has been carried out by an international research team consisting of researchers from the University of Southern Denmark, Michigan State University (United States), Leeds University (United Kingdom), and Audencia Business School (France). The research team has met physically at research meetings twice every year to report the status of ongoing activities, discuss various topics, interact with business people, and plan and review research results and further proposals. Between the meetings, research activities have taken place, including data collection, data processing, and writing of publications for research conferences as well as practical and scientific journals. During ReCoE, a number of PhD students have been produced, and still some projects are ongoing. During the research meetings, these young scholars also have sought exposure to scientific discussions and feedback on their individual ongoing projects. The overall ReCoE project has been divided into five work packages (WPs), with a principal research question to lead each WP:

WP 1: Supply chain analysis (actors, drivers, barriers, etc.)
Principal research question: How is the current OWT industry composed in terms of actors, activities, and relationships?

WP 2: Supply chain innovation and business models
Principal research question: How can business models in the OWT industry be changed through supply chain innovation?

WP 3: Assessing ambidexterity
Principal research question: How do companies in the OWT industry

maintain competitiveness through a proper balance between exploitation and exploration?

WP 4: Global requirements for SMEs
Principal research question: What are the global competence requirements for SMEs in the transformation process?

Because of heavy consolidation within the industry, which has reduced the number of SMEs, this WP has been changed to focus on Industry 4.0.

WP 5: Reconfiguring the OWT supply chain
Principal research question: What is the most competitive configuration of the wind energy sector with a view to competing with fossil fuels?

1.3 Relevant research

Throughout its duration, the ReCoE project pursued a research strategy that emphasizes both theoretical and practical relevance. In recent years, academic research has to an increased extent been evaluated on where the research is published. Accordingly, scientific journals are being ranked in terms of their degree of esteem. However, different ranking lists exist, such that the same scientific journal can be ranked differently among the different lists. Thus, the rankings of the journal targeted as the outlet for disseminating research results is often used as a measure for scientific quality. A potential danger of too much focus being placed on highly ranked journals is that such research might be conducted at the expense of being practically relevant.[5] An increased volume of research is published, but the question is how practically relevant is the research and whether it, in fact, has an impact.[6] Practical relevance can be operationalized in different ways and is concerned with how research influences practical decision-making.[7] An important element in conducting and disseminating practical, relevant research is engaging with practitioners to avoid the problem of knowledge production (securing practical relevance of the research question in focus) and the problem of knowledge translation (ensuring that results are disseminated in ways that are understandable and applicable for practitioners).[8] The ReCoE project is built on the belief that theoretical and practical relevance are not mutually exclusive. The aim is to disseminate some of the results in highly ranked outlets and some in lower-ranked journals as well as to disseminate research with practical impact in practically oriented outlets. The present book is an example of this aim.

Endnotes

1 Mortensen, M. and Arlbjørn, J. (2012), "Inter-organizational supplier development: The case of customer attractiveness and strategic fit", *Supply Chain Management: An International Journal*, Vol. 17 No. 2, pp. 152-171.

2 Arlbjørn, J.S., de Haas, H. and Munksgaard, K.B. (2011), "Exploring supply chain innovation", *Logistics Research*, Vol. 3 No. 1, 1-18.

3 Narasimhan, R., Mahaptra, S. and Arlbjørn, J.S. (2008), "Impact of relational norms, supplier development and trust on supplier performance", *Operations Management Research*, Vol. 1 No. 1, pp. 24-30.

4 Trott, P. (2012), *Innovation Management and New Product Development*, Prentice Hall, London.

5 Narasimhan, R. (2018), "The fallacy of impact without relevance – reclaiming relevance and rigor", *European Business Review*, Vol. 30 No. 2, pp. 157-168.

6 Stentoft, J. and Freytag, P.V. (2018), "Guest editorial: Journal rankings and the notion of "relevance" within business research", *European Business Review*, Vol. 30 No. 2, pp. 94-100.

7 Stentoft, J. and Rajkumar, C. (2018), "Balancing theoretical and practical relevance in supply chain management research", *International Journal of Physical Distribution & Logistics Management*, Vol. 48 No. 5, pp. 504-523.

8 Van de Ven, A.H. and Johnson, P.E. (2006), "Knowledge for theory and practice", *Academy of Management Review*, Vol. 31 No. 4, pp. 802-821.

2.
The offshore wind energy sector

2.1 Wind energy is clean and pollution-free and a growth sector

In Europe, fossil fuels (coal, natural gas, and oil) and renewable sources were responsible for 43 percent and 29 percent respectively of all gross electricity generation in 2016 (www.eea.europa.eu).[1] The EU Renewable Energy Directive requires the EU to fulfil at least 20 percent of its total energy needs with renewables and at least 20 percent of its transport fuels with renewable sources by 2020. By 2030, the EU aims to achieve at least 27 percent renewables in final energy consumption.

Offshore wind is a low-carbon, renewable source of energy. Since the first offshore wind farm (4.95 MW capacity) in the world was commissioned in 1991 in Vindeby, Denmark,[2,3] much has happened in the offshore wind industry, which today has grown into a multibillion EURO and global industry. In 2018, 409 new OWTs were connected, adding an additional 2,649 MW of net offshore wind capacity to the grid and leading to 18,449 MW of total installed capacity based on 4,543 grid-connected turbines across 11 countries in Europe[4] such as the United Kingdom, Germany, Denmark, Belgium, Finland, and France. The United Kingdom and Germany have been the leading installers in recent years, with 85 percent of the newly added capacity (See Figure 2.1). The goal is to achieve 25-GW capacity by 2020.

Figure 2.1 Annual offshore installations by country and cumulative capacity (MW)

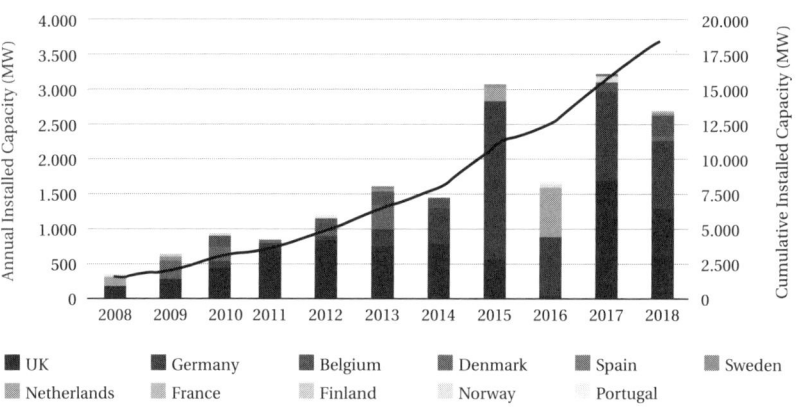

Source: Windeurope, (2019, p. 7)[4]

However, the industry is global, with markets outside Europe developing. It is predicted globally that 15 GW will be installed every year for the next 10 years, mainly driven by the Asian markets.[5] For example, China installed 1,164 new MW, accumulating to 2,788 in 2017.[6] Other markets include Vietnam, Japan, South Korea, the United States, and Taiwan. China has set itself a national 2020 target of accumulated 5 GW, and in addition three Chinese provinces (Jiangsu, Guangdong, and Fujian) have set individual ambitious targets accumulating to 7.5 GW in 2020.[6] Japan's wind industry has called for a target of 10 GW of offshore wind in 2030. Although the government has not yet set a specific target, Ørsted has just signed a memorandum of understanding (MoU) with the Japanese company Tepco.[7] Taiwan has also set ambitious 2025 targets of 5.5 GW and raised the 2030 targets to 10–17 GW of offshore wind,[6] and forecasts predict Taiwan to be the second largest offshore wind market in Asia.[5]

A wind turbine converts kinetic energy (wind) into three-phase AC electrical energy. An OWT typically consists of a foundation, tower, blades, and nacelle unit. Inside the nacelle unit is a generator, gearbox, rotor, main shaft connecting the generator to the blades, bearings, and control system. All components that do not belong to the turbine unit are called balance of plant (BoP), which could take up to 30 percent of the wind farm's capital cost. Many wind turbine manufacturers also manufacture blades. Monopiles are still the main structures used in foundation design. At the bottom of the tower is a power takeoff system (transmitting wind energy to electrical using generators) that connects electricity to offshore and then onshore substations, which in turn supply energy to national grid systems. An offshore substation contains mainly switchgears, reactors, transformers, cables, water tank, platforms, accommodation, and a control room. A Yaw system is used to orient the nacelle to the wind direction during operation. A 5-MW OWT can cost up to 7 million Euro, the nacelle for a 5-MW turbine itself costs around 3 million Euro, and the steel tower alone could account for up to 1.2 million Euro.[8] Nowadays, wind turbines are 8 MW, with a blade length of 80 m and steel tower height of up to 120 m. However, most recently, 10-MW turbines have been marketed.

Siemens Gamesa renewable energy and MHI Vestas Offshore Wind are still the OWT manufactures chosen for European installations per se, supplying 62.2 percent and 33.3 percent of capacity in 2018, respectively. However, other competitors such as GE Renewable Energy and Senvion are active in the European market.[4]

Compared with onshore wind power, offshore wind power is more complex and costlier to install.[9] The costs increase because of longer distances to shore; more difficult operations and maintenance; rising material, commodity, and labor costs; more-expensive foundations; and difficult integration to electrical networks.[9,10] The advantages of offshore wind farms are, among others, more space, a stronger wind at sea, larger size, and reduced negative visual and noise impact because locations are far from shore. However, the location of offshore wind farms is associated with a certain type of NIMBY effect—"not in my back yard." Recently, there have been discussions in Denmark about mayors that would like to hinder the construction of offshore wind farms close to their city because they suggest that it disturbs the ocean view and thus can affect the tourism business negatively. Other so-called social gaps[11] are the impact of offshore wind farms on nature,[12] wildlife,[13] and shipping and navigation.[14]

2.2 Innovation focus and industry life cycle

Most industries develop through various life cycle phases. As competitive conditions change through the phases, different strategies and business models are needed. Witcher and Chau (2010)[15] identified the industry life cycles phases as Introduction, Growth, Shakeout, Maturity, and Aging. The early phases focus on exploration, flexibility, and technology innovation. The latter stages are more concerned with process innovation standardization, cost, and detailed documentation.

Abernathy and Utterback (1978)[16], in their work on innovation and technology development, identified three phases. First is the fluid phase, which is dominated by technological and market uncertainties. In this first phase, manufacturing relies on craftsmanship, and almost no process innovation takes place. The following phase is the transitional phase. This phase introduces a battle for the dominant design followed by less differentiation, and mass production and standardization start to emerge. In this second phase, competitors are still many but are declining in number. The third phase, the commoditization phase, is dominated by incremental innovations and increased focus on cost. The work of Abernathy and Utterback (1978)[16] is illustrated in Figure 2.2.

Figure 2.2 The degree of product and process innovations over time

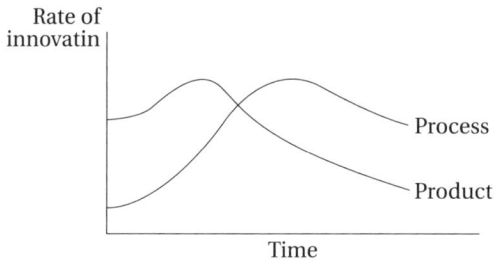

Source: Abernathy and Utterback (1978)[16]

The phases of innovation and the industrial life cycle are simplified in Table 2.1.

It may be argued that the offshore wind industry, since Vindeby in 1991, has moved out of the fluid phase and into the transitional phase and to some degree is peeking into the commoditization phase. In 2011, the industry was still seen as a rather immature industry compared with many other industries. Much has happened in the last decade, and the industry has matured. However, it is still characterized by a low level of intercompany integration between the actors, a low degree of transparency, and a low level of value chain perspective. But different parts of the offshore wind value chain have different maturity levels. For example, the service and maintenance part is less mature than, e.g., the manufacturing of wind turbine generators. And even then, the dominant design is settled for the wind turbines but not to the same degree as for foundations.

Table 2.1 Early and mature innovation phases

	Early innovative phases	Later mature phases
Strategic focus	Exploration	Exploitation
Primary innovational focus	Product innovation	Process innovation
Type of innovation	Radical innovation	Incremental innovation, improvements in quality
Primary competitive factor	Development capability	Price/cost
Distribution of industry	Local	Global
Products characteristics	Customization, with many different designs	Heavy standardization in designs
Degree of documentation	Minor and informal	Formal and detailed
Level of competition	Many small firms, local	Fierce and global, classic oligopoly
Organization	Entrepreneurial, organic structure	Traditional hierarchical structure
Process	Flexible and inefficient	Efficient, capital intensive and rigid
Threats	Old technology, new entrants	New technologies and firms bringing disruptive innovations

Source: Abernathy and Utterback (1978)[16]; Trott (2012)[17]; Witcher and Chau (2010)[15]

The above does not mean that the actors should only focus on process innovations at the expense of product innovations. It is not an "either/or" but rather a "both/and."

2.3 Offshore wind farms in five phases

Offshore wind farms are developed and constructed in five major phases. The first phase is planning and development (consent). In this phase, wind farm developers, various governmental agencies, consultants, survey companies, and major OWT manufacturers work together to perform feasibility studies, planning, environmental surveys, coastal process surveys, station surveys, seabed surveys, front-end engineering and design (of the turbine and other major systems), and human impact studies. The second and third phases involve production, installation, and commissioning. Typically, substructures must be built onshore closed to the site. Then, foundations are built into the seabed, followed by the installation of steel towers, nacelle, and the blades. Major components for the foundation and steel towers are typically manufactured in factories onshore. Blades, nacelles, rotors, generators, and gearboxes are also manufactured onshore and transported to the site for installation. The third phase involves the use of transportation (components and crews) and installation vessels, and weather conditions can make the installation more expensive. The fourth phase is operations and maintenance. This phase is typically carried out by the wind farm manufacturers or consortia and passed over to the developers/owners some years later. Finally, after many years, the offshore wind farm can be decommissioned and dismantled. After more than 25 years in operation, Vindeby was decommissioned and dismantled in 2017.

Each of the above phases of a wind farm life cycle involves many different supply network partners throughout the project. At the same time, each new project or farm is different, with new supply network partners from project to project within each phase. This makes managing the projects even more complex. The top five offshore wind connectors in 2018 were Ørsted (17 percent), E.ON (11 percent), Global Infrastructure Partners (9 percent), Equinor (7 percent) and Macquarie Capital with 6 percent. Together the five accounted for more than 50 percent new installed capacity in 2018 (estimated by Windeurope, 2019).[4]

2.4 Levelized CoE

Levelized cost of energy (LCOE) is equal to total costs over lifetime divided by electricity produced over lifetime. LCOE consists of mainly capital (CAPEX) and operating cost (OPEX). LCOE calculation does not consider the total actual economic costs of individual primary sources. Society's cost of electricity (SCOE) was proposed to account for subsidies, transmission costs, variable costs, environmental risk, and societal and employment effects. Steel is the most commonly used material for manufacturing towers. Recent auctions in Brazil, Canada, Germany, India, Mexico, and Morocco have resulted in onshore wind power LCOEs as low as USD 0.03/kWh. The offshore wind energy sector has seen significant reduction of LCOEs between 2000 and 2017. The main drivers for cost reduction are technology improvement, competitive procurement, supply chain efficiency, and learning experienced by leading developers and manufacturers. OWTs cannot generate energy when there is no wind. On an LCOE basis, offshore wind still seems more expensive than other energy sources such as solar and onshore wind. However, when offshore wind energy is generated close to the time it is required for consumption, it becomes very valuable.

Sector maturity is one of the main challenges when of cost reduction in offshore wind farm projects. The cost of capital is a major driver of LCOE. The cost of producing an offshore wind farm can be reduced by increasing experience. Firms with more experience are better at avoiding waste and reducing the costs of errors. The increase in volume can also drive costs down because of the economy of scale. The use of production assembly lines can also help in reducing manufacturing costs. While some of the platform technologies mature, a stabler and higher-volume production environment will help further drive down costs. By pursuing standardized components and systems, the cost of operations and maintenance can also be reduced. The ways offshore wind projects are contracted can likewise affect LCOE.

Supply chain constraints are another major factor affecting the cost of an offshore wind farm. CAPEX can be broadly divided into wind turbine, BoP, and financial cost. During the early years, the LCOE of offshore wind farms increases mainly because of an increase in CAPEX, driven by supply chain constraints for components (e.g., OWT generators) and services (e.g., installation). The cost of components may increase because of increasing demand for technology innovation and the costs of raw materials. Like many raw materials, steel is used for producing tower foundations and many substructures. However, steel prices are volatile. Moreover, fluctuation in currency exchange may drive up costs. The cost of procuring raw materials may increase because of a lack of maturity and political stability. Capacity constraints may occur because of misalignment between government policy and funding structure and investment of the industry in capacity and new technology. For instance, the lack of appropriate installation vessels could cause delays in installation and add costs to offshore wind projects. The cost of operations has also increased because of changes in technologies and operations and maintenance philosophy (toward a more proactive maintenance). The real total cost of decommissioning offshore farms is still an unknown factor.

Industry learning is supposed to help significantly reduce cost. However, the offshore wind sector has been troubled by a lack of suitable and trained technical and installation staff. This increases the cost of transporting staff to different sites. Moreover, the ways offshore project contracts are designed and awarded can restrict industry-wide learning. The use of competitive bidding teaches firms to compete in their industry, but it restricts the sharing of best practices. An offshore wind developer subcontracting many parts of the project to many different contractors and manufacturers increases coordination cost and potentially reduces opportunities for firms to learn from each other. When the composition of these contractors and manufacturers changes from one project to another, it may increase the speed of learning among consortium members, but it also may restrict industry-wide learning.

Endnotes

1 European Environmetnal Agence (EEA) (2018) *Overview of Electricity Production and Use in Europe*, https://www.eea.europa.eu/data-and-maps/indicators/overview-of-the-electricity-production-2/assessment-4, Accessed March 8, 2019.

2 Barthelmie, R.J., Courtney, M.S., Højstrup, J. and Sanderhoff, P. (1994), *The Vindeby Project: A Description – Risø-R-741(EN)*, Risø National Laboratory, Roskilde.

3 Korsgaard, M. (2016) "Farvel til verdens første hav-vindmøller", *Berlingske*, https://www.berlingske.dk/virksomheder/farvel-til-verdens-foerste-hav-moeller, Accessed March 8, 2019.

4 Windeurope (2019) "Offshore Wind in Europe: Key trends and statistics 2018", *Wind Europe Intelligence*, published February 2019, Brussels.

5 www.gwec.net: https://gwec.net/global-offshore-wind-summit-taiwan, Accessed March 9, 2019.

6 GWEC (2018), *Global Wind 2017 Report: Annual Market Update 2017*, Global Wind Energy Council, Published April 208, Brussels.

7 Richard, G. (2019) https://www.windpoweroffshore.com/article/1523285/orsted-signs-japanese-offshore-wind-mou, Accessed March 9, 2019.

8 UK Government (2010) Value breakdown for the offshore wind sector, https://assets.publishing.service.gov.uk/government/uploads/system/uploads/attachment_data/file/48171/2806-value-breakdown-offshore-wind-sector.pdf, Accessed March 8, 2019.

9 Bilgili, M., Yasar, A. and Simsek, E. (2011), "Offshore wind power development in Europe and its comparison with onshore counterpart", *Renewable and Sustainable Energy Reviews*, Vol. 15 No. 2, pp. 905-915.

10 Stentoft, J., Narasimhan, R. and Poulsen, T. (2016), "Reducing cost of energy in the offshore wind energy industry", *International Journal of Energy Sector Management*, Vol. 10 No. 2, pp. 151-171.

11 Bell, D., Gray, T. and Haggett, C. (2005), "The 'social gap' in wind farm sitting decisions: Explanations and policy response", *Environmental Politics*, Vol. 14 No. 4, pp. 460-477.

12 Kaldellis, J.K. and Zafirakis, D. (2011), "The wind energy (r)evolution: A short review of a long history", *Renewable Energy*, Vol. 36 No. 7, pp. 1887-1901.

13 Saidur, R., Rahim, N.A., Islam, M.R. and Solangi, K.H. (2011), "Environmental impact of wind energy", *Renewable and Sustainable Energy Reviews*, Vol. 15 No. 5, pp. 2423-2430.

14 Snyder, B. and Kaiser, M.J. (2009), "Ecological and economic cost-benefit analysis of offshore wind energy", *Renewable Energy*, Vol. 34 No. 6, pp. 1567-1578.

15 Witcher, B.J. and Chau, V.S. (2010), *Strategic Management: Principles and Practice*, Cengage Learning, Andover.

16 Abernathy, W.J. and Utterback, J.M. (1978), "Patterns of industrial innovation", *Technology Review*, Vol. 80 No. 7, pp. 40-47.

17 Trott, P. (2012), *Innovation Management and New Product Development*, Prentice Hall, London.

3. Supply chain innovation framework

Supply chain innovation is "a change (incremental or radical) within a supply chain network, supply chain technology, or supply chain process (or a combination of these) that can take place in a company function, within a company, in an industry or in a supply chain to enhance new value creation for the stakeholder" (Arlbjørn *et al.*, 2011, p. 8).[1] The supply chain innovation framework integrates innovation and business models along with SCM practices. Supply chain innovation employs a content perspective and is concerned with the process of innovation and the management of innovation processes. The product of an innovation process is seen as the innovation content, whereas a process perspective is how innovations are carried out. The process and content perspectives influence each other; for instance, the content of innovation may affect the way in which the process is organized and vice versa. The supply chain innovation framework makes clear the content of supply chain innovation and makes it operational.

Supply chain innovation consists of three content components: (1) supply chain business processes, (2) supply chain network structure, and (3) supply chain technology. Supply chain innovations are not static and are typically triggered by companies' dynamic interaction with their business environments. Consequently, the framework suggests a dynamic process around and interaction with the specific content elements as a recognition for a need to change (e.g., long lead times, high supply chain costs, and low service levels).

Understanding the necessity of change is related to redefining the company's business model, which helps in recognizing market segments, formulating the value proposition, characterizing the structure of the value chain, disclosing the position of the firm in the value network, evaluating cost structure and profit potential, and articulating a competitive strategy to gain advantages over competitors. The recognition of the necessity should then initiate a process of analyzing current practices along with proposing new solutions that can enhance performance. The acknowledged new solutions should be implemented, and in due course, a new recognition for improvements will emerge. In connection with the definition of supply chain innovation mentioned earlier, the work is done to increase new value creation for the customer.

Figure 3.1 Supply chain innovation framework

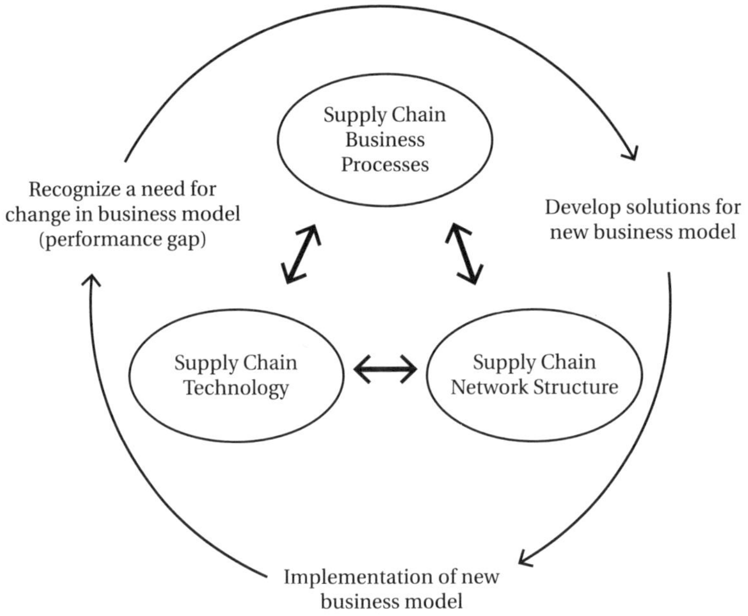

Source: Arlbjørn et al. (2011)

The first element, the supply chain business process, is associated with the activities that create a specific measurable output and are often cross-functional in nature. Business processes can be defined as "A structured, measured set of activities designed to produce a specified output for a particular customer or market" (Davenport, 1993, p. 5).[2] To implement both efficient transactions and structured interfirm relationships, it is essential to implement customer-oriented business processes within and across members of the supply chain. Hence, this is the aim of innovations in supply chain business processes. Supply chain business processes include customer relationship management, supplier relationship management, customer service management, demand management, order fulfillment, manufacturing flow management, product development and commercialization, and returns management.

The second element, supply chain technology, denotes technologies that are utilized in isolation or in combination with other technologies to make supply chain innovations. Hence, the technology component is not associated with the relevant technology itself but in the novel use of technology within the context of the supply chain. With the help of supply chain technology, firms may actively involve their supply chain partners (e.g., customers, suppliers, etc.). Supply chain technologies include, e.g., planning and execution systems, identification systems, communication systems, analytics technology, electronic marketplaces, advanced manufacturing technologies, advanced materials, big data, and drones.

The third element, supply chain network structure, recognizes the members of the supply chain, the structural dimensions, and the different types of process links. The structural element is concerned with the horizontal structure (number of tiers across the supply chain), the vertical structure (the number of suppliers/customers represented within each tier), and the horizontal position of the company (e.g., close to the point of origin of raw material vs. close to private consumers). Supply chain network structure includes internal functions, customers, suppliers, third-party providers (e.g., logistics providers), competitors, consultants, universities, and public agencies.

Supply chain innovation helps in value delivery and capture.[3] Value delivery signifies what a firm delivers that is of value to external partners (e.g., faster delivery to customers, supply development programs targeting specific suppliers, and online customization to customers). Value capture signifies how the company internally captures the value through supply chain innovation (e.g., cost reduction, high-quality maintenance, transparency in procurement processes, supply consistency, and improved effectiveness, as well as flexibility in internal processes of storing, handling, and packaging).

Endnotes

1 Arlbjørn, J.S., de Haas, H. and Munksgaard, K.B. (2011), "Exploring supply chain innovation", *Logistics Research*, Vol. 3 No. 1, 1-18.

2 Davenport, T.H. (1993), *Process Innovation: Reengineering Work Through Information Technology*, Harvard Business School Press, Boston.

3 Munksgaard, K.B., Stentoft, J. and Paulraj, A. (2014), "Value-based supply chain innovation", *Operations Management Research*, Vol. 7 No. 3-4, pp. 50-62.

SECTION II

4. Supply chain management practices

In addition to technology improvement and the use of competitive procurement, supply chain efficiency is another major driver for reducing the levelized cost of energy (LCOE) in the offshore wind industry (OWI). Sometimes, increases in CAPEX and OPEX are caused by supply chain constraints, including the lack of efficient supply market; the poor coordination of supply and demand, which leads to fluctuation in commodity prices and a lack of resources (e.g., installation vessels, engineers, etc.); and the ways supply chain relationships are formed and contracted that prevent learning among developers, manufacturers, and suppliers.

For nascent industries with relatively immature supply chain management (SCM) practices, there are silos between functional departments within organizations, a lack of information sharing across the supply chain, and a reliance on a transactional approach to managing buyer–supplier relationships. These issues could lead to a lack of effective knowledge flows and therefore prevent innovation within the supply chain. A matured supply chain, such as those in the automotive sector, is characterized by intense information sharing, frequent interactions and long-term relationship commitment, and a focus on collaboration to drive innovation and efficiency.

In this section, we argue the OWI can transit to a more matured state in SCM practices such that it is possible to accelerate innovation required to drive costs down. In this section, Narasimhan and Stentoft provide a comprehensive framework of SCM best practices that might help OWI. In the framework, three major groups of SCM practices—i.e., innovation, industrialization, and partnering—are recommended to enable supply chain innovation in OWI. The framework can be used to benchmark maturity among OWI supply chains.

As is pointed out, partnering relationships can be sources of innovation for OWI. In the second article, Hennelly and Wong present case studies on how new interfirm relationships are triggered and formed due to compatibility and complementary. The case studies illustrate how new relationships between UK OWI suppliers and their suppliers and customers can be formed successfully or disrupted because of asymmetric or a lack of complementarity in product, market, and technology. The article demonstrates the importance of compatibility in corporate culture and complementarity in the technical market as triggers for making progress in new interfirm relationships. More importantly, compatibility and complementarity can be shaped by both buyers' and suppliers' frequent interactions, sharing of information, demonstration of commitment, and investment in the new relationships.

In the third article, Narasimhan and Martinez-Neri address the need for greater utilization of supply chain integration (SCI) in the OWI. The authors focus on developing a context-dependent understanding of how a transformation into a systems integrator and an engineering–procurement–construction (EPC) supplier to a client is enabled by SCI. Finally, through conceptual clustering, authors identify design and manufacturing, sourcing, and governance as three principal factors.

Reducing cost of energy (CoE) in the offshore wind energy industry: The promise and potential of supply chain management [1]

Ram Narasimhan
Emeritus of Michigan State University and the ReCoE project

Jan Stentoft
Department of Entrepreneurship and Relationship Management
University of Southern Denmark

Idea in Brief
In this paper we focus on how offshore wind industry can transition to maturity in supply chain management (SCM) practices to promote innovation. We discuss this by addressing:

- *Innovation*

- *Industrialization*

- *Partnering*

We discuss SCM practices that enable supply chain innovation.

---

[1] This paper is based on Stentoft, J., Narasimhan, R. and Poulsen, T. (2016), "Reducing cost of energy in the offshore wind energy sector: The promise and potential of supply chain management," *International Journal of Energy Sector Management*, Vol. 10 No. 2, pp. 151-171.

1. Introduction

The purpose of this paper is to discuss how supply chain management (SCM) practices can reduce costs in the offshore wind industry (OWI). We provide a conceptual framework to show how SCM practices can be used in the wind industry to decrease the CoE. This SCM framework draws on successful applications of SCM in other industries. The discussion focusses on three streams of thought: *innovation, industrialization, and partnering*. We discuss each of these aspects highlighting a set of practices relating to them.

2. Supply chain innovation

Supply chain innovation is defined as "a change (incremental or radical) within a *supply chain network*, supply chain technology, or supply chain process (or a combination of these) that can take place in a company function, within a company, in an industry or in a supply chain in order to enhance new value creation for the stakeholder."[1]

In this paper, we discuss SCM practices that have been utilised successfully in mature industries to pursue the twin objectives of innovation and cost reduction. Our aim is not to suggest that these practices are easily transferrable to the OWI. Rather, our intention is to discuss their general applicability in OWI.

The OWI supply network draws upon the knowledge and skills of diverse industries, such as electric components (e.g., turbine components), cables and controllers, and towers. Some of these industries are large-scale manufacturers; others are smaller with significant power differentials between firms. These characteristics can also be seen in the automotive and aerospace supply chains (for example, aircraft engine manufacturers have considerable power and influence in dealing with Boeing). Therefore, transfer of best practices can be a useful strategy for rapid deployment of supply chain management practices in the OWI. OWI can seek to transfer best practices from other industries, such as the automotive and home appliance industries, and from project-oriented industries such as aircraft manufacturing. Although best practices in SCM can be potentially useful in each of the OWI phases, the greatest potential might be in the early phases of a project. Next, we discuss the conceptual framework that develops the promise and potential of SCM practices in the OWI.

3. Conceptual framework

Figure 1 is a conceptual framework showing how SCM practices relate to reducing cost of energy. The framework also depicts where 'maturity models' and benchmarking can be useful in implementing these practices in the wind power industry.

Figure 1. SCM practices for reducing cost of energy in the offshore wind industry

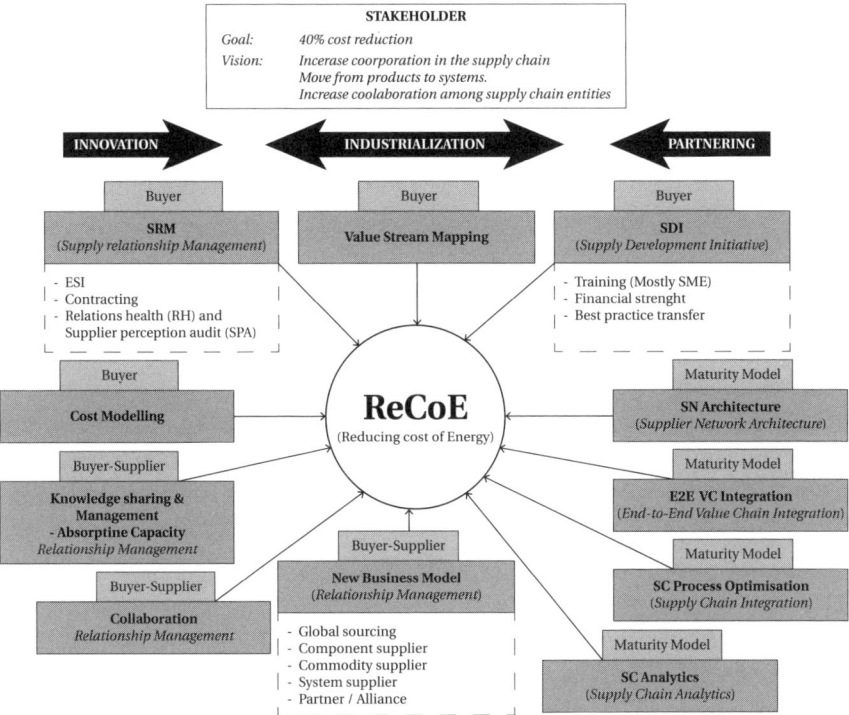

Source: Stentoft, J., Narasimhan, R. and Poulsen, T. (2016), "Reducing cost of energy in the offshore wind energy sector: The promise and potential of supply chain management," International Journal of Energy Sector Management, Vol. 10 No. 2, pp. 151-171.

The framework in Figure 1 focuses on three interdependent aspects of reducing cost in OWI: *innovation, industrialization, and partnering*. These three aspects encompass supply chain business processes, supply chain technologies, and supply chain network structures.

3.1 Innovation

Innovation is fundamentally knowledge-based. In today's business environment, knowledge is dispersed in the global footprint of firms.

The ability of firms to acquire, assimilate, and exploit knowledge for innovation (i.e. absorptive capacity) is critical. Firms that achieve superior innovation performance do so by achieving a high degree of *integration with their suppliers*.

Value chain integration: Value chain integration is an aspect of strategic sourcing. Value chain integration entails clear articulation of the firm's sourcing strategy, establishing goals and priorities for SCM efforts, a high degree of information exchange and communication, and utilisation of information technology to increase end-to-end visibility in supply chains.[2] In mature industries, value chain integration has led to superior cost and responsiveness (innovation) performance. Notable examples are Dell's pull production system in the computer industry and Esquel's system in apparel manufacturing. Supplier integration leads to close collaboration with suppliers, capturing what has been termed 'relational rent'.

In addition, integration has enabled firms such as GM and Boeing to transition to system integrators wherein key supplier partners have full responsibility for systems and subsystems. In this model, the manufacturer relies on the product, and process capabilities of principal suppliers. For example, GM relies on Lear Corporation for seating systems, whereas previously bought seat parts independently. Transitioning to 'systems buying' has enabled automotive firms to accelerate product development, reduce cost, align strategic goals across the value chain, and innovate more quickly. Thus, as the OWI increases its reliance on innovative and capable suppliers for strategic components that underlie new technologies and innovation, implementing value chain integration best practices would prove useful.

Knowledge management, knowledge sharing, and absorptive capacity: Knowledge management, and knowledge sharing, have been at the heart of collaborative relationships in SCM. Knowledge flow in supply network is facilitated by supply network design and architecture, relational networking, frequent communication, and information exchange. Raytheon, a major U.S. defense-systems contractor, has used supplier knowledge effectively for product technology and process innovation. Annual supplier council meetings are held by the firm to let the suppliers know where Raytheon is heading in terms of new products and new technologies. These meetings communicate Raytheon's technology strategy to suppliers and enable the suppliers to discern where their own technology investments might be most useful for Raytheon. Thus, Raytheon's effective information and knowledge sharing with suppliers results in greater absorptive capacity for both parties. Similarly, the OWI can increase innovation and reduce CoE through knowledge management in supply chain operations.

Value stream mapping: Value stream mapping is designed to eliminate waste in supply chain operations and thus maximise value. Supply chain operations in the OWI are complex. Two main differences distinguish the OWI from mature industries. First, the lifecycle of a wind farm is relatively long (30 years or more). Second, the time needed to construct a wind farm is several years, compared to days or hours for autos or home appliances. The longer lifecycle has four distinctly different phases involving many diverse organisations. Value stream mapping can be used to analyze these supply chains to identify and eliminate non-value adding activities and redesign the activities for maximum productivity and efficiency. Value stream mapping of the supply chain could eliminate waste in terms of time, movement, material flow, and efficiency of decision making, thus contributing to a reduction in CoE.

Supply network architecture (SNA): A supply network encompasses sourcing and supplier selection, the degree of autonomy given to tier 1 suppliers, the design of the supply network, the degree of influence of the focal firm on its supply network, contract management, and the degree of personal and professional ties among network members.[3] The influence of direct ties and indirect ties among alliance partners in supply networks can positively influence the innovation output of firms and reduce the cost of wind energy.

Supply chain analytics: Supply chain analytics has considerable potential for innovation in product, process, and supply chain operations. Although firms capture data on all aspects of business, including supply chain operations, few firms are mature enough to fully exploit their data resources for innovation. Current advances in analytics have enabled firms to extract customer and supply market intelligence from both qualitative and quantitative data as well as from internal and external data. KPMG refers to this as 'massively open business intelligence'.[4] Firms in the wind power industry could use external data and analytics to pursue innovations that could potentially reduce CoE. Next, we discuss the second aspect of the conceptual framework, industrialisation.

3.2 Industrialization

In this paper, the industrialization concept is defined to be the stage at which an industry or a firm is in the *maturity curve* of SCM practices. Repetitive manufacturing firms are higher on the maturity curve. As firms implement SCM practices in phases, their SCM capabilities increase, giving them a potential for greater value creation. Maturity models position a firm in one of four states ranging from a 'buying' perspective to 'partnering' and strategic sourcing. Each stage in the maturity model implies distinctly different SCM capabilities. The maturity models also reflect the shifting role of the SCM function from procurement to a focus on strategy, superior value creation, innovation, and market responsiveness at the mature stage of partnering with suppliers. Industrialization in the mature industries utilises cost modeling, supplier development initiatives, and supply chain process optimization.

Cost modeling: Cost modeling in mature industries is a common practice. Under cost modeling, the firm develops an independent understanding of the cost structure of the component or system that it is buying without relying on a supplier quote. Prior to this approach, early in the maturity cycle, firms negotiated a cost reduction without a comprehensive understanding of the cost structure. Without a complete understanding, sourcing decisions will be myopic and suboptimal. This approach is sometimes referred to as 'should cost' modeling. Strategic cost modeling emphasizes the segmentation of procured components and systems into strategic and nonstrategic groups and related SCM processes. Identification of cost avoidance opportunities as opposed to cost reduction opportunities is sought in the strategic cost modeling approach.

Further, clean sheeting is a new approach to cost modeling in which the firm develops a cost structure for the component or system *by assuming best practices and sourcing from world class suppliers and not necessarily from suppliers currently in its supply network*. The ability to gather supply market intelligence is essential in this approach.

Supplier development initiative: The supplier development initiative (SDI) is a common practice in mature industries. SDI encompasses training personnel in cost modeling and statistical process control, implementing quality management and continuous improvement practices, assisting in implementing new process technology, and offering financial assistance to ensure solvency. For example, Raytheon helped one of its suppliers to implement six sigma and lean manufacturing to achieve impressive quality and cost performance.

Supply chain process optimisation: Supply chain process optimisation refers to executing SCM processes with maximum efficiency, thereby reducing wait time for internal customers and execution times for processes, increasing responsiveness to internal and external partners, and increasing accuracy of process outcomes, thus enhancing productivity and standardization. Purchase order placement is an example. Intel, winner of the MSU-Richter Award for excellence in SCM in 2014, achieved impressive gains by employing information technology (IT) to optimize its purchase order placement process (ISM-MSU Richter Awards, 2014).

3.3 Partnering

The third aspect of the conceptual framework in Figure 1 is partnering. Firms that rank higher on the maturity curve of SCM practices actively pursue supplier partnering. However, partnering does not necessarily imply long-term contracts. Partnership in mature industries is characterised by joint development of product and technology, sharing of product and technology strategy with the supplier, specific investments made by the supplier exclusively for the buying firm, flexible contracts, high degree of IT integration and integration with the supplier processes, commitment of specialized skills and human capital by the supplier, reliance on the supplier partner for innovation performance, deep relationship, and collaboration with the supplier partner.

Buyer-supplier (B-S) relationship: Practitioners in mature industries agree that B-S relationship management must stress collaboration, joint problem solving, high level and frequency of information exchange, concern for the supplier's profit, early supplier involvement, and lack of emphasis on power over suppliers. B-S relationship management depends on the establishment of trust and commitment in the relationship. Trust and commitment reduce relational stress, potential for conflict development, and supplier opportunism and increase productive collaboration between transacting partners. In the presence of trust and commitment, firms experience superior cost, quality, and innovation performance. Firms in mature industries use supplier segmentation and develop different business models appropriate for each segment. Segmenting the supply chain and managing the B-S relationship via practices tailored for each segment has led to superior cost performance in mature industries. For example, one classification scheme that could be used to manage buyer-supplier relationships involves classifying suppliers as commodity suppliers, component suppliers, system suppliers, or partnership/strategic alliances.

Best practices from mature industries could be transferred to the wind power industry to achieve cost reduction.

Collaboration: Collaboration is the watchword in business exchange in today's competitive environment. Firms in mature industries seek to achieve 'customer of choice' status, also known as 'earned preferential treatment' from their suppliers[5] studied relational health in the automotive industry for more than a decade, and their data show that firms that achieve superior cost, quality, and innovation performance have a high relational health index relative to their competition. Best practices exist in mature industries, which could be transferred to the wind power sector to achieve similar results.

Supplier relationship management's (SRM) core principles include the practice of relational norms, supplier perception audits, annual supplier councils, strategic integration through early supplier involvement (ESI), and deep relationship development with suppliers, leading to relational health. Relational norms lie at the heart of SRM. Justice practices—relational justice (evidenced by supplier involvement in key decisions and joint problem solving), procedural justice (flexibility in handling conflicts and resolving disputes), and distributive justice (concern for supplier profit and gain sharing)—associated with relational norms are helpful in establishing trust and relational commitment.[6] Similarly, justice practices could be helpful in reducing CoE in the wind power sector. Supplier perception audits are useful to identify areas that need improvement as firms seek to develop deep relationship with their suppliers.

In this section, we discussed SCM practices that could be useful for reducing CoE. In this context, developing familiarity with maturity models in different industries and benchmarking for transferring best practices could be highly useful to the wind power sector.

4. Conclusion

Transforming the OWI requires industrialization utilizing maturity models and best practices for use by the OWI. Configuration of SCM practices most valuable in each phase of the lifecycle of an OWI should be identified and implemented. It would be useful to identify the different configurations of practices so that resource deployment could be maximally beneficial for achieving cost reduction. The conceptual framework of this paper should help identify specific practices that are likely to be beneficial in different OWI projects. Contextual differences should be considered in assessing the suitability and efficacy of these practices.

Endnotes

1 Arlbjørn, J.S., de Haas, H. and Munksgaard, K.B. (2011), "Exploring supply chain innovation", *Logistics Research*, Vol. 3 No. 1, pp. 3-18.

2 Narasimhan, N. and Kim, S.W. (2002), "Effect of supply chain integration on the relationship between diversification and performance: Evidence from Japanese and Korean firms", *Journal of Operations Management*, Vol. 20 No. 3, pp. 303-323.

3 Narayanan, S. and Narasimhan, R. (2014), "Governance choice, sourcing relationship characteristics, and relationship performance", *Decision Sciences Journal*, Vol. 45 No. 4, pp. 717-751.

4 Gupta, A. (2014), "Supply chain analytics", *Executive Summit Presentation*, Michigan State University, East Lansing, U.S.A.

5 Henke, J.W. and Zhang, C. (2010), "Increasing supplier driven innovation", *Sloan Management Review*, Vol. 51 No. 2, pp. 41-46.

6 Narasimhan, R. and Narayanan, S. (2013), "Perspectives on supply network enabled innovation", *Journal of Supply Chain Management*, Vol. 49 No. 4, pp. 27-42.

Formation of new interfirm relationships: Case studies of offshore wind firms[1]

Patrick A. Hennelly
Institute for Manufacturing, Cambridge University, UK

Chee Yew Wong
Leeds University Business School, University of Leeds, UK and the ReCoE project

Idea in Brief
New interfirm relationships can be sources of innovation for the offshore wind industry (OWI). New interfirm relationships are triggered and formed by compatibility and complementarity. We study the formation of new relationships between OWI suppliers and their suppliers/customers:

- *Compatibility in corporate culture and complementarity in the technical market are important for triggering new interfirm relationships;*

- *Compatibility and complementarity can be shaped by both buyers and suppliers' frequent interactions, sharing of information, demonstration of commitment, and investment in new relationships.*

1. Introduction

The offshore wind industry (OWI) is relatively immature. It has no widely accepted and standard technologies. Meanwhile, the sector needs to significantly reduce cost and be independent from state fund-

---

1 This paper is based on Hennelly, P. and Wong, C.Y. (2016), "The formation of new interfirm relationships: A UK offshore wind sector analysis," *International Journal of Energy Sector Management*, Vol. 10 No. 2, pp. 172-190.

ing. Collaboration across OWI supply chains is thought to help save cost and standardize the sector. This involves forming new interfirm relationships, including searching for more cost-effective or more innovative suppliers. In some countries, politics drives the use of local contents. Thus, OWI firms need to demonstrate willingness to develop a new local supply base. However, in the OWI, the formation of new interfirm relationships is troubled by typically high market risk and political uncertainty.

This research is important because the establishment of new interfirm relationships or alliances in the OWI sector is known to be difficult. Many firms have failed to expand their initial explorative relationships with suppliers new to the OWI. It is important to learn how OWI firms build up relationships with new suppliers, especially during the early stage of the relationships. The literature has provided little knowledge about how firms interact and make decisions at the awareness and exploration stages of the new relationship, especially under significant political and technological uncertainties. Compatibility and complementarity are known as important ingredients for forming a successful partnership. However, the literature assumes compatibility and complementarity present automatically without efforts toward investing in communication, information sharing, and trust building. Before two firms formally interact, little is known of how the perceived levels of compatibility in business value and practices and complementarity in resources affect information sharing, trust building, and commitment. The formation of an alliance requires trust developed through a process of assessing motives and behaviors of the opposite parties. Understanding of these nuances helps OWI firms better manage their new supplier relationship development processes.

2. Conceptual framework

When a supplier in the OWI establishes a new relationship with their suppliers or customers, they may follow the relationship life cycle model outlined by Dwyer et al. (1987)[1], commonly known as "DSO theory," which explain how the interfirm relationship life cycle evolves over time through five stages: *"awareness," "exploration," "expansion," "commitment/maturity,"* and *"dissolution."* As an interfirm relationship evolves from one stage to another, it typically starts with low relational norms, which change gradually over time. The rate at which the different relationship stages progress can be triggered by interactions between the buyer and suppliers over time. It is the reinforcing interactions between triggers (complementarity and compatibility) and enabling factors that trigger movement between stages.

As shown in Figure 1, the first trigger is compatibility. Compatibility "gives match quality through similarities—capabilities can be combined to create value because they are similar or share a standard interface."[2] Compatibilities in OWI products, markets, and technologies create relatedness between firms. Compatibility in organizational cultures and capabilities between partner firms can lower coordination costs and assist expectation management and behavioral control. They stabilize the relationship and increase the levels of tolerance through a "social glue" that helps overcome temporary periods of disequilibrium. Without compatible values, norms, and cultures, the effects of socialization can diminish, potentially leading to a vicious circle of mistrust and conflict.

Figure 1. A framework of interfirm relationship triggers and enabling factors

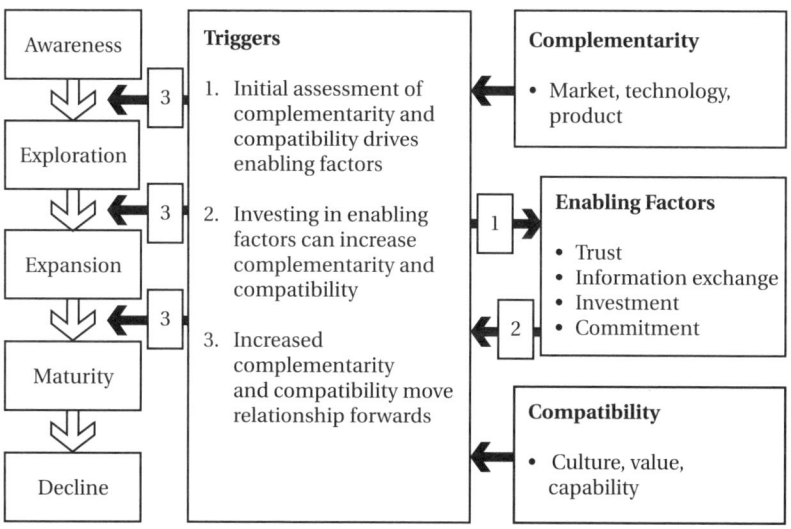

The second trigger is complementarity. OWI firms form relationships with new partners because of resource complementarity—unidentical resources (e.g., technology, product, market) that "complement" each other. OWI firms need to examine partners' resource profile when forming new interfirm relationships. Resources from partners can be combined with own resource sets to create a resource bundle that provides unique competitiveness. Resource complementarity helps in learning new and valuable capabilities, creates mutual interdependency, and facilitates the formation of alliances. Resource interdependence helps reduce the chances of opportunism in an alliance where by allowing both partners to perceive that there is "value" in the relationship.

3. Case companies

We purposely study two sets of dyadic relationship, one from a customer perspective and the other from a supplier perspective. From a customer perspective, the first three case studies (cases 1-1, 1-2, and 1-3) examine how a UK gearbox manufacturer, MOCO, attempted to establish new relationships with three suppliers under the hope that an OWI firm (SACO) would win some OWI contracts in the UK using MOCO's gearbox. The key informants are key account managers, director, supply chain manager, and technical product manager of MOCO.

From a supplier perspective, the second set of cases (cases 2-1, 2-2) involves a UK steel manufacturer, TACO, that attempted to establish a new relationship with two customers (SICO and WTCO) to supply steel structures for wind turbines and towers. Data was collected through unstructured interviews using the framework in Figure 1, in which we mapped how the relationships unfold over time along the DSO life cycle model, as well as the roles of compatibility, complementarity, and other factors.

3.1 Case 1-1: MOCO and COCO (supplier)

Quality issues led to dispute and decline of relationship

MOCO required a foundry that could provide castings for their gearbox. Very few foundries in the UK could supply a casting of the required size. COCO was a UK casting manufacturer that was founded over 100 years ago and had a large facility. Capable of large and heavy graphite-rich castings, COCO supplied to numerous industries. COCO was considered a sole supplier in the UK by MOCO; alternative suppliers were Europe-based or beyond Europe. COCO was a supplier of DACO, who acquired MOCO. Though there were existing relationships, managers from MOCO did not know managers from COCO until MOCO decided to consider COCO for casting for the OWI orders. There was uncertainty initially because COCO was about to go into administration. After being taken over by a new owner, COCO was able to convince MOCO to place an order because a strong, positive bond was created between the new owner and staff at MOCO. Because of the quality issues of the castings MOCO received from COCO, MOCO later lost their trust in COCO and decided to subcontract some of the orders to another company, who machined the component and sent it back to MOCO facilities. This made it extremely difficult to attribute quality problems to either COCO or another company and created disputes among the three companies.

3.2 Case 1-2: MOCO and SKCO (supplier)
Technical knowledge incompatibility led to decline
SKCO is one of the largest bearing manufacturers in the world, with lots of experience in OWI sector. As SKCO served almost half of the sector, OWI was a small part of SKCO's revenue. SKCO provided technical complementarity to MOCO because MOCO was not experienced in making bearings for OWI. The technical capability of SKCO was world leading. However, there was a significant gap in technical knowledge, leading to technical knowledge incompatibility. There was an earlier interaction between the two firms, but progress was not made, because of changes at MOCO. MOCO later attempted to reestablish the relationship, and MOCO quickly made an order because of their confidence in SKCO's reputation and capability. However, because of a dispute about machine or design error for the bearings, SKCO sent staff to prove that the problem was created after the bearings were delivered to MOCO. Later, it was concluded that the errors occurred when MOCO installed the bearings onto the raceways for housing the bearings supplied by another supplier, VICO. Failing to install and test the bearings in the raceways means MOCO's client would not pay, and MOCO was not able to pay SKCO's invoice. Even though there was good will to resolve the technical issues, the financial dispute terminated the relationship.

3.3 Case 1-3: MOCO and OTCO (supplier)
Lack of market complementarity led to decline
OTCO is a family-owned Germany gearbox manufacturer with much experience in the OWI. OCTO was valuable for MOCO, as it offered technical, product, and market complementarities. OCTO could develop prototypes for MOCO to venture into the OWI sector. MOCO trusted the capability of OCTO because of its consistency in quality and delivery performance. OCTO, however, did not find any complementarity MOCO could offer. Thus, OCTO kept MOCO at arm's-

length. OCTO provided training to MOCO but preferred to only deliver orders to MOCO without much interaction. As western European firms, there were some levels of compatibility but little friendship between the two firms. MOCO used to purchase from OTCO, but the order was canceled by its client SACO. MOCO had to cancel its order to OTCO, and the relationship was terminated. OTCO demanded MOCO to pay for all materials purchased for the order.

3.4 Case 2-1: TACO and SICO (customer)
Market complementarity drives expansion of relationship

TACO was a large steel manufacturer in the UK, located not far from UK offshore wind farms. TACO had no experience providing steel structures to OWI (experience in only onshore). Pressured by rising and fluctuating prices in iron and raw materials, the steel industry was declining when OWI started to pick up in the UK. Thus, TACO was hopeful in becoming a major steel supplier to tower fabricators and turbine manufacturers. In 2010, TACO invested in a "wind tower hub" containing machineries and facilities, aiming to make themselves an attractive supplier. TACO had improved its production quality and logistics capabilities to attract the attention of SICO (a major turbine manufacturer). After meeting at an exhibition in 2009, the two companies continued meeting. TACO would purchase SICO's new systems and process technologies to use in their steel mills. SICO had a choice of many steel suppliers apart from TACO, but TACO's main advantage was its proximity to UK offshore wind farms and the potential for reducing logistics costs. Since 2009, the two companies had tried to build trust and common working procedures together. In 2011, TACO secured an order from SICO for 25,000 tonnes of high-quality profiled steel plate that would be used to build 150 onshore wind towers. However, SICO was not entirely satisfied by the initial delivery. The two companies created a joint quality initiative, which costly to TACO. Because of tensions about quality issues, the trust level and two-way communication had declined. After delivering the first order to SICO, TACO did not receive another order as they had hoped. This was mainly because SICO had not received an order for UK wind farms. TACO instead used the new capabilities to negotiate with other tower fabricators, even though they still failed to compete on price.

3.5 Case 2-2: TACO and WTCO (customer)
Multiple compatibility and complementarity drive expansion of relationship
WTCO was a specialist supplier of wind turbine towers based in the UK. WTCO also supply towers to SICO. The relationship between TACO and WTCO first began in 2002. TACO and WTCO already had an indirect relationship with each other in 2008 when TACO supplied onshore turbine manufacturers who would then contract WTCO to do the fabrication. When TACO and WTCO met in 2013 at a conference, both companies were new to the OWI. WTCO wanted to design wind tower solutions from scratch. TACO's priority at this stage was to invest much of their time and knowledge into developing WTCO's capabilities and complementary resources to gain their trust. Several visits by staff from both sides, a supplier open day, and technical knowledge exchange took place. Discussions regarding future pipelines also took place so TACO could have a more thorough idea of WTCO's order book. WTCO suggested two areas for improvement: quality of the product and delivery performance. TACO further demonstrated how they attempted to improve quality performance. TACO proposed signing a service-level agreement, whereas WTCO wanted a "softer" and more flexible approach to the contractual relationship. Upon demonstration of goodwill and willingness to share information, mutual trust was built. Both parties were eventually willing to take risks and invest in the relationship. TACO received first and second orders from WTCO. Both companies continue to work together to deal with political uncertainty. With a strong mutual understanding, once the political uncertainty was over, the two companies have continued to trade and work together.

4. Conclusion
The five cases show that building up new interfirm relationships in the OWI can be affected by different types of compatibility and complementarity. Case 1 illustrates how MOCO's lack of quality-management capability led to poor relationships with new suppliers. Quality issues can lead to dispute and seriously destroy trust and will eventually deteriorate relationships. Case 2 illustrates how the lack of technical incompatibility can lead to a decline in a new interfirm relationship. Even though SKCO appeared to complement MOCO's lack of technical capability, the quality product SKCO supplied to MOCO was not installed properly, leading to dispute and termination of the relationship. Case 3 illustrates a situation of one party that is high-

ly capable and already successfully supplying to OWI feeling a lack of complementarity by supplying to MOCO. This incompatibility and the fact that OTCO had other channels to markets led to a lack of commitment to building up close a relationship and transferring knowledge. Case 4 shows how market complementarity can lead to commitment from both parties to invest in the relationship, especially the supplier TACO by developing new facilities and capabilities, even though it was very costly. However, in addition to political uncertainty, tensions about quality issues remained a critical factor that prevented the relationship to mature. Finally, in case 5, the presence of both compatibility and complementarity drove the expansion of the new relationship between TACO and WTCO.

On reflection, compatibility in terms of cultural similarity made it easier to communicate and build trust. Trust was further enhanced by frequent communication and visits. However, similarities in culture were not enough to promote the expansion of new relationships. Despite a similar national culture, differences in technical capabilities, value, and quality expectations made agreeing on quality and technical issues difficult. The lack of technical compatibility made it harder to work on the same page. Perceived complementarity in technical capabilities promoted attempts to expand the relationships through initiating small orders. However, complementarity with suppliers that are hard to substitute created an asymmetric interdependency. Complementarity that was asymmetric restricted the progression of new relationships. Quality issues prevented new relationships to reach the expansion stage.

This study helps managers in OWI firms and similar sectors to improve their capabilities in establishing new suppliers. Even though some potential suppliers or customers may initially seem compatible in terms of culture, it is important to assess quality and technical compatibility. This is why some large OWI firms qualify new suppliers through very high quality and technical standards. Another lesson learned is that balancing the complementarity is important for promoting equal efforts in sharing information and investing in the new relationships. While governments from many countries argue the importance of supply chain collaboration, standardization, and localization, it is important to note that many new relationships fail to go past the expansion stage because of a lack of skills in managing compatibility and complementarity. In short, here are some important decision logics for forming new interfirm relationships:

- If there is significant asymmetry in complementarity, the party that has a better alternative will invest less in the relationship;

- If there are significant and multiple complementarities, both parties are likely to invest more in the relationship, leading to increased complementarity and compatibility;

- Even though there may be potential complementarities, lack of technical knowledge compatibility and quality standards can add risk to the new relationship;

- For "systems" suppliers, it is important to assess the potential suppliers' capabilities to manage upstream in their supply network, as well as their technical knowledge and quality standards.

Even though this case study is based on the OWI sector, it applies to firms operating in uncertain environments and seeking to establish new suppliers. Most managers would consider building up relationships with new suppliers based on initial perceived complementarity in market or technical capabilities and perceived compatibility in culture. The study shows that when initial perceived compatibility and complementarity are asymmetrical, both sides may not necessarily put equal effort into the new relationship. The willingness to share information and invest in the relationship can somehow increase the perceived compatibility and complementarity by both sides. Most managers would quickly expand the new relationships by placing some initial orders. The study shows it is important to first assess technical and quality compatibility. When technical capabilities and quality expectations significantly differ, misunderstanding and dispute could occur. Moreover, when there is asymmetry in technical or market complementarity, the interdependency is likely to be imbalanced. Managers could address asymmetrical complementarity by offering additional benefits to the parties with lower perceived complementarity.

Endnotes

1 Dwyer, F.R., Schurr P.H. and Oh, S. (1987), "Developing buyer-supplier relationships", *Journal of Marketing*, Vol. 51 No. 2, pp. 11-27.

2 Mitsuhashi, H. and Greve, H.R. (2009), "A matching theory of alliance formation and organizational success: Complementarity and compatibility", *Academy of Management Journal*, Vo. 52 No. 5, pp. 975-995.

Transformation to systems integration in the wind power industry-efficacy of supply chain integration[1]

Ram Narasimhan
Emeritus of Michigan State University and the ReCoE project

Ivan Fransisco Martinez Neri

Idea in Brief
This article addresses the efficacy of supply chain integration as a means by which an OEM in the wind power industry can transform itself into a "system integrator". We draw upon the experiences of firms in other industries that have achieved such a transformation under competitive and cost reduction pressures. Based on a case study, the article

- *Discusses the three strategic aspects of transformation – design and manufacturing, governance and sourcing and their constituent dimensions,*

- *Identifies the supply chain management practices that enable supply chain integration and the organizational structural/infrastructural changes that are needed for each strategic aspect, and*

- *Identifies what is needed by way of change management practices to effect the transformational changes that are needed.*

- *The pros and cons of transforming to a system integrator are noted.*

---

1 This article is based on Martinez Neri, I. and Narasimhan, R. (2018), "Supply chain innovation in the offshore wind power sector: Strategic transformation from a line manufacturer to a systems integrator", Unpublished Paper, ReCoE Project, University of Southern Denmark.

1. Introduction

Offshore wind farms (OWFs) have attracted the interest of investors as reliable, low-risk, long-term investments with predictable yields. Stakeholders other than utilities would like an increase in the availability of these investments by means of Engineering-Procurement-Construction (EPC) projects.1 Among the entities who can offer such EPC projects are utilities, OEMs (e.g. turbine manufacturers), cable installers, substation operators and firms responsible for operation and maintenance. Firms in various industries have successfully transformed themselves into system integrators utilizing *supply chain integration* (SCI) as a strategy. We explore the efficacy of SCI in the offshore wind industry (OWI), which can contribute to reducing the cost of wind energy. The objective of this paper is to delineate how SCI can aid transformation of a firm into a system integrator in the wind power industry. Specifically, the paper addresses: what dimensions of SCI are important to the context of the OWI and how a firm in the OWI should pursue integration from its current state? How should the concomitant organizational transformation and change management be pursued? To address these questions, we utilize a case study and analogical reasoning.

We draw upon the experience of Boeing, a major aircraft manufacturer, that transformed itself into a systems integrator in response to market and cost pressures, and global supply chain challenges. By means of a comparative analysis, we develop a transformation framework for firms in the wind power industry to become systems integrators. Such transformation could present an opportunity to reduce the cost of energy.

2. System integrators

In EPC projects, a company or consortium executes a major project under contract from the client. They are technically complex, multi-disciplinary, involve large capital and are mostly one-off, non-recurrent endeavors. Like EPC projects, OWFs are projects that are executed using supply chain partners from previous projects and new suppliers. An established WTG manufacturer can fulfill the role of an EPC contractor, as these OEMs receive the most benefit from the transformation to systems integrators. For other OEMs such as cable suppliers, foundation manufacturers, and substation providers, system integration might still be a viable strategy, although the revenues from the offshore wind sector represent only a minor share of their overall revenue. In the remainder of this article, we consider WTG manufacturers as they are most likely to take the initiative to become EPC providers by transforming themselves into system integrators.

When becoming systems integrators, firms do not abandon their traditional manufacturing strength, instead adopt hybrid organizational structures that lie between the two archetypes. These types of organizations emphasize *flexibility, modularity, standardization of interfaces, and the ability to integrate the multiple systems*. The systems integrator oversees coordinating and aligning the subsystems provided by external suppliers to deliver a functional system consistent with project goals. In this business model, the resources of an OEM can be used in synergy with the members of its supply network to reduce costs. Supply chain integration facilitates this synergistic exploitation of resources to realize project objectives.

There are noteworthy examples of businesses that have used SCI to provide integrated solutions and to become more involved in the life- cycle of a product. To reduce the cost of energy in the OWI, such life cycle perspective and SCI can be beneficial. In the computers and electronics industry, IBM initially emphasized in-house manufacturing capabilities. By the middle of 1980s, however, a new business model emphasizing SCI was required due to market challenges, as various clients demanded integrated systems, of which IBMs components were only a part.[2] The transformation of Cisco into a system integrator emphasizing end-to-end (E2E) integration is another example. This has also happened in project environments, including oil and gas[3], aircraft manufacturing, and military systems. Systems integrators in addition to the design and manufacture of different components, also develop integrative capabilities that are needed to coordinate the network of subsystem suppliers.

3. Supply chain integration

SCI refers to the strategic practice in which an organization and its supply network partners collaborate to accomplish synergies in all phases of a project through cooperation, increased exchange of information, collaborative planning and material flow coordination. Supply chain integration requires a supply chain that is aligned strategically, tactically and operationally to benefit all members. Such alignment gives commonality of purpose to all actors in the supply chain. SCI engages material, human capital, information and knowledge resources of all actors in a supply chain to a common purpose. SCI touches design and manufacture of a product, governance of relationships, and the structure of a supply chain. Broadly, SCI encompasses strategy integration (aimed at alignment of goals across the supply chain; for example, supplier enabled innovation), operational integration (aimed at operational priorities), decision integration (aimed at cooperation and coordination across the supply chain), logistics integration, and information integration (to increase visibility and velocity of information across the supply chain, data analytics and metrics integration). SCI can be a catalyst for organizational transformation into a system integrator. The primary drivers of such transformation, of course, are market and strategic considerations. In general, SCI can promote innovation, reduce cost and increase profitability. Given the need to reduce the cost of energy in OWI, SCI might prove to be a viable approach.

4. Case study

We selected the development of the Boeing Dreamliner as a suitable case study. First, the magnitude and complexity are comparable in terms of costs per project, the number of subsystems to be interconnected, and the nature of the company prior to the transformation. Additionally, Boeing had similar market pressures that forced the company to innovate by means of integration in its supply network. The case of Boeing illustrates how collaboration and coordination of a network of global suppliers can optimize the results for the company including cost reduction. We analyzed detailed information on Boeing from secondary data sources to identify strategic, tactical and operational aspects of its transformation and identified supply chain management practices and processes that enabled its transformation.

The impetus for the transformation of Boeing arose from the pressure from airlines to help reduce their capital and operating costs through increased fuel efficiency and technological innovations. There was intense competition from Airbus, which emphasized closer working relationship with its supply network and distributed manufacturing. These challenges stimulated innovation in Boeing, not only in the development of new jetliners, but also in its supply chain practices. Boeing drastically reduced its supplier base and transferred a large share of the risk and the cost of building airplanes to the suppliers. Boeing outsourced 70 percent of the development and production activities of the Dreamliner. It became a focal manufacturer in charge of integrating the components and subsystems produced by suppliers. Boeing developed strategic partnerships with 50 tier-1 suppliers, who simultaneously served as integrators of the subsystems provided by tier-2 suppliers.[4]

Boeing credited *communication, collaboration and coordination* as central in this strategic transformation. Boeing's *communication* was facilitated by a *web-based platform* that provided visibility, better control, and the integration of processes, which in turn enhanced information integration across its supply network. This web-based tool improved coordination of decisions, such as engineering changes, modifications in the bill-of-materials, etc. At Boeing, the *willingness to share information* played a central role in reaping the benefits of the large investments made in integrating information by means of IT infrastructure. Boeing was able to decrease the negative impact of unforeseen events and take *corrective actions* more quickly.

Collaboration is a process that involves cooperative activities among the members of a supply chain and it leads to mutual benefits. The development of new collaborative tools at Boeing was essential for supply chain integration. It facilitated *early supplier involvement* in the project, which resulted in a more efficient development and production of the new airplane. By increasing collaboration with its suppliers, Boeing reduced the development time as well as improved the overall performance of its supply chain. Boeing's cooperation was characterized by an increase in the intensity of communication and a collaborative attitude with its partners in the supply chain.

As the share of outsourced components was increased significantly, Boeing had to increase its *coordination* capabilities to maintain control over outsourced components with increased visibility into its suppliers' processes and capabilities. Apart from increased visibility across the supply chain, high levels of coordination and collaboration enhanced trust and commitment among its partners. Boeing used an initiative called "Global Partners" to move from strategic sourcing to a long-term vision of strategic relationships with suppliers. This initiative enabled Boeing to manage its suppliers by: (1) measuring the performance of suppliers with a scorecard; (2) developing long-term strategic relationships with key suppliers; and (3) promoting the *self-regulation* of the supply chain by establishing *supplier councils* to make suppliers accountable to each other. In self-regulation, the partners became accountable to each other and worked in a collaborative way rather than waiting for Boeing to solve an issue with each partner individually whenever a problem arose.

Boeing's suppliers delivered complete subsystems to reduce development time and Boeing also maximized cost reduction by shifting production to strategic partners around the world. These partners were asked to take additional responsibilities, such as the financial risks of development. In five years, the company decreased its supplier base from 3,800 to 1,200 suppliers. For the Dreamliner program, Boeing was more open to innovations and suggestions from suppliers than before. Instead of providing detailed specifications for components, Boeing exploited the suppliers' expertise during the development of the Dreamliner by asking them to provide innovations and solutions. This also led to a reduction in transaction costs and further integration of tier-1 and tier-2 suppliers, thereby expanding the supplier's scope of work, as these tier-1 suppliers oversaw integrating the subsystems provided by tier-2 suppliers. Partners brought suggestions and solutions to Boeing to help in the design of a better product and the company considered the *early and deep involvement* of these partners as essential for performance improvements in the Dreamliner project. The enablers of SCI found in Boeing's case were: *Information sharing and information integration (communication). Collaboration, Coordination, Commitment and Trust, Relational Governance, Early Supplier Involvement, Supplier Councils and Supplier Innovation.*

The strategic transformation of Boeing into a systems integrator was a break from its past practice of developing new jetliners. Here, we should note that such a transformation as that adopted by Boeing was not accomplished without some problems. Specifically, it has been reported that Boeing did experience problems dealing with a large number of sub-suppliers. Transformation to system integrator at the scale attempted by Boeing is fraught with supplier management risks due to the scale and scope of such outsourcing. The problems encountered by Boeing were acknowledged by the CEO of Boeing. An initiative such as the one adopted by Boeing has the potential to create relational risk, non-performance risk and opportunism risk due to the size and scope of the supply network and its global footprint. Given these risks, it is essential to pay attention to governance issues that are essential for becoming a system integrator. The case of Boeing provides useful insights into what an OEM in the wind power industry could do to move from a line manufacturing environment into an integrator of systems via SCI.

5. Transformation framework

The case of Boeing provides insights into what a company in the OWI could do to move from a line manufacturing environment into an integrator of systems via SCI. Figure 1 clusters lessons learned from the case study regarding SCI enablers along with the strategies into three strategic dimensions to be addressed by a company to transform itself into a system integrator in the OWI.

Figure 1. Strategic dimensions of transformation

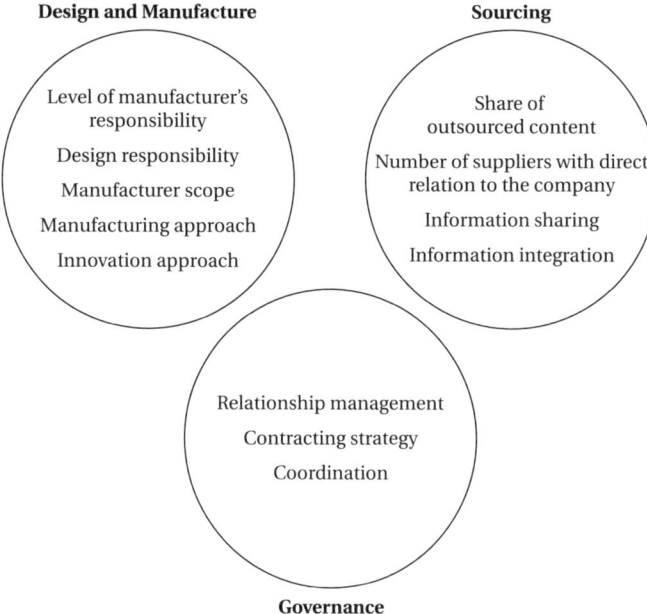

Source: Martinez-Neri and Narasimhan (2018)

In Tables 1, 2 and 3, we describe the framework for this strategic transformation. This enables an analysis of the present state of the industry and of the assumed situation of most existing OEMs, the desired state for an EPC provider, the SCI enablers, SCM processes, structural, and infrastructural changes needed to bring about this transformation.

Table 1. Design and manufacture strategy

Aspect	Desired State	Current State	SCI/SCM Enablers	Structural/ Infrastructural Changes Needed
Level of manufacturer's responsibility	The strategic suppliers provide complete subsystems	Design, manufacturing and installation are dispersed and not integrated	Supplier integration. Early supplier involvement, supplier management	Information Sharing, IT, Organizational Restructuring
Supplier's scope	Tier-1 suppliers responsible for complete sub-system	Currently, OEMs don't recognize or have no knowledge of complete subsystem requirements	Supplier risk assessment and management, supplier management, Supply chain innovation	Creation of new responsibilities, Establishing new lines of communication, IT, Knowledge acquisition
Construction Approach	Subsystems arrive at the project site to be assembled by the systems integrator	The subsystems are assembled at the project's site from components.	Early supplier involvement, Supplier development initiatives	New responsibilities, New lines of communication, New reporting relationships, Integration practices
Innovation Approach	Supplier driven innovation	Innovation is from the utilities and some of the suppliers; OEMs have experience in involving suppliers in innovation	Supply chain integration, Innovation sourcing	Supply market intelligence, innovation incentives, flexible contracts, Risk taking

Table 2. Sourcing strategy

Aspect	Desired State	Current State	SCI/SCM Enablers	Structural/ Infrastructural Changes Needed
Outsourced Content	Outsource major share of the product as subsystems	Components outsourced to OEMs (e.g., foundation providers, cable manufacturers. Some OEMs have experience in outsourcing	Supplier integration. Early supplier involvement, supplier management	Information Sharing, IT, Organizational Restructuring
Number of suppliers with direct relation to the systems integrator	Few strategic tier-1 suppliers have direct relationship	OEMs have no experience with strategic suppliers of the balance of plant (BoP) or the supporting activities (e.g. accommodation, transfer of personnel, etc.).	Supply network design, knowledge management, supplier segmentation,	New responsibilities, SRM software, Strategic sourcing, Talent management
Information Sharing	Strategic supplier engagement	No formal strategy, Meetings occur as needed	Trust-based governance, Dedicated project team	New responsibilities, New lines of communication, New reporting relationships, Knowledge management
Information integration	Web-based system	No integrated systems between the utilities which construct the OWFs and the suppliers.	Supply network architecture, supply chain integration	Joint problem solving, Process integration, Dedicated teams, New organizational responsibilities

Transformation to systems integration in the wind power

Table 3. Governance strategy

Aspect	Desired State	Current State	SCI/SCM Enablers	Structural/Infrastructural Changes Needed
Relationship Management	Partnering with Tier-1 Suppliers	Limited use of Partnering Relationships	Contract Management, Supplier Management Relational Governance	Information Sharing, IT, Organizational Restructuring
Contracting	Risk and gain Sharing Tier-1 become system suppliers	No risk sharing Cost/performance based contracts	Contract Management, Supplier Management	New responsibilities, SRM software, Supplier Councils
Coordination	Strategic supplier engagement	No formal strategy, Meetings occur as needed	Trust-based governance, Dedicated project team	New responsibilities, New lines of communication, New reporting relationships, Knowledge management

6. Change management

For an OEM to become an EPC provider, it must acquire some specific skills and follow the structural and infrastructural changes suggested in Tables 3, 4 and 5. An OEM must change its mindset from internally focused management and internally driven processes to much more open, externally driven processes emphasizing a cooperative structure. Such a dramatic process in change management will call for an unlearning process at the organizational level and among all individuals. The process may need a dramatic change of the perspectives among management personnel.

First, the company must develop the supply chain architecture to make a subjective representation of the strategic suppliers, their capabilities, and the operations and processes involved in the construction of an OWF. The EPC candidate must map, control, coordinate, optimize, and visualize the structure of this construction chain, its flow of materials, human resources, subsystems, exchange of operational as well as strategic information, and all the finances involved in the endeavor. At this early stage of development, the company can also use supply chain design concepts to define the supply chain infrastructure, the manufacturing facilities, assembly sites, means of transportation and installation schedules to develop the project within the specified time and budget. Overall supply chain design refers to the network configuration that will be used to complete the project.

Supply chain design is also concerned with the capabilities to be developed by the EPC-entrant. For this, the candidate will have to acquire knowledge from the industries that will supply the rest of the subsystems for the OWF. These industries have their own characteristics that differentiate them from the rest of the OEMs. All these new capabilities must be considered before the initial contracts are signed, as very specific knowledge of the industries is required to know what to include in the contract, its provisions, and so on.

As the supply chain design involves long-term decisions, it is important to decide which suppliers will be selected as strategic partners to integrate them early in the development of the project. To foster supplier integration, the EPC candidate must allow the linking of some of its internal resources and capabilities to those of its strategic suppliers. As a focal company, the systems integrator must create a mutual vision, common goals and strategies to be shared with its strategic partners. The integration of suppliers will require the company and its partners to be willing to share information regarding strategic decisions, capabilities, and processes, as well as the sharing of resources. This process is challenging and will require continuous joint efforts from the members of the alliance.

The utility companies currently handle up to 500 different contracts when building an OWF, but there are many activities that could be grouped into one contract. There are currently companies that are willing to offer the complete package of designing, manufacturing, and installing the foundations and the EPC candidate should look for such partners to provide subsystems. The provision and installation of subsea cables is also possible, as is the provision of the complete offshore substation together with its supporting structure. Other potential services include getting the accommodation vessel and all transfer vessels as one package as well. This will help the EPC candidate to reduce the number of interactions with suppliers to a few strategic tier-1 partners.

As part of this integration, the EPC provider will have to share its technical, financial, and operational knowledge with the chosen strategic suppliers. Sharing of vital information will require the company to have a different strategic mindset in which it has to deal with and integrate with industries other than its own and from a different position. In order to carry out this process, the company should follow a multidisciplinary approach that involves evaluating risks in the flow of materials, information and finances in the supply chain. This requires knowledge of multiple echelons in the network that are also represented by different industrial contexts that are not familiar to the OEM. During this evaluation, the future integrator of systems should rely on the use of supply chain risk management processes and tools.

Another way to mitigate the risk across the supply chain and through the life-cycle of the wind farm is to follow the early supplier involvement approach. This will help the systems integrator to reduce the completion time of the project, as it will help avoid potential mistakes, decrease the risk of deficiencies in the subsystems, and avoid unnecessary allocation of resources to fix these deficiencies. Additionally, the involvement of suppliers will help the EPC firm to get the most out of the supplier's technological capabilities and it fosters the integration of those capabilities into the project's supply chain.

Supplier development is an initiative that the EPC-entrant will undertake with its suppliers of subsystems up to a certain degree, as most of the strategic suppliers are well established and experienced companies in the sector. This initiative is better addressed to the medium and small suppliers that will provide supportive services, as well as those suppliers that have experience in other industries unrelated to the offshore wind power sector with the aim of improving their performance, technology and strategies to fit OWI's needs. Supplier-driven innovation (i.e., "Exploration") as well as the adoption of innovations from suppliers (i.e., "Exploitation"), brings new capabilities and features to the company's extended scope without having to invest in generating these ideas within the company. The OWI has a challenge in this regard since for most potential strategic partners, except the WTG manufacturers, the OWI represents at most 10–15 percent of their revenue, which means supplier interest in investing in innovations in this sector is low. Supplier-driven innovations should still be pursued since the OWI represents an opportunity to acquire new knowledge that can be exploited in the industries where the supplier has a larger presence.

The transformation to a system integrator has its pros and cons. Succinctly stated, the pros are: the potential for cost reduction (through close collaboration with the supply network) and supply chain innovation (due to deeper and effective relationship with suppliers, better alignment of strategic goals, information sharing and knowledge management) and superior responsiveness to a client (via cost reduction and, higher level of customization and innovation). The cons are: complexity and scope of supply chain operations (e.g. size and scope of supply network, global manufacturing footprint), degree of commitment needed to effecting change (e.g. unlearning legacy perspectives) and increased supply chain risk such as: opportunism risk, supply disruption risk, and non-performance risk.

7. Conclusion

This paper sought to address the need for greater utilization of supply chain integration in the OWI, which is currently experiencing industry and market pressures. Governmental subsidies are set to expire, adding a sense of urgency to increase the performance of the sector.

Our objective was to develop a context dependent understanding of how a transformation into a systems integrator can be pursued in the OWI and it is enabled by SCI. We have identified the key aspects of such transformation and how such transformation can be pursued. Through conceptual clustering we have identified *design and manufacturing, sourcing and governance* as three principal factors. Further, we have identified the constituent dimensions of these principal factors in terms of supply chain integration (and management) related processes. The framework presented in this paper and Tables 3-5 together are useful for OEMs in the OWI.

Endnotes

1 ReNews (2015), "Danish minister puts costs ball firmly in industry court", *reNews Live*, 9 March, p. 2.

2 Gerstner Jr, L.V. (2009), "Who says elephants can't dance?, Zondervan.

3 Berends, K. (2007), "Engineering and construction projects for oil and gas processing facilities: Contracting, uncertainty and the economics of information", *Energy Policy*, Vol. 35 No. 8, pp. 4260–4270.

4 Tang, C.S. and Zimmerman, J.D. (2009), "Development and supply chain risks: The Boeing 787 case", *Supply Chain Forum: An International Journal*, Vol. 10 No. 2, pp. 74–86.

5.
Innovation fostering practice

This section contains articles that discuss innovation-fostering practices and their role in enabling supply chain innovation in the offshore wind industry (OWI). Achieving superior innovation performance requires more than investments in research and development (R&D). Fundamentally, innovation is enabled by increasing a firm's absorptive capacity through knowledge acquisition, retention, dissemination, and knowledge exploitation. Thus, knowledge creation and use lie at the heart of innovation success. Increasingly, firms have recognized the importance of leveraging knowledge residing in the supply network and suppliers' innovative capabilities as part of their innovation strategies. Pursuing such an open innovation strategy, however, requires carefully constructed internal and external strategies. Internally, firms need to invest in R&D, practice effective knowledge management to capitalize on codified and tacit knowledge, adopt flexible approaches to knowledge exploitation, and foster an innovation culture that encourages creativity and risk taking. Externally, firms must engage with the innovation ecosystem embedded in the supply network, establish multiple pathways for exchange of knowledge and innovation ideas, develop deep supplier relationships, and adopt governance practices that emphasize ambidexterity – flexibility and control over innovation efforts. Collectively, these initiatives are referred to as innovation-fostering practices (IFPs).

The first article in this section addresses fostering innovation in offshore wind power (OWP) projects. It delineates the unique considerations that characterize complex wind power projects. Much has been written in manufacturing contexts regarding IFPs. These practices, despite their value in promoting innovation, cannot be transferred to the OWI without recognizing the contextual uniqueness of OWP. A contextually anchored framework with practical value is presented. The second article addresses the quintessential question: whether supply chain innovation leads to tangible benefits. Based on empirical analysis of data, this article demonstrates that supply chain innovation does pay off in terms of economic and innovation performance. The third article introduces the important role governance plays in the OWI context. It argues that relational governance must be practiced along with contractual governance, which currently dominates buyer–supplier relationships in the OWI. Transitioning to relational governance that recognizes and exploits the unique aspects of OWP requires organizational changes (decision making, innovation practices, etc.) as well as interorganizational changes in information flows and knowledge exchange.

Collectively, the three articles in this section present useful ideas concerning IFPs of potential value to OWI firms.

Fostering supply chain innovation in offshore wind power (OWP) projects: Context and a framework[1]

Ram Narasimhan
Emeritus of Michigan State University and the ReCoE project

Lone Kavin

Idea in Brief
This paper presents some ideas for fostering supply chain innovation in offshore wind power projects. A set of innovation fostering practices are discussed, which have proven useful in manufacturing contexts. Specifically, the paper suggests:

- *That innovation is driven by three sets of business processes - Project Development and Management (PDM), Supplier Relationships Management (SRM) and Supply Chain Transactions Management (SCTM),*

- *That contextual differences influence the efficacy of these innovation fostering practices, and*

- *Practical principles that can be used to promote innovation*

---

[1] This paper is based on Kavin, L. and Narasimhan, R. (2018), "An investigation of contextual influences on innovation in complex projects," *Innovation and Supply Chain Management: Relationship, Collaboration and Strategies,* Springer International Publishing, pp. 51-77.

1. Introduction

This executive brief addresses the question – whether "proven" innovation fostering practices in global manufacturing contexts be effective in large, complex OWP projects. We share with you some ideas that might be worthwhile considering. They are based on a synthesis of ideas from the manufacturing industry and a case study of large Engineering, Procurement and Contracting (EPC) firm (e.g. Ørsted and key suppliers in its network in the OWP industry), done for ReCoE project at SDU. This brief is intended to provoke debate and discussion in the context of OWP. The ideas contained in this brief are suggestive and not to be construed as conclusive.

Fostering innovation within a complex OWP project context where both the design and engineering activities are driven by the EPC firm is different from a manufacturing context in important ways. Instead of coping with demand uncertainty, interaction with new suppliers and commitment to a project become the primary concerns. The innovation process in a complex project context is thus typically initiated based on an "innovation pull" where a client, external to the supply network, initiates a project. The project activities, in general, are concerned with identifying and utilizing knowledge and capabilities of suppliers to fulfill project needs. The supply network structure is often designed by the client and characterized by multiple supply network actors involved at different times. This affects the configuration of the supply network as the EPC firm often relies on competitive bidding to accomplish every new project at the lowest possible cost, resulting in distinctly different supply networks for each project. Thus, a new supply network is set up each time a client initiates a new development project.

In a complex project context, the business processes will focus on achieving efficiency in delivering a customized solution to a specific client based on the requirements. In this context, the value-creating activities are related to performance, flexibility, and innovativeness. This is complicated due to the *temporary* organization created from a project coalition of different firms engaged in the successful completion of delivering the customized solution related to time, financial, and technical goals. *Integrating business processes* and creating an efficient flow of transactions by managing reciprocal interdependencies among suppliers (i.e. multiple nodes in global networks), is therefore an important feature in a complex project context.

We elaborate on the business processes that are central to promoting innovation in OWP projects. We assert that the integration of these practices will be fundamentally useful in promoting supply chain innovation.

Innovation in Offshore Wind Power (OWP) projects is driven by three sets of business processes - *Project Development and Management (PDM), Supplier Relationships Management (SRM) and Supply Chain Transactions Management (SCM)* (see Figure 1).

Figure 1. Three sets of business processes in offshore wind power (OWP)

> **Business Processes**
>
> Project Development and Management (PDM)
> - Contracting and Contract Management (CC)
> - Technology Competence (TC)
> - Interface Management (Risk)(IFM)
> - Innovation Management (INM)
>
> Supplier Relationships Management (SRM)
> - Lead Supplier Management (LSM)
> - Strategic Supplier Engagement (SSE)
> - Commitment and Trust (CT)
> - Supplier Advisory Council (SAC)
> - Knowledge Management (KM)
>
> Supply Chain Transactions Management (SCTM)
> - Integration Management (INTGNM)
> - Information Exchange (IE)

2. Project development and management

Principal components of PDM are Contracting and Contract management, Technology Competence, Interface management (Risk) and Innovation Management. Contracting and Contract Management (CC) are aspects of control in managing supply networks. While contracting affords maximum control over transactional interactions and overall project objectives, it does not necessarily conduce to achieving high levels of innovation. Externally oriented and flexible management practices across the supply network, the different phases of the project and across projects makes it more likely for the EPC firm to capture and use the ideas and technologies affecting innovation. For instance, the EPC firm uses different contract structures to control the diverse sub-deliverables throughout the project. The contracts are however project specific and linked to the time, cost, quality and innovation objectives of a single project, not obligations across projects, which can affect innovation performance. Fostering transfer of best innovation ideas across projects through flexible interactions with supplier network is fruitful. Flexibility in managing interactions in supply network is necessary for fruitful knowledge exchange and deep supplier relationships, which have been shown to underpin effective supply chain innovation. Flexibility is built upon a foundation of integration across planning, procurement, sourcing, and logistics in terms of strategy, process, technology and metrics. The underlying principle that emerged during our ReCoE investigation with respect to CC was that *control and flexibility are complementary*.

Technology Competence (TC) is a requisite for an EPC firm to promote and exploit innovation in its supply network. TC is acquired through knowledge exchange, knowledge acquisition and creation of knowledge cells established through network interactions. To capture, share and use knowledge from suppliers in the innovation process, the EPC should interact dynamically with the industry and external sources of knowledge (e.g. universities, consultants, professional associations and consortia) domestically and internationally, to acquire tacit and explicit knowledge.

Most innovation projects within supplier firms are triggered by former projects or acquisition of new capabilities. Each supplier tries to identify and codify their existing knowledge and use their data and information in operationally useful ways. However, they do not share their codified knowledge; only relational knowledge is shared if different suppliers collaborate on several projects.

Knowledge on each OWP project is "stored" at the separate suppliers. Due to different project managers on each project and complex retrieving systems, data and new knowledge are seldom used in new projects or across the supply network. To counter this tendency, the EPC firm, as part of the tender, can require multiple technological solutions along with a price for each of the solutions to be delivered, utilizing the so called "portfolio approach". One informant at an EPC firm in the ReCoE project stated: *"to promote innovation, we require the bidders to submit at least three different ways of solving their part of the final solution … so that in reality it becomes a portfolio of offers from each supplier"*.

By encouraging suppliers to use a "probe and learn" strategy (i.e., knowledge acquisition through "innovation experimentation"), the EPC firm could promote network-based learning by extending learning across the suppliers in the network. To achieve this, the EPC firm must facilitate collaboration among key suppliers. This approach is particularly useful in complex project contexts where innovation is discontinuous when viewed across various projects. The "probe and learn" strategy differs from the typical approach in manufacturing where innovation is often pursued with a few stable partners. However, in a complex project context, stable relationships with suppliers might not exist. Knowledge Management practices must enable technological change through efficient information flows. This is also necessitated by the length of the project, complexity and the uncertainty related to the innovation outcome. In contrast to the repetitive manufacturing context, the *"uncertainties of the market are not important"* in the project context as innovation needs are defined by the requirements of the client. The underlying principle is that TC requires purposive management action to promote and facilitate knowledge flows across the network to foster a high degree of <u>network-based learning</u>.

Interface Management (IFM) addresses the manner, means and methods of interacting and managing network exchanges. IFM must recognize the contribution of supplier collaborations and promote exchange of innovative ideas. Such ideas can be exchanged routinely or ad hoc in a formal or informal manner, in innovation incubation meetings scheduled for that purpose or continually through web portals and social networking. The ReCoE project investigation indicated that it is important to *create a platform for idea exchange through multiple pathways*. An idea platform can enable increased velocity of information flow across the supply network and promote "end-to-end transparency" in supply networks. To be effective, such idea platforms must be founded on trust and commitment among exchange partners in the supply network.

Our investigations reveal that Innovation Management (INM) in OWP context should utilize *closed* (emphasizing control and internal value appropriation) and *open* (emphasizing flexibility and opportunistic utilization of external, heterogeneous knowledge) innovation approaches. The responsibility to utilize such combined approaches must be fostered in the network. This has been referred to as ambidexterity in pursuing innovation. As one executive put it "…innovation by all, all the time in all aspects (of business)". In multi-tier supply networks, the EPC firm should anchor this effort to *promote ambidexterity in innovation*.

3. Supplier relationship management (SRM)

Principal components of supplier relationship management are: lead supplier management (LSM), strategic supplier engagement (SSE), commitment and trust, supplier advisory council (SAC) and knowledge management (KM). Lead supplier management entails a partnering relationship with first-tier suppliers to foster innovation and structuring responsibilities for control and coordination. As OWP industry matures, the depth and breadth of supply networks can be expected to shrink aided by consolidation among the network actors, increased modularization enabled by innovation and a move to a business model that emphasizes system integration. Partnerships with lead suppliers can be the trigger and coalescing point for network-based innovation.

Strategic supplier engagement refers to engaging suppliers early in innovation efforts and in project coordination in OWP networks. Value of such engagement has been proven in pharmaceutical, consumer products and manufacturing industries. Can it be equally beneficial in OWP contexts? It can be, if supplier segmentation is followed by engagement with strategic suppliers with high innovation capabilities. "Strategic suppliers" in the OWP context needs to be understood as those suppliers that can contribute to cost reduction through innovation from a lifecycle perspective of an OWP project. The manner, timing and extent of such engagement should be clearly identified early in OWP projects. Building *commitment and trust* is relatively more difficult in OWP context. The case study done as part of the ReCoE project suggests that fostering innovation and network-based learning through collaboration and knowledge exchange can be incentives where incentives based on volume are absent, leading to commitment and trust. Commitment and trust development should underpin relationship management across the network. Supplier Advisory Council and Knowledge Management are practices that have proved effective in manufacturing contexts and they can be helpful to OWP firms in building trust and commitment.

4. Supply chain (transactions) management

Two practices within Supply Chain Management (SCM) merit special attention – integration management and information exchange. Integration of lifecycle perspectives in the design, construction and operation of OWP should be actively pursued to promote innovation. This is aided by frequent and effective information exchange and involvement of key actors in each phase, during the project development phase.

Integration management has to do with managing network interactions and transactions connected with the project. Intensity of network interactions is greater in manufacturing due to previous experiences and interactions with a stable set of suppliers and partnering relationships. In contrast, the intensity of interactions with specific suppliers in an OWP project environment is likely to be lower. Each project's unique requirements would have a bearing on the supply network involved in it. During the ReCoE project, the CEO of an assembly and installation firm (a sub-supplier in the OWP network) observed that intensity of interactions might be considerably lower in OWP networks since they are governed primarily by contractual agreements. Contractual governance should be complemented by relational governance aimed at building commitment, trust and transparency.

The *heterogeneity* of information, motivation and resources is higher in an OWP project network, where the suppliers belong to different industries with diverse knowledge and capabilities. Therefore, the EPC-firm cannot rely on past interactions as do focal firms in manufacturing networks but must promote purposive networking to a greater degree in each complex project, taking into consideration the unique project requirements and different set of network actors. The ReCoE data suggest that knowledge gained through networking can, however, improves learning and innovation performance in both contexts. The case study data suggest that the EPC-firm in OWP projects engages in networking activities in different networks supporting turbine manufacturing, electrical infrastructure, foundations and power transmission. In contrast, in manufacturing the focal firm typically interacts with tier 1 suppliers only who, in turn, manage sub-suppliers and lower tier suppliers. The objectives of the EPC firm are to utilize both explicit and tacit knowledge within not only its own network or industry, but also in *peripheral or complementary industries* to effectively manage interactions and transactions. Effective information exchange is key to integration management. Integration should encompass project goals and objectives, development of compatible processes, a common platform to exchange information and ideas, common applications and data analytics, incentives for innovating and multiple pathways for problem resolution.

5. Putting it all together

These practices deduced from the investigation done for the *ReCoE* project are antecedents for pursuing the twin aspects of "exploitation" and "exploration" of innovation. Exploitation is generally seen as utilizing internal knowledge and a firm's absorptive capacity. Exploration, in contrast, involves search for new knowledge. Often, this search for new knowledge involves the supply network. Our investigation included case studies, literature review, interactions with practitioners and, qualitative and quantitative data analysis. Pursuing exploration and exploitation concurrently has been referred to as "ambidexterity". Ambidextrous firms have been shown to have superior innovation performance. Research done in the ReCoE project also shows that *supply network structure* and *innovation culture* play a key role in pursuing ambidexterity for superior innovation performance.[1 2 3]

Supply network structure encompasses the type of network that is designed (centrally controlled by the EPC firm, Shared power and responsibility among supplier partners, connectivity among supply network actors etc.), type, mode and frequency of information exchange, and governance (contractual, relational or both governance modes). Networking, in projects requires more extensive efforts to select and integrate suppliers with different knowledge sets and is done at the start of each project. The *heterogeneity* of information, motivation and resources is higher in a project network, where the suppliers belong to different industries with diverse knowledge and capabilities. Therefore, the EPC-firm cannot rely on past interactions as do focal firms in manufacturing networks but must promote purposive networking to a greater degree in each complex project, taking into consideration the unique project requirements and different set of network actors. This is also necessitated by lower network intensity and lower level of trust among suppliers due to the absence of past interactions. The ReCoE data suggest that knowledge gained through networking can, however, improve learning and innovation performance in OWP contexts.

The objectives of the EPC firm should be to utilize both explicit and tacit knowledge within not only its own network or industry, but also in *peripheral or complementary industries*. During the ReCoE project investigations, the CEO of an electrical infrastructure firm (a sub-supplier in the network) observed: *"…Danish Research Consortium for wind power was created, with representatives from major universities, industrial companies, and even small industries along with us…,"* which underscores the need for integrating different industrial and academic networks. Networking across industries is likely to be more due to the high complexity of the integrated solution sought in a complex project context such as the design, installation, operation and maintenance of an off-shore wind park.

Promoting a strong innovation culture is an enabler of ambidexterity and hence superior innovation performance. Due to the need for *system-wide integration* of innovations in projects, there is a greater need to integrate the knowledge and technical skills of the sub-suppliers and to *foster collaboration among diverse suppliers* – large versus small, domestic versus international, same versus different industry and different levels of knowledge asymmetry. This implies that primarily, it is the EPC firm that is responsible for promoting collaboration across the supply network and in multiple tiers of the supply network. Such collaboration is fundamental to fostering an innovation culture. Therefore, the organizational structure in OWP projects must be able to cope with high level of uncertainty induced by information asymmetry associated with the different technologies and the constraint of being "locked-in" by decisions taken in earlier phases of the project, without stifling creativity.

In a complex project context, it is necessary to occasionally change the organizational structure to respond to the changing and uncertain nature of the project. For example, the CEO of assembly and installation firm told us that this was the case with the Anholt site where it was not possible to fasten anything to the sea bed. To install the turbines and the electrical infrastructure, it was necessary to use the knowledge and experiences within the network based on ad hoc teams and external support functions illustrating adaptations and fluidity of organizational structures. Absorptive capacity pertaining to organizational structures must be higher in a complex project context to recognize and react to contingencies and exploit new information by internalizing and synthesizing it with knowledge resting in the network. Thus, organizational structure must be fluid to adapt to these varied requirements without adversely impacting the innovation outcome; the degree of adaptation required in terms of organizational structures is much lower in a manufacturing context due to the relative stability of technologies, relationships and the supply network. Innovation culture is promoted by increasing absorptive capacity in the network, promoting network-based learning, encouraging risk taking, increasing collaboration, fostering commitment and trust, and setting up incentives.

Innovation culture and supply chain structure interact to create an environment in which ambidexterity can be successfully pursued for superior innovation performance.

These principal findings from the ReCoE project are encapsulated in the conceptual framework shown in Figure 2. The framework can be useful for guiding thinking and executive action in practice.

Figure 2. Findings from the ReCoE project

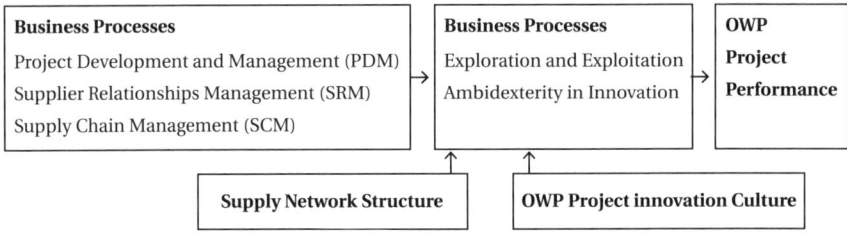

6. Conclusion

This executive brief has discussed a few practical ideas for promoting supply chain innovation in OWP projects. OWP projects are unique due to their complexity and unique characteristics. In ReCoE project, we sought to understand to what degree principles from the manufacturing sector might or might not translate to the OWP context. Our findings suggest that the practices outlined in this executive brief would be useful in promoting innovation. Practical lessons/principles that emerge from our discussions are:

- Recognize *Control and flexibility* are complementary
- Foster a high degree of *network-based learning*
- Create a platform for *idea exchange*
- Promote *ambidexterity* in innovation
- Implement *strategic supplier engagement*
- Develop *Integration across the network*
- Promote *innovation culture*

The conceptual framework developed in this brief and these principles can be useful for promoting supply chain innovation in complex OWP projects.

Endnotes

1 Kavin, L. and Narasimhan, R. (2018), "An investigation of contextual influences on innovation in complex projects", In: Moreira, A.C., Ferreira, L.M.D.F. and Zimmermann, R.A. (Eds.). (2018), *Innovation and Supply Chain Management*, Cham, Switzerland, Springer, pp. 51-77.

2 Kavin, L. and Narasimhan, R. (2017), "An investigation of innovation: The role of clock speed," *Supply Chain Forum: An International Journal*, Vol. 18 No. 3, pp. 189-200.

3 Stentoft, J. and Rajkumar, C. (2018), "Does supply chain innovation pay off?", In: Moreira, A.C., Ferreira, L.M.D.F. and Zimmermann, R.A. (Eds.). (2018), *Innovation and Supply Chain Management*, Cham, Switzerland, Springer, pp. 237-256.

Supply chain innovation practices optimize market and operational performance[1]

Jan Stentoft
Department of Entrepreneurship and Relationship Management
University of Southern Denmark

Christopher Rajkumar
Department of Entrepreneurship and Relationship Management
University of Southern Denmark

Idea in Brief
In this paper, we focus on the link between supply chain innovation (SCI) and market and operational performance. SCI is unfolded through the components of business processes, network structure, and technology. We discuss this by addressing

- *SCI practices;*

- *Market and operational performance; and*

- *Do SCI practices pay off?*

We discuss SCI practices' payoff in terms of improved market and operational performance.

---

[1] This article is based on Stentoft, J. and Rajkumar, C. (2018), "Does supply chain innovation pay off?", In: Moreira, A.C., Ferreira, L.M.D.F. and Zimmermann, R.A. (Eds.). (2018), *Innovation and Supply Chain Management*, Cham, Switzerland, Springer, pp. 237-256.

1. Introduction

In today's dynamic market settings, industries are required to meet necessities such as faster time to market of new products and services, consistency in deliveries, and cost reduction to remain competitive. Competitiveness is measured through various parameters related to products, processes, services, quality, time, and delivery performance. Accordingly, the supply chain is considered a major source for achieving competitive advantage. There are various reasons to explore the supply chain as an innovation object with regard to both (1) initiatives that could improve the overall turnover and (2) initiatives that could improve the bottom line in terms of costs reductions. The business environment today has acquired increased volatility, uncertainty, complexity, and ambiguity (VUCA) and demands a dynamic focus on supply chain designs and redesigns, for which reason supply chain innovation (SCI) practices are desired. Moreover, companies' product as well as service innovations necessitate the practice of SCI. Firms are also aware of the need for SCI to maintain and/or further develop competitiveness.

SCI undoubtedly has become the most essential feature for any firm to survive in today's dynamic and competitive marketplace. Innovation processes are vital both from a single-firm perspective and from a network perspective with a focus on shared processes. The area of supply chain, in general, covers high-cost impact in many firms and includes much complexity regarding the reason for a continued need to innovate to remain competitive. Firms still have not much explored the role of SCI in developing overall firm performance in terms of both market and operational performance. SCI helps the firms sustain their position in their market by providing innovative, next-generation products, processes, and services. Therefore, this can support firms in sustaining their performance at an optimum level. SCI suggests that firms organize the three major components—business process innovation, network structure innovation, and technology innovation—to achieve a competitive edge and sustain superior performance by satisfying the needs of customers and suppliers. Furthermore, SCI can be considered as an important capability that helps firms in sustain their overall performance in terms of market and operational performance.

This paper recommends SCI as an innovative capability and aims to advance the understanding of SCI practices through exploring how SCI, together with the three components of business processes, network structure, and technology, pays off in terms of market and operational performance. This paper is built on data gathered through a questionnaire-survey that was distributed among Danish manufacturing firms with at least 50 employees in autumn 2016. The survey questionnaire was developed to test how different aspects of SCI affect different performance outcomes. A gross of 1,580 firms was selected, and an email with a link to the electronic questionnaire was sent to all participating firms. This process finally resulted in 187 firms who provided valid responses.

2. Supply chain innovation practices

SCI is considered as "a change (incremental or radical) within a supply chain network, supply chain technology, or supply chain process (or a combination of these) that can take place in a company function, within a company, in an industry or in a supply chain to enhance new value creation for the stakeholder."[1] It is a known fact that SCI has become the most crucial aspect for any firm to survive in today's dynamic and competitive marketplace. It can be believed that firms are knowledgeable about the necessity to progress supply chain strategies, to encourage supply chain transformations through the utility of SCI practices, and to make it a reality for improvement projects to challenge scarce resources in busy daily operations. For these reasons, SCI practices should be observed as an innovative capability, as it helps in increasing the supply chain knowledge pool and achieving a competitive advantage. SCI embeds innovation, business models, and supply chain management (SCM) practices. SCI can be stimulated through firms' continuous dynamic collaboration as well as communication within their business environments.

As mentioned, SCI embraces three essential components: supply chain business processes, supply chain network structure, and supply chain technologies.[1] Supply chain business processes integrate activities that create a distinct value to the customers (output in terms of products, processes, and services). To put into practice effective business and interfirm relations, it is important to implement customer-oriented business processes within firms and among supply chain partners. Supply chain business processes include eight processes: customer relationship management, supplier relationship management, customer service management, demand management, order fulfillment, manufacturing flow management, product development and commercialization, and returns management. Supply chain network structure incorporates supply chain partners, a variety of process networks, and structural dimensions. The structural aspect manages both horizontal and vertical structure besides the horizontal position of the firm. Supply chain process networks concentrate on different degrees of resources engaged for integrating and managing processes among supply chain partners. Supply chain network structure could be acknowledged through effective networks that entail knowledge resources as well as core competences to progress the ability of the firm to sustain a long-term relationship with supply chain partners and create new value. Supply chain network structure includes eight network structures: internal functions, customers, suppliers, third-party providers (e.g., logistics providers), competitors, consultants, universities, and public agencies. Supply chain technologies are possibly practiced separately or together with other technologies or with the other components, like business processes and network structure, to realize SCI. This supply chain technology, particularly, includes not only relevant technology but also innovative use of the technology within the supply chain context. Through supply chain technology, firms can actively involve their supply chain partners (e.g., customers, suppliers, etc.) and offer increased product variety. Supply chain technologies include nine technologies: planning and execution systems, identification systems, communication systems, analytics technology, electronic marketplaces, advanced manufacturing technologies, advanced materials, big data, and drones. Figure 1 presents the overall framework of SCI practices.

SCI typically can be stimulated through firms' active and continued collaboration with their business/market environments. The most common drivers triggering SCI may be extended lead times, increased supply chain costs, and reduced service level. On the contrary, SCI particularly formulates the firm's value proposition to (1) recognize new market segments and (2) review the design of the value chain to attain an advantage over competitors. Acknowledging the necessity of adapting to changes in the dynamic market environment then makes possible a process of evaluating current practices as well as suggesting innovative/new solutions that enhance the overall performance of the supply chain. Subsequently, the accepted innovative/new solutions need to be implemented, which in turn will further identify the need for improvements. Defining the SCI and designing framework for SCI is realized to be a new value creation for the customer.

Figure 1. SCI Framework

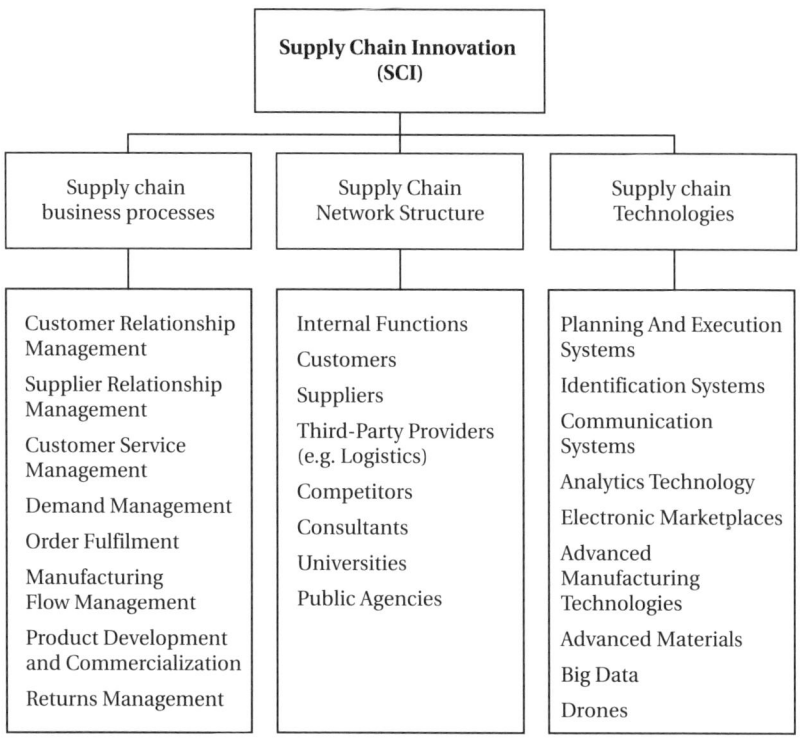

3. Performance—market and operational

In today's dynamic market environment, SCI, along with other practices, manages the firms in effectively sustaining their competitive position and share. This in turn helps sustain the firm's overall performance at an optimal level. Firm performance describes the practice of evaluating the firm's competence and effectiveness, and it is crucial for effective firm management. Firm performance has, in literature, been used in several ways. However, this paper considers two categories—market-based and operational-based performances—and proposes that SCI, which includes business process, network structure, and technology, makes possible superior market-based and operational firm performance.

Market performance measures increase firms' capability to evaluate the dynamic condition of the market and to precisely forecast the benefits along with performance. It can be argued that market performance results in superior customer value and profits. Firms should evaluate their market-based capabilities like customer-driven development, cross-functional integration, customer value, customer responsiveness, information sharing, and supply chain leadership. Market-based performance measures are not subjective to firm-specific characteristics; in lieu, they are more about external-oriented characteristics. Market-based performance includes market goals like meeting customer needs together with market share, competitive advantage, customer loyalty, brand equity, etc.

Operational performance depends on the activities that promote consistency, responsiveness, productivity, lower costs, and efficiency. Operational-oriented performance measures disclose internal-oriented attributes and assist the supply chain in continuously succeeding in today's dynamic markets. Operational performance can be seen as service-level abilities that lead to supply chain quality, supply chain efficiency, supply chain productivity, supply chain costs, and supply chain reliability. Operational performance influences supply chain production planning and long-term firm perspectives. Furthermore, high operational performance can be captured through networking with suppliers and customers. Operational-based performance is associated with operational efficiency, process reliability, responsiveness, agility, costs, capacity utilization, etc.

4. Implications—do these SCI practices pay off?

Based on this paper, SCI practices in many ways improve both market and operational performance. In view of the components of SCI for improving performance, (1) market-based performance needs networking with third-party logistics, consultants, universities, and electronic marketplace technology; and (2) operational-based performance needs networking with competitors, consultants, universities, and electronic marketplace technology.

That is to say, SCI does pay off; however, on the basis of this paper, more focus is on operational performance than on market performance. SCM is rather customer-driven, supply-driven, and market-driven; therefore, it is surprising to observe less importance placed on market performance. This paper recommends that firms start to focus impartially on both operational and market performance. Furthermore, this paper argues that market-oriented firms will experience increased customer focus, which in turn helps in customer satisfaction and synchronized marketing to advance the competitiveness and market share as well as profit orientation. Firms should try to prioritize market-based performance, as it increases their existing market-oriented capabilities. Most notably, it is believed that market-oriented performance assists firms in modifying their firm and network capabilities on the basis of their opportunities for future firm performance. In contrast, on the basis of this paper, firms are continuing their emphasis on operational performance; however, there is still potential for further improvement.

Regarding the business process component, among others, supplier relationship management influences only operational performance and not market performance. Most of the earlier surveys and research have focused more on operational performance measures than on market performance measures. This could be the reason for less implication with respect to business process and market performance. Another explanation for this could be that it might be easier to relate and isolate an innovation effort of a specific business process toward operational performance than toward market performance. Improved market performance might also be caused by factors other than business process innovations. In contrast, operational performance improvements might have a stronger and more direct relation to business process innovations. Nevertheless, this paper argues that firms should not only consider operational performance as long-term; instead, they should perceive both market performance and operational performance as long-term objectives.

In regard to the network structure component, among others, network with third-party provider logistics, network with consultants, and network with universities influence market performance; and, for example, network with competitors, network with consultants, and network with universities influence operational performance. Therefore, in general, the network structure component influences both market and operational performance. This is interesting, since an earlier empirical study on this SCI framework[2] found that the network structure component received the lowest mean value of 3.3 (on a 5-point Likert scale) on respondents' perceptions of the component's importance in creating SCIs.[3] The technology component received an average of 3.5, and the business process component received an average of 3.8. The new findings of the survey reported in this paper indicate that firms have become aware of the fact that they are dependent on their network actors' relationships to obtain both market and operational performance improvements.

Finally, the technology component has no influence on market performance, maybe because it is difficult to determine that a specific technology is the reason for improved market share and customer loyalty. Another explanation could be that firms still need to develop the strategic links between technology strategies and market performance. On the contrary, the technology component influences operational performance. Accordingly, it is understood that firms do perceive their technology innovation efforts, and this effort controls their operational performances. For instance, the more reliable the processes, the better the cost performance and improved responsiveness.

Considering the individual components of SCI, this paper conveys that there is more attention given to the network structure component than to business process and technology. SCI should include all three components, and firms should focus on all three components equally to experience SCI. However, at the moment, firms are not focusing much on business process and technology pertaining to market performance. It is great that firms understand the importance of networking with their supply chain partners to innovate and achieve greater performance in terms of market and operational performance. This paper insists firms should now begin to realize the importance of business process and technology as they relate to market performance. This paper claims firms should start focusing equally on all three components of SCI to achieve higher performance in terms of both market and operational performance. To achieve continuous growth in both market and operational performance, firms should establish strong business process practices and employ robust technologies. It is understood that firms are not utilizing the entire available network. Firms again should recognize the value in the supply chain network to experience greater innovation and firm performance. Most importantly, taking all three components of SCI into account, SCI does pay off in terms of market and operational performance; however, the strongest relationship is for operational performance.

5. Conclusion

As measured in this paper, the overall SCI paradigm does pay off in terms of market and operational performance. Operational performance has the most prominent association with SCI, which indicates that firms are aware that they need to innovate with their supply chains to lever their competitive factors. It is motivating to notice that firms' innovation efforts also influence market performance, which indicates that the firms have understood the importance of operating and developing market-oriented supply chains. This paper recommends that firms observe SCI in connection with business process, network structure, and technology innovation to realize superior performance in both market and operational performance. This paper also informs firms that they are not focusing on market performance measures at the moment. Therefore, to achieve long-term objectives, firms should not just pursue SCI and measure operational performance only; instead, they must strategically integrate all the components of SCI and measure both their market and operational performance.

Endnotes

1 Arlbjørn, J.S., de Haas, H. and Munksgaard, K.B. (2011), "Exploring supply chain innovation", *Logistics Research*, Vol. 3 No. 1, pp. 3-18.

2 Arlbjørn, J.S. and Paulraj, A. (2013), "Special topic forum on innovations in business networks from a supply chain perspective: Current status and opportunities for future research", *Journal of Supply Chain Management*, Vol. 49 No. 4, pp. 3-11.

3 Arlbjørn, J.S., Mikkelsen, O.S., Munksgaard, K.B., Schlichter, J. and Paulraj, A. (2013), *Konkurrencekraft gennem Supply Chain Innovation [Competitiveness through Supply Chain Innovation]*, Department of Entrepreneurship and Relationship Management, University of Southern Denmark.

Innovation-processes in green industries: The role of governance

Ram Narasimhan
Emeritus of Michigan State University and the ReCoE project

Idea in Brief
This paper discusses innovation fostering practices in general terms and assesses their efficacy in OWP projects. The unique role played by trust, control and governance in the OWP context are highlighted. Prescriptions are offered for promoting and managing innovation are offered. Specifically,

- *A conceptual model for increasing innovation performance highlighting the role of governance and innovation fostering practices is presented*

- *Innovation fostering practices are influenced by trust, control and governance in OWP context in unique ways*

- *The salient aspects of governance include social control, behavior control, goodwill-based trust and competence-based trust.*

- *Governance in OWP interacts with supply network to increase the absorptive capacity of the lead firm and it increases the efficacy of the innovation fostering practices*

1. Introduction

This paper focuses on how innovation-fostering-practices of firms are influenced by *trust, control and governance* mechanisms in offshore wind power (OWP) industry. OWP context is part of the green industry initiatives of nations. Its importance is expected to grow as nations increasingly pursue green initiatives to combat climate change and reduce dependence on fossil fuels. OWP is characterized by a multi-layer, complex supply network assembled to deliver a specific set of solutions for a focal firm. The entire network is characterized by firms that have varying degrees of innovation capability and drawn from diverse industries. The Engineering Procurement and Contracting (EPC) firm such as Ørsted acts as the focal firm in charge of constructing the supply network, contracting, governance and promoting innovation. Although, this context bears similarities to a repetitive manufacturing context, the project orientation of offshore wind farms, legacy systems and management practices, and unique characteristics of the supply network render transferring best practices from the manufacturing context problematic. This paper discusses innovation fostering practices in OWP projects. The role played by trust, control and governance in the OWP context is highlighted. Prescriptions are offered for promoting and managing innovation.

The unique aspects of OWP context pertain to open versus closed-innovation, network-ties, controlled versus flexible approaches, formal versus informal knowledge-management systems, external knowledge integration and absorptive capacity.

2. Innovation-fostering-practices

"Innovation-fostering-practices" can be defined as practices that improve performance of the *innovation-processes* of a focal firm. They consist of many complementary and related concepts concerned with the supply-network of firms involved in innovation. They encompass network-connections, organizational-learning, and flexible control mechanisms to integrate the efforts of suppliers with different responsibilities, capabilities and knowledge bases. Each link in the supply network transmits new and different information, which means superior knowledge-assimilation is the basis for improving innovative performance.

When engaging the supply-network in the innovative process, *absorptive capacity* of the focal firm and other firms in the network is an important factor affecting the innovation-outcome. Absorptive capacity is the ability of a firm to recognize, assimilate and apply new external knowledge to achieve innovation objectives. This capability enables the EPC firm to make better use of external resources and to identify the best partners across the supply-network. The EPC firm in the OWP context must rely on its absorptive capacity in configuring the supply network, aligning the objectives of network partners, integrating knowledge flows and in promoting network-based learning for innovation. Additionally, innovation-fostering-practices employed by the EPC firm must embrace a definition of supply-network strategy that includes innovation.

Innovation fostering practices fall into three categories:[1]

- Management Practices
- Knowledge Management Practices
- Organizational Practices

Management practices pertain to setting an innovation agenda, implementing an innovation protocol, opportunistic surveillance of the supply network for innovation and stressing innovation in supplier management. It also includes configuring the supply network (supply network design, integration of information flows among network partners, governance practices etc.). Knowledge management practices relate to seeking external knowledge, knowledge acquisition, retention and dissemination, and knowledge exploitation. Organizational practices include creating an innovation culture, encouraging risk taking in knowledge exploitation, and organizational integration for creating multiple pathways for new knowledge to flow through the supply network.

For firms to capture, develop, share and effectively use knowledge from suppliers at any point in the innovation-life-cycle, *knowledge-management-practices* are essential.[2] Identification and codification of existing (tacit or explicit) knowledge forms the basis for using data and information, contextualizing it and giving it meaning, which is important to make it relevant and operationally useful. Another important aspect of knowledge-management-practices is how knowledge is stored and retrieved and how it is shared and distributed within and across the supply-network.

In addition to knowledge-management-practices, *organizational practices* are important to improve supply-network enabled innovation. Networking is a common way of exchanging information and material-resources to get easy access to sources useful in implementing new ideas. Additionally, the infrastructural practices of training employees in the importance of innovation, how innovation works in the firm and basic innovation-skills and use of innovation-tools are essential. Further, organizational-structures should incentivize and promote innovation as they impact how firms learn and integrate knowledge both internally and with customers or suppliers. The organizational-fostering-practices at the EPC firm should focus on changing the culture of how to do business in the company. Data collected as part of the ReCoE project suggests that the EPC company should create a common understanding of innovation – the goals, tools and processes. The firm should support continuous learning, the power of dreaming, and recognize that people are essentially creative and have the talents, abilities, and the need to create and innovate. Finally, to increase innovative performance, organizational-structures must facilitate channels of communication for innovative ideas to flow through the supply network and must create the capacity to integrate them.

Management practices should develop a creative climate. Management practices should emphasize training to encourage risk-taking and to promote employee-engagement with both internal colleagues and suppliers on innovation. As the traditional culture characterized by internal R&D and protection of intellectual-property still dominates, middle-management is generally reluctant to take risks. Top-management must implement and encourage risk-taking as part of creating an innovation culture. Incentives should be put in place to promote innovative thinking.

The innovation-fostering-practices at the EPC firm should include *networking* and *open innovation*-practices with suppliers, consultants, universities and research institutions. The EPC firm should acquire external knowledge through research seminars, industry fairs and conferences and interactions with potential new suppliers or sub-suppliers. To facilitate the adoption of open innovation, the EPC firm should pursue employee empowerment and creating an innovation culture. To accomplish these, a major manufacturing firm transformed every aspect of its business to promote continuous innovation by employing a "rational framework" and emotional drivers to manage the innovation-process. The "rational framework" is dynamic that includes strategic-architecture, management-systems, "the idea-pipeline" (I-pipe), the innovators and innovation-mentors ("I-mentors"), execution and results. The company sees its strategic-architecture as the road-map of its innovation-effort. The EPC firm in OWP can adapt some of these ideas to pursue innovation in its context.

3. Role of governance

Governance in the OWP context must recognize the *innovation ecosystem*. The innovation ecosystem is essentially a network of alliances among the firms that comprise the supply network.[3] These ecosystems emphasize extensive collaborations among a widely "diverse partners who combine their individual technologies and/or services into innovations". The principal role of the EPC firm is to *align the goals* of the supply network firms within the innovation ecosystem. Governance in this context should recognize that innovation ecosystems are not just a compendium of several bilateral agreements. Governance processes must promote ability of the focal entity to manage the supply network and its ability to influence and control the ecosystem.

Governance practices influence how the EPC firm interacts with its supply network to manage information and knowledge flows. Configuration of the supply network by the EPC firm must take into account governance mechanisms, the need for control and flexibility, and alignment of innovation goals through trust and commitment. "Alignment stimulators" such as trust and commitment are influenced by governance mechanisms. See Table 1 for alignment stimulators and practices that underpin the "governance types".

Table 1. Alignment stimulators and practices

Governance type	Practices
Output control	Alliance Contract
Social Control	Innovation leadership Partner expectation management Trust development
Behavioral control	Alliance Norms Open discussion and Communication Commitment Trust development Leadership
Goodwill trust	Commitment Leadership Internal organizational support Open communication
Competence trust	Sourcing decision Innovation department Resource allocation; Reputation of supplier

Source: Adapted from Cobben and Roijakkers (2018)[3]

Control is an essential aspect of governance. Control has two aspects – "external (output) measure-based control and internal value-based control."[4] The former relates to the establishment of formal rules, procedures and policies to measure and reward desirable outcomes. The latter refers to the establishment of organizational norms and values, behavior and culture that lead to higher levels of collaboration and desirable outcomes. Accordingly, in the conceptual model, governance is shown to influence the supply network and innovation fostering practices.

In contrast to rule (contract) based control, establishment of *trust* is considered a flexible form of control and governance. "When trust-based governance mechanisms are used, every partner is allowed to join, leadership is decentralized, and cultural differences are valued leading to more long-term relations."[5]

Trust has two aspects – competence-based trust and behavior-based trust. The former relates to the ability of the alliance partner to deliver performance according to specifications in the contract. The latter from of trust cannot be based on contract specifications. As shown in Table 1, it is based on leadership, organizational processes, commitment and communication. It should be noted that these aspects of governance complement the innovation fostering practices to promote superior innovation performance.

4. Conceptual model

The conceptual-model shown in Figure 1 depicts the essential role of governance in fostering innovation. This model was developed based on case studies conducted in the manufacturing sector as part of the ReCoE project.

The model depicts the core relationship between new knowledge and innovation performance. New knowledge is acquired through the supply network and integrating external knowledge with the absorptive capacity of the firm. Innovation fostering practices moderate the influence of new knowledge on innovation performance. Governance in working with the supply network increases the absorptive capacity of the EPC firm. The innovation fostering practices – management practices, organizational practices and knowledge management practices – are also influenced by governance in OWP context. Innovation fostering practices aided by governance allow the firm to convert new knowledge into innovation performance.

Figure 1. Conceptual model of innovation process in green industries

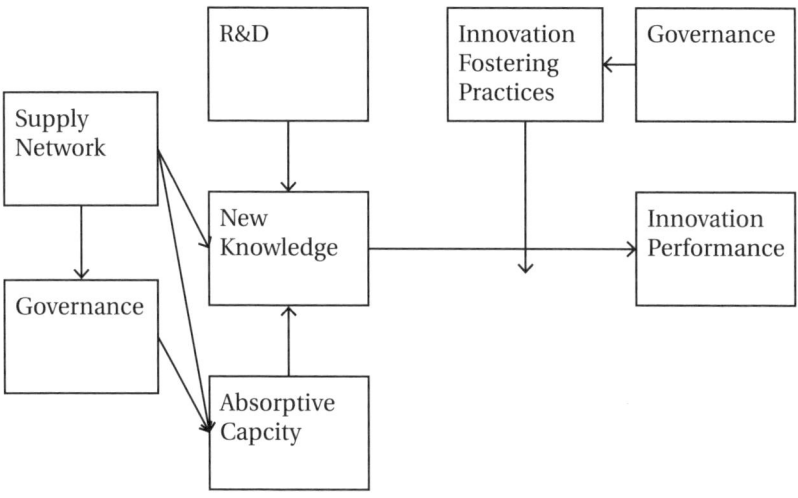

Source: Adapted from Kavin and Narasimhan (2017)[1]

5. Conclusion

From a practical point of view,

- OWP firms must create *new knowledge* through external knowledge integration.

- they should adopt appropriate innovation fostering practices throughout the innovation cycle from idea generation to execution.

- innovation success relates to the firm's ability to integrate complementary knowledge and technology of suppliers into a project, and the firm's degree of openness, which influences management, knowledge-management and organizational fostering-practices.

- the central role of governance in the OWP innovation ecosystem should be recognized.

Aligning the innovation goals across the supply network is essential to achieve supply network enabled innovation. In this regard alignment stimulators relate to EPC leadership, effective communication, trust and commitment development, and establishing alliance norms (e.g., norms of reciprocity, gain sharing etc.).

Endnotes

1 Kavin, L. and Narasimhan, R. (2017), "An investigation of innovation processes: The role of clock speed", *Supply Chain Forum: An International Journal*, Vol. 18 No. 3, pp. 189-200.

2 Narasimhan, R. and Narayanan, S. (2013), "Perspectives on supply network–enabled innovations", *Journal of Supply Chain Management*, Vol. 49 No. 4, pp. 27–42.

3 Cobben, D. and Roijakkers, N. (2018), "The dynamics of trust and control in innovation ecosystems", *International Journal of Innovation*, Vol. 7 No. 1, pp. 1-25.

4 Das, T.K. and Teng, B. (2001), "Trust, control, and risk in strategic alliances: An integrated framework", *Organization Studies*, Vol. 22 No. 2, pp. 251-283.

5 Man, A.d. (2006), "Alliantiebesturing. Samenwerking als precisie-instrument", Koninklijke Van Gorcum BV: Assen.

6.
Supply network strategies

This section of the book documents the research by Project ReCoE into supply networks, including the challenges of how to manage the supplier relationships that make up supply networks and the strategies employed to manage supply networks as a whole. As supply networks are tied together through buyer–supplier relationships, effective relationship management is the first step in developing effective supply networks.

The first chapter in this section deals with the big picture. Thomas Johnsen, Ole Stegmann Mikkelsen, and Chee Yew Wong look into the "Strategies for managing complex supply networks in the offshore wind power industry." Much has been written about different types of interorganizational networks, including supply networks, and researchers tend to describe any network as inherently complex and difficult to manage. However, as executives within the offshore wind power (OWP) sector will testify, OWP supply networks are much more complex and difficult to manage than, for example, those found in the automotive or high-tech sectors. Not only do OWP supply networks concern highly complex product–service systems, but they also involve a long life cycle, from installation and manufacture to operations and maintenance of often remote and inaccessible wind farms. There is a lot more to wind power than the visible part of the systems—i.e., the wind turbines—especially when the turbines rely on building foundations at sea and connecting to power stations and substations. Based on in-depth case studies, our research into OWP supply networks formed the first part of Project ReCoE by creating a general understanding of the nature of OWP supply networks and analyzing what makes them so complex to manage.

The second chapter in this section is by Christopher Rajkumar and Jan Stentoft. They take a closer look at supplier relationship management (SRM), providing insights into the relevance, barriers, and benefits of SRM. Through a survey of Danish companies, they investigate the types of models or methodologies that companies rely on for SRM. This survey goes beyond the OWP industry to take a wider look at SRM across the Danish manufacturing industry. Whereas the survey indicates a general appreciation of the importance of SRM, it also shows that there is a long way to go in many companies before supplier relationships are managed in a structured manner. In sum, there is an exploited value potential in the supplier relationships of many companies both within and outside the Danish OWP industry.

Strategies for managing complex supply networks in the offshore wind power industry[1]

Thomas Johnsen
Audencia Business School

Ole Stegmann Mikkelsen
Department of Entrepreneurship and Relationship Management
University of Southern Denmark

Chee Yew Wong
Leeds University Business School, University of Leeds, UK and the ReCoE project

Idea in Brief
In this chapter, we focus on how offshore wind power developer firms can design different strategies to manage their highly complex supply networks. We do this by discussing:

- *Sources of supply network complexity;*

- *Results from case study analysis; and*

- *Strategies for managing complex supply networks.*

---

1 This chapter is based on Mikkelsen, O.S., Johnsen, T.E. and Wong, C.Y. (2017), "Strategies for managing complex supply networks: Initial case study findings from the offshore wind power industry", *Proceedings of the 26th IPSERA Conference*, 9-12 April, Budapest/Balatonfured, Hungary.

1. Introduction

The purpose of this chapter is to explore the different strategies companies in the offshore wind power (OWP) industry can apply to manage their highly complex supply networks. We report on our case study analysis of OWP supply networks to shed light on sources of complexity in OWP supply networks, and we present two OWP supply network strategies: (1) *control and intervention* and (2) *coordination and delegation*.

2. Supply chain or supply network?

Before we can begin to understand sources of complexity in supply networks, we need to define supply networks and how these are different from supply chains.

The notion of a "supply chain" offers a powerful metaphor to understand the strong interdependencies of supply chain actors. "Supply chain" also implies a simple linear structure from the ultimate raw material extractor to the end customer. This metaphor is easy to understand, but in reality, supply chains are highly complex, and the phrase "supply chain" is an oversimplification. For this reason, supply chains are better understood as networks.

Using the word *network* instead of *chain* is especially relevant in industries producing complex products because a high number of product components dramatically increases the number of suppliers. Industries that are based on so-called complex product-service systems involve technologically complex products as well as a range of different services. Typically, product-service systems have long life cycles that require extensive operations and maintenance services over years or even decades in use. Consider, for example, the ship building, aerospace, oil and gas, and OWP industries. More importantly, a key difference between typical (e.g., fast-moving consumer goods [FMCGs], automotive) supply networks and supply networks in complex product-service systems concerns the nature of focal firms and the different actors involved.

We can draw from an existing definition of supply networks:[1]

> "*A supply network […] includes all companies that take part directly or indirectly in supplying industrial inputs to a focal company with or without that company's knowledge.*"

In contrast, another prominent definition includes not only the upstream (supplier-facing) network but also the downstream (customer-facing) network:[2]

> "Sets of supply chains, describing the flow of goods and services from original sources to end customers".

The logic of defining supply networks from the end customer instead of a focal (or central) actor extends from definitions of supply chains that do exactly the same, emphasizing the ultimate goal of supply chain management: delivery of value to end customers. In practical terms, and within an OWP context, this distinction is less important because the end customer (business customer) is not a retailer but an organization responsible for project management of wind farms or "developers."

3. Supply network complexity

The literature measures supply network complexity as a function of

- The *number of suppliers* in the supply base;

- *Supplier differentiation*: the degree to which suppliers vary in terms of organizational culture, size, location, technology, etc.

Such structural complexity can also be analyzed by distinguishing between horizontal complexity, vertical complexity, and spatial complexity:

- *Horizontal complexity*: the number of different entities in the same level;

- *Vertical complexity*: the number of levels in the system;

- *Spatial complexity*: the number of operating locations.

Complexity is also affected by the number of *interfaces* among actors. Companies across many industries have deliberately sought to reduce complexity arising from the number of interfaces through tiering, ultimately by designing modular products that enable modular supply networks.

Modularization of product design enables modularization of tasks and decreases overall interdependencies among supply network actors. This is widely applied in the PC or automotive industries. By delegating tasks through modularization, companies reduce the number of contact points that need to be managed and thereby reduce the operational "load" borne by the focal company.[3] Supply network complexity is therefore a result of both structural complexity and complexity resulting from the interorganizational relationships within the supply network.

Less is known about how *dynamic* characteristics affect supply network complexity. In industries characterized by long product-service life cycles, supply networks actors usually do not cease their role once the product has been delivered but continue to perform different roles, for example, in ongoing operations and maintenance. Here, we can draw from the field known as *Procuring Complex Performance* (PCP). PCP focuses on the challenges of managing total supply chain operations during the life cycle phases of a major program, including design, building, service support, and disposal.[4] PCP addresses the particular challenges in industrial sectors that face high levels of complexity and focus on securing both products and services over a long period of time. PCPs tend to be capital-intensive public–private collaborations in which there is an increased risk of oligopolistic market conditions and frequent political interference. These factors all add to supply network complexity.

Much of the literature on complex supply networks focuses on the number and diversity of actors and the relationships between these. As shown by PCP, there are other potential sources of complexity in OWP, including *political and regulatory influences* and the often *conflicting goals of stakeholders*. In the following section, we give some insights into our research on OWP supply networks to illustrate the kind of supply network complexity this industry faces and how different focal firms—so-called developers—seek to reduce and manage this complexity.

4. Insights from the OWP Industry

Our study focuses on an industry that is not only rapidly growing but also truly complex: offshore wind power (OWP). The OWP industry is widely regarded as strategically important in many countries for moving away from fossil fuels and toward renewable energy. However, one of the key challenges for the OWP industry is that it is relatively new and immature. OWP supply chains are obviously complex as a result of, for example, the size and diversity of the supply base.[5]

Trying to understand OWP supply chains by relying on existing supply chain management frameworks is problematic because best practices derived from, for example, the FMCGs or automotive industries do not readily apply in OWP. Most importantly, OWP supply chains are not controlled by a single powerful focal company. They are *distributed* and characterized by many actors trying to control them.[6]

Studying OWP supply networks, we can immediately observe several characteristics that make supply networks complex and dynamic. An offshore wind project goes through four distinct phases: project development and concession, installation and commissioning, operations and maintenance, and decommissioning. Typically, actors change from phase to phase. Furthermore, the industry is exposed to changes in political decisions that impact market and industry uncertainty and dynamics.

Political influences are evident, not least through the demand for local content that influences geographical location decisions. The increased size of offshore projects and the fact that projects move further and further offshore and into deeper waters add to the challenges in planning and managing the supply network, particularly during the installation phase. Each OWP project is unique. As one industry participant in our study said, "*Every site is different—tower, foundation etc. … different products and circumstances for every project.*"

In general, the industry suffers from a lack of industry-wide standards, which drives up both complexity and cost. Fast changes in technology add further complexity. As a participant in one of our executive forums said, "*… missing economies of scale in general in the business, because [the high] speed of technology development and high investments and low quantities… CoE [cost of energy] is the target, but technology is moving so fast that it is hard to deal with that.*"

In the following sections, we briefly introduce two case studies to illustrate different strategies that are used to manage these complexities.

4.1 Case study 1: Alpha supply network

Alpha is a major OWP developer operating across many different markets. The many supply network actors it relies on are scattered globally but mainly concentrated in northern Europe. In this case, supply networks are controlled on two fronts: from Alpha and from large wind turbine suppliers. Foundation manufacturers and array cable and installation companies all have less power, as their products or services are more or less standardized, and they are all heavily dependent on Alpha and turbine manufacturers. There have recently been some changes in this dynamic as new wind turbine manufacturers have entered the market, thus giving developer firms more alternatives.

Being a large and financially strong company with long-term internal expertise on offshore wind projects, Alpha can take a large amount of risk. Perceiving itself as excelling in managing complex projects, Alpha manages supply network activities through detailed multicontract management, including contracts directly with selected second-tier suppliers, e.g., by specifying steel manufacturers for foundations, and they produce detailed component specifications for suppliers to follow.

4.2 Case study 2: Beta supply network

Beta is a smaller developer firm. As a recent entrant in the offshore wind industry, Beta has less power within the supply network. Beta faces many of the same complexities and challenges as Alpha. Its supply network is basically the same although operating within a narrower geographical market. Typically, Beta interacts with three or four suppliers in each project that in turn coordinate and control subtier suppliers. Beta is exposed to increased project sizes, but because of its limited financial size, Beta cannot take on the very large projects.

Beta's business model and strategy is based on risk avoidance and management. Projects need to be financed up front with a traditional split of own equity and external funding of 30/70. Beta calculates all risks into projects up front before securing investment. Consequently, suppliers—especially turbine manufacturers—representing approximately 40 percent of CAPEX, must be "bankable," i.e., using proven technology.

Beta has contractual relationships with first-tier suppliers but seldom engages with the second-tier suppliers and beyond. Its strategy to decrease complexity and risk is to use systems-sourcing arrangements, delegating responsibility to tier 1 suppliers for coordination tasks such as installation and detailed planning. For example, the turbine supplier is responsible for installation, including crew and vessels. One manager at Beta stated, "… *we have an opinion about who the [tier 1 suppliers] use as tier 2 suppliers and the level of quality etc., but the supplier the [tier 1 suppliers] choose is secondary. We do not want to take upon us risk by interfering …*"

4.3 Comparisons

Based on the two supply networks researched, we identify a variety of supply network complexity sources related to structural, life cycle, relational, integration, and technology complexity. Table 1 shows the sources of complexity identified.

Table 1. Sources of complexity

Complexity dimension	Source of complexity
Structural	Physical size of wind farms and components Deep water installation Political stakeholder influence—e.g., demand for local content Governmental regulations Diverse suppliers (size and geographical)
Life cycle	Product-service system spanning long life cycle Suppliers and service providers change over life cycle
Relational	Distributed power: not one actor controlling supply network Interconnected supply network actors Customer intervention in supplier choice Modularization and standardization at early state
Integration	Lack of logistics capacity Lack of knowledge sharing
Technology	Fast-changing technology

5. Strategies for managing complex supply networks

Our results illustrate two different ways of managing supply network complexity. The Alpha supply network emphasizes tight control coupled with multitier contracting with suppliers. Alpha uses tight control over its supply network, extending deep into its supply network. We can label this an *interventionist strategy*.[7] Beta, in contrast, manages its supply network through fewer contracts with its tier 1 suppliers, delegating authority to them to manage sub-suppliers. This suggests a cascading, or *delegation strategy*, in which the focal firm takes on a coordination role.

Building on research, we therefore suggest a classification of two different complex supply network strategies in Figure 1.

Figure 1. Strategies for managing complex OWP supply networks

Supply Network Control & Intervention	Dimension	Supply Network Coordination & Delegation
Detailed interface management with tight control	Governance approach	Delegated systems sourcing – modylarity
Intervention beyond 1st tier e.g. for supplier selection	Power use	Delegates responsibility to 1st tier. Engage with only few 1st suppliers
Risk taking approach Interface risk adaption on complex projects.	Risk sharing approach	Risk distribuation approach Rely on supply network partners to carry risks in vturnkey contracts
Project factory approach Seeks optimization of projects	Project portfolio management	opportunistic selective approach. No pipeline —one off tenders
Detailed multi, and multi-level, contracting	Contract management	Few contracts Mainly with 1st tier suppliers

The control and intervention strategy exemplified by Alpha is based on engagement in multisourcing and multitier arrangements. The goal is to govern and control all the interfaces in the project, including technology interfaces, sometimes even employing crews for wind farm installation. The focal (developer) firm specifies lower-tier suppliers and activities through which the focal firm exerts its power throughout the supply network. The focal firm takes upon itself the risk of coordination errors but at the same time aims to reduce cost through a supply network intervention and control strategy, seeking to optimize interfaces to exploit its project management capabilities.

In contrast, a delegated supply network strategy, as exemplified by Beta, relies on systems-sourcing arrangements with a small number of first-tier suppliers. The focal firm assumes a coordination responsibility and empowers and delegates to suppliers, distributing risk further down the chain to first-tier suppliers. This is an attempt to mimic a modularization approach—as operated, for example, in the automotive industry—that aims to decrease the number of interfaces and interdependencies.

In deciding on these two alternative strategies, we urge managers to consider the firm's supply network position, the complementarity of technologies accessible from different supply network actors, and the method with which the focal firm controls the suppliers in the network. These factors will influence a firm's ability to capitalize on innovations through its supply network.[8] Whereas intervention in suppliers' operations is a way to control supply networks and thereby reduce risk, a delegation strategy may be more likely to facilitate technological innovation by empowering suppliers to pursue innovative solutions.

6. Conclusion

This chapter has discussed generic strategies for managing complex supply networks, focusing on the OWP industry. This industry is of strategic importance to many countries that have invested heavily in reducing reliance on fossil-based fuels and shifting toward renewable energy sources. The industry is truly complex not only because of the size of the product-service systems involved, which means large supply bases, but also because of the changing phases that involve development, installation, and operations and maintenance. Supply networks change over the course of these phases, posing different challenges within and across each phase. OWP supply networks are *distributed* because of the number of actors that try to control them. Importantly, complexity is high because of the nature of these actors (e.g., political stakeholders).

The OWP industry has a long way to go before it resembles the modular structure found in, for example, the automotive industry, and the nature of the OWP industry may not easily develop in that direction, as power is more distributed among typical supply network actors and political stakeholders.

Endnotes

1 Choi, T.Y., Dooley, K. and Rungtusanatham, M. (2001), "Supply networks and complex adaptive systems: Control versus emergence," *Journal of Operations Management*, Vol. 19 No. 3, pp. 351-366.

2 Harland, C.M. (1996), "Supply chain management: Relationships, chains and networks", *British Journal of Management*, Vol. 7, pp. 63-80.

3 Choi, T. Y. and Krause, D.R. (2006), "The supply base and its complexity: Implications for transaction costs, risks, responsiveness, and innovation", *Journal of Operations Management*, Vol. 24 No. 5, pp. 637-652.

4 Caldwell, N. and Howard, M. (2011), *Procuring Complex Performance: Studies of Innovation in Product-Service Management*, Taylor & Francis Group, New York.

5 Corbetta, G., Pineda, I. and Moccia, J. (2014), *The European Offshore Wind Industry - Key Trends and Statistics 2013*, EWEA *European Wind Energy* Association.

6 Andersen, P.H. and Drejer, I. (2008), "Systemic innovation in a distributed network: The case of Danish wind turbines", *Strategic Organization*, Vol. 6 No. 1, pp. 13-46.

7 Johnsen, T.E. (2011), "Supply network delegation and intervention strategies during supplier involvement in product development", *International Journal of Operations & Production Management*, Vol. 31 No. 6, pp. 286-708.

8 Narasimhan, R. and Narayanan, S. (2013), "Perspectives on supply network-enabled innovation", *Journal of Supply Chain Management*, Vol. 49 No. 4, pp. 27-42.

Supplier relationship management in the light of competitiveness and hard benefits[1]

Christopher Rajkumar
Department of Entrepreneurship and Relationship Management
University of Southern Denmark

Jan Stentoft
Department of Entrepreneurship and Relationship Management
University of Southern Denmark

Idea in Brief
In this paper, we focus on firms' perception of the understanding, importance, and practice of supplier relationship management (SRM) among firms. We discuss this by addressing:

- *understanding, importance, and practice of SRM among firms;*
- *the perceived relevance and current status of SRM;*
- *whether there is a special model/methodology for SRM;*
- *the degree of ability in measuring hard benefits of SRM efforts; and*
- *the major barriers for working with SRM.*

We discuss SRM as a value-added function.

---

1 This paper is based on Stentoft, J. and Rajkumar, C. (2017), "Supplier relationship management is important for competitiveness but it is difficult to measure its hard benefits," *Dilf Orientering*, Vol. 54 No. 3, pp. 10-17.

1. Introduction

Today, in view of the fact that the complexity of the products, processes, and services together with the demands of the customers have considerably increased, and firms cannot solely perform all activities, firms are therefore increasingly collaborating with external partners as well as actively involving their supply chain partners (for example, suppliers, stakeholders, etc.) to sustain their competitiveness. Moreover, a high percentage of added value is realized outside the buying firm, and the supply chain partners are thus playing a significant role in developing products, processes, and services. This, in turn, conveys that a buying firm will not have substantial growth unless they exercise strong network relationships with their supply chain partners. For this reason, it is crucial that buying firms recognize the right supply chain partners who are competent, innovative, and willing to participate in all their efforts. The recognized supply chain partners, subsequently, should be actively as well as strategically involved in developing new products, processes, and next-generation services. Here, the role of the sourcing function is considered to be important and strategic in nature to envision the firm's overall objectives; to identify, select, involve, and evaluate the supply chain partners; and to help firms together with their supply chain partners in achieving and sustaining their competitiveness. Ultimately, this is a continuous process and requires pertinent management. Supplier relationships need to be continuously managed, monitored, and measured to encourage strategic collaboration and to achieve the needs of the buying firm. Accordingly, supplier relationship management (SRM) is very important for firms for continuous supply management in today's dynamic and competitive environment. In support of effective and long-term relationships, it must be advantageous for all participants, the buying firm and the supply chain partners.

The purpose of this paper is to provide insights, based on the results of the mini-survey of the Danish Supply Chain Panel, on the following:

- understanding, importance, and practice of SRM among firms;

- the perceived relevance and current status of SRM;

- whether there is a special model/methodology for SRM;

- the degree of ability in measuring hard benefits of SRM efforts; and

- the major barriers for working with SRM.

In brief, on the basis of the results of the mini-survey of The Danish Supply Chain Panel, the paper attempts to convey that SRM is crucial for sustaining competitiveness, but it is difficult to measure its hard benefits.

2. Supplier relationship management

SRM is viewed as one of the most important aspects of supply chain management (SCM) and is intended to integrate the management of relationships among supply chain partners. SRM represents the mechanism of engaging in activities of establishing, balancing, monitoring, evaluating, and terminating relations with upstream supply chain partners to create as well as enhance potential value in relationships. SRM helps in progressing mutually beneficial relationships with strategic supply chain partners who deliver next-generation innovation and competitive advantage. SRM practices develop a shared perspective to enable effective communication between buying firms and supply chain partners and increases the efficiency of the processes related to acquiring goods and services, materials management, inventory management, etc. SRM is considered an extensive approach and helps incorporate active supplier involvement (engagement) in the development of new products, processes, and services, which allows the buying firm to benefit from their supply chain partners' capabilities and technology to deliver innovative and competitive products, processes, and services.

The main characteristics of a successful SRM include trust, communication, knowledge exchange, benchmarking, and sharing of best practice. Supplier management is considered as perhaps one of the most crucial issues in sustainable SCM, and activities concerning supplier development bring about enhancements in the overall performance as well as shared competitiveness of the supply chain networks. SRM could be an instrument facilitates, within the context of sustainability, delivery against multiple objectives; however, SRM is particularly important in the areas demanding control over activities outside the direct control of the focal (buying) firm. Therefore, SRM promotes shared value creation based on trust, active communication, and continuous collaboration with a limited number of supply chain partners. One of the most important objectives of SRM is leveraging supplier capabilities. Acquiring access to unique knowledge, resources, and capabilities is an integral part of this objective. Another important objective of SRM is cost reduction. This could conflict with the focus on value creation; however, reducing the overall cost is still a key necessity.

SRM is, of course, not a new paradigm; however, it has always remained embedded within the sourcing function. SRM manages:

- the assessment of supplier's capabilities in view of the firm's overall business strategy,
- decisions on the activities to engage in with various suppliers and organizations, and
- execution of all interactions with the supplier network to increase the value realized through the collaboration.

SRM has a major impact on overall performance and achieving sustainable competitiveness. In general, SRM could be considered a value-added function that helps in developing collaborative benefits along with the supplier network through a more strategically focused sourcing function.

3. Practical considerations—SRM

The insights acquired from the results of the mini-survey of The Danish Supply Chain Panel will be discussed concisely from a practical perspective. This panel includes voluntary senior supply chain managers from an array of Danish companies.

3.1 Organizational understanding of SRM

Considering firms' understanding of SRM, Figure 1 indicates that top management is not giving considerable attention to the strategic importance of SRM (with an average score of 2.68 on a five-point Likert scale where 1 = to a very low degree and 5 = to a very high degree). In addition, Figure 1 notes that the other functions within the organization are not understanding and acknowledging the work done to advance SRM. However, for effective SRM practice, it is essential that the top management team should focus on the importance of SRM as well as support their firms in taking new initiatives. Not only top management but also the other functions within the organization should try to understand the strategic importance of SRM to encourage the effective practice of SRM and thus enhance strategic collaboration with their supplier network.

Figure 1. Organizational understanding of SRM

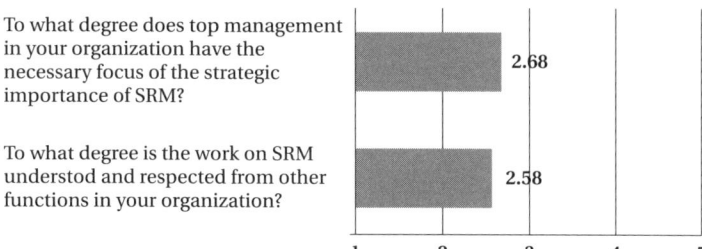

Source: Stentoft and Rajkumar (2017)[1]

3.2 Pursuing various SRM practices

In view of the fact that there are various SRM practices available, firms not only should be aware of those practices but also should pursue those practices effectively to exploit new opportunities and strengthen their strategic collaboration. Therefore, it is important to understand to what degree firms pursue various SRM practices. Figure 2 indicates that firms to a great extent work differently (conscious about time and purpose) with their suppliers depending on the segmentation—for instance, standard (armslength), bottleneck, leverage, and partnership-like (with an average score of 3.08 on a five-point Likert scale where 1 = to a very low degree and 5 = to a very high degree). Some of the firms approach their suppliers differently based on a structured segmentation of suppliers (with an average score of 2.90). Further, Figure 2 notes that, to a certain extent firms are working with selected suppliers with whom they consciously accomplish supplier development efforts and cooperative product development projects (with an average score of 2.90). Apart from these practices, firms to some extent are evaluating the performance of their suppliers depending on the relationship (with an average score of 2.60) and managing supplier risk management profiles in relation to SRM efforts (with an average score of 2.58).

Figure 2. Pursuing various SRM practices

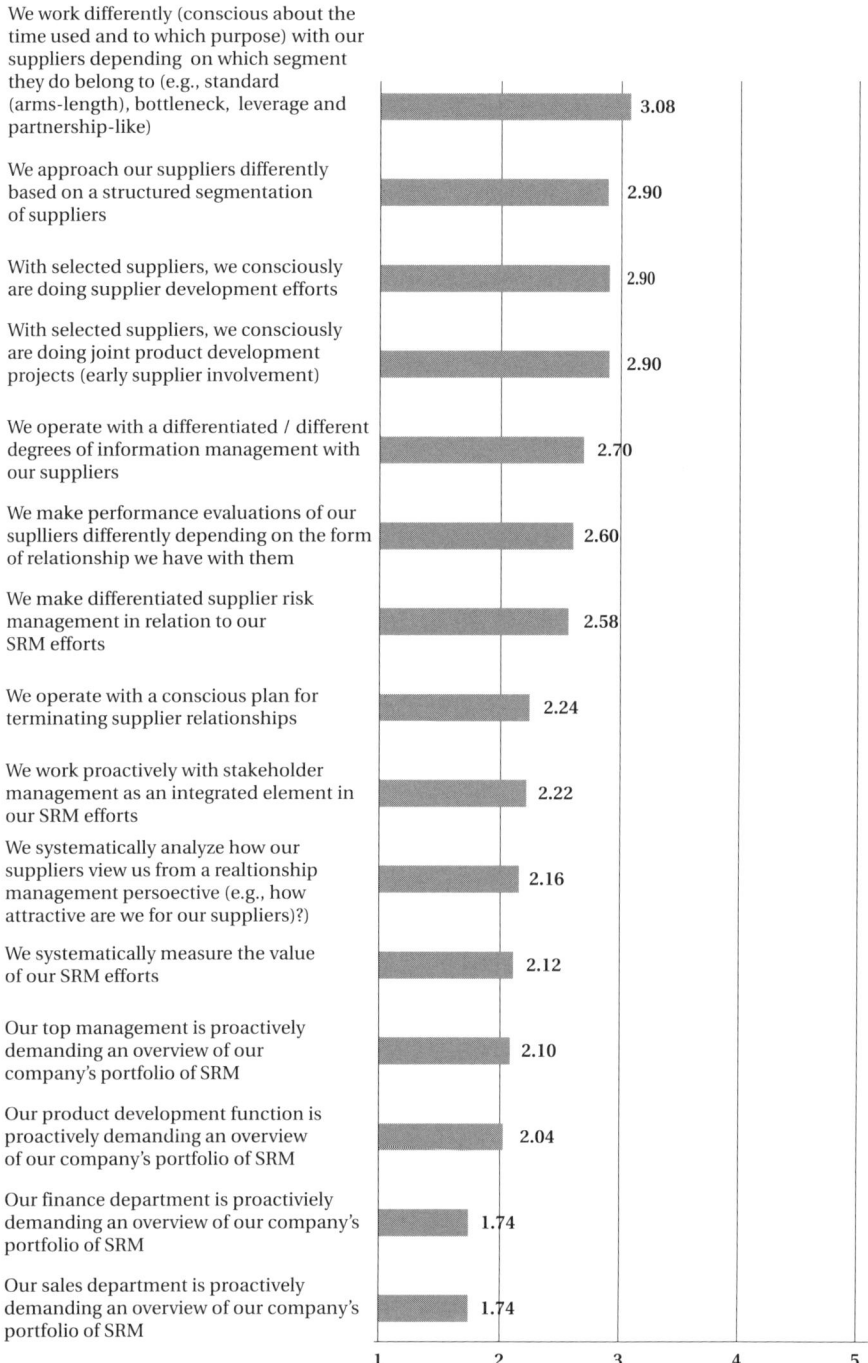

Source: Stentoft and Rajkumar (2017)[1]

On the other hand, from Figure 2, it can be seen that firms barely operate with a conscious plan for terminating supplier relationships (with an average score of 2.24), work proactively with stakeholder management as an integrated element in their SRM efforts (with an average score of 2.22), systematically analyze how their suppliers view them from a relationship management perspective (with an average score of 2.16), and systematically measure the value of their SRM efforts (with an average score of 2.12). As stated earlier and based on Figure 2, it is evident that the top management is not promoting SRM and proactively demanding an overview of their company's portfolio of SRM (with an average score of 2.10). Thus, firms need to start focusing on SRM practices by at least, for example, having the product development function, finance, and sales departments proactively demanding an overview of the company's portfolio of SRM (see Figure 2).

3.3 Perceived relevance and current status of SRM

It is important to envision how companies understand the relevance of SRM and formally work with SRM. Figure 3 indicates that even though the firms recognize the relevance of SRM (with an average score of 3.72 on a five-point Likert scale where 1 = to a very low degree and 5 = to a very high degree), they are not formally or actively practicing SRM (with an average score of 2.80). Therefore, there is certainly a gap between the perceived relevance and the actual practice of SRM.

Figure 3. Perceived relevance and current status of SRM

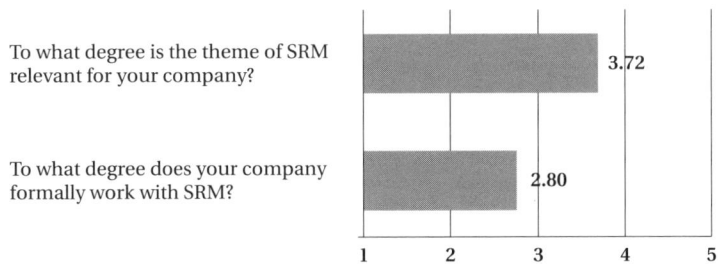

Source: Stentoft and Rajkumar (2017)[1]

An effective practice of SRM will lead to long-term supplier relationships, and it is important for the sourcing department to be responsible for SRM within each organization not only to understand the importance and benefits of SRM but also to actively practice SRM.

3.4 Utilization of special model/methodology for SRM

It is pertinent to perceive whether firms have any special model or methodology for working with SRM (e.g., a segmentation model such as Kraljic, 1983).[2] Figure 4 indicates that the vast majority of firms do not practice any distinctive model or methodology for working with SRM (80 percent of companies). On the contrary, there are very few firms (20 percent of companies) following a special model or methodology for working with SRM (see Figure 4). This could be an indication that in the future, more firms might use a formalized model or methodology for working with SRM. The benefit of a specific model and/or methodology is that it can help structuring the work. Firms in this study that answered "yes" to using a specific model or methodology were provided with an option to mention the models or methodologies used. Some of the models or methodologies mentioned were a global sourcing model within our corporation, homemade, Microsoft XRM, a combination of more models that give a company a specific approach, Kraljic's segmentation model as a basis for a differentiated approach to SRM, and structured supplier evaluation.

Figure 4. Utilization of special model/methodology for SRM

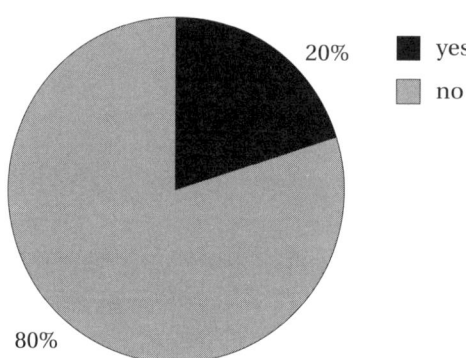

Source: Stentoft and Rajkumar (2017)[1]

Furthermore, among the 10 firms that mentioned that they follow Kraljic's segmentation model, six firms indicated that they use this segmentation model at the supplier level, one firm indicated that they use it at the item level, and three firms indicated that they use it at both the supplier and the item level.

3.5 Measuring hard benefits of SRM efforts

It is also relevant to understand to what extent firms can measure the benefits of SRM efforts. Figure 5 indicates that firms do not have adequate ability to measure the benefits of their SRM efforts (with an average score of 2.28 on a five-point Likert scale where 1 = to a very low degree and 5 = to a very high degree)). Although it could be assumed from Figure 5 that firms do understand the importance of evaluating the benefits of their hard efforts taken toward SRM, they might not have the appropriate capability for measuring the hard benefits of SRM efforts.

Figure 5. Degree of ability to measure hard benefits of SRM efforts

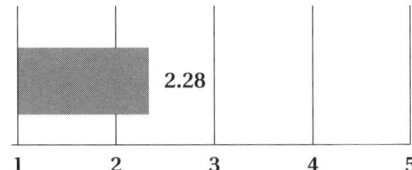

A common saying is "if you cannot measure it, you cannot manage it." Hence, firms need to realize the importance of having adequate abilities to measure the benefits of their hard work in order to appreciate their efforts as well as to continuously sustain their performances. Some of the practices that are used to measure the hard benefits are represented in Table 1.

A common saying is "if you cannot measure it, you cannot manage it." Hence, firms need to realize the importance of having adequate abilities to measure the benefits of their hard work in order to appreciate their efforts as well as to continuously sustain their performances. Some of the practices that are used to measure the hard benefits are represented in Table 1.

Table 1. Examples of practices to measure har benefits

Operational	Strategic	Financial	Others
- Lead times - Daily service - Manual list of delivery performance - On Time In Full (OTIF) - Supply ability - Delivery performance - Follow up on delivery security	- Measured through stable supply, fast responses from suppliers, successful strategy execution, and constant "cost-out" benefits - Quality - Subjective evaluation on supplier/item based on six criteria, which are weighted among each other: price highest, cost reduction, delivery performance, product quality, dialogue, and knowledge sharing - Change in supplier quality and delivery - Supplier audits	- Measuring the percentage of total spend that originates from strategic suppliers - Net Working Capital - Change in estimated total cost of ownership - Logistical costs - Financial risk - Price benchmark/management	- Excel sheets - Measured by subjective criteria - Direct, easy, and quick communication - Ongoing development of working procedures - Number of meetings with suppliers, orders placed, and claims

3.6 Main barriers for working with SRM

Firms need to recognize and analyze the major barriers for working with SRM. Accordingly, firms were asked to evaluate the relevancy of barriers for effectively working with SRM practices. Figure 6 indicates that lack of time (more focus on daily operations) is the topmost barrier for working with SRM (70 percent of the companies). The second topmost barrier for working with SRM is lack of methods to make the benefits visible (38 percent of the companies), and the third topmost barrier for working with SRM is lack of appropriate performance measures (28 percent of the companies). The two latter barriers correspond to the findings in Figure 5, on the lack of ability to measure hard benefits. If companies cannot measure, how can they make the benefits visible? In addition, 24 percent of the companies indicated that too much silo mentality, lack of internal competencies, and lack of management focus/attention are further barriers for working with SRM. Some of the companies (22 percent) also indicated that the lack of alignment among corporate strategy and sourcing strategy is a potential barrier for working with SRM.

Figure 6. Main barriers for working with SRM

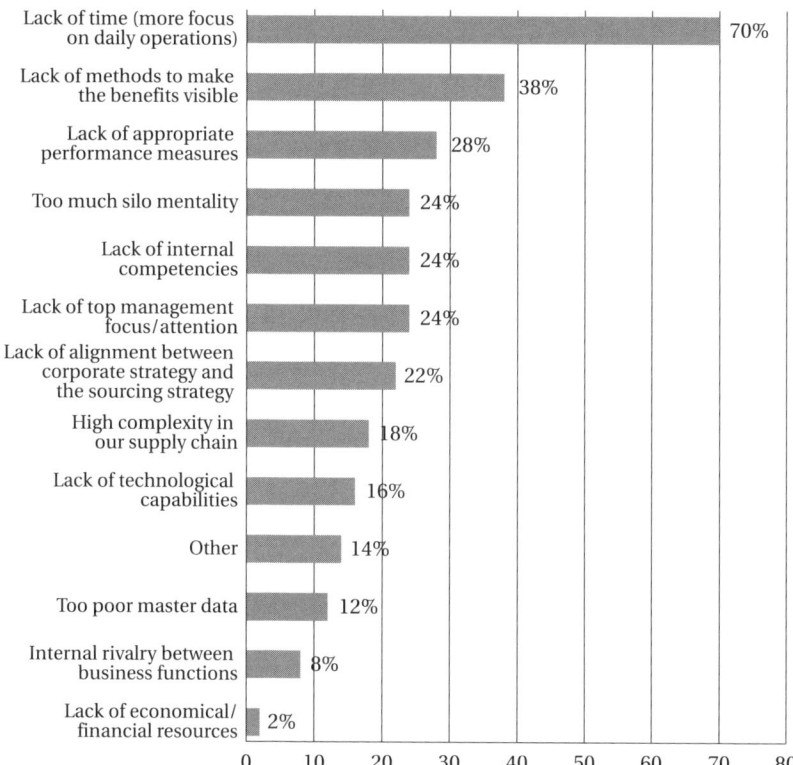

Source: Stentoft and Rajkumar (2017)[1]
Note: Companies have each marked three barriers.

The "other" barriers mentioned by the companies for working with SRM include:

- establishing a shared holistic view of the entire value chain,

- other projects being prioritized, and

- onboarding internal stakeholders.

3.7 Value addition from supplier network

As mentioned earlier, a high percentage of value adding is realized outside the buying firm. Therefore, it is important to understand how much value adding is sourced from the supplier network. Figure 7 indicates that among 50 companies, 20 percent of the respondents indicated that 0–20 percent of the value adding is sourced from the supplier network, 12 percent indicated 21–40 percent, 10 percent indicated 41–60 percent, 14 percent indicated 61–80 percent, and 12 percent indicated more than 80 percent. On the other hand, it is surprising that almost 32 percent indicated that they do not have any knowledge about how much of the value is sourced.

Figure 7. Value addition from supplier network

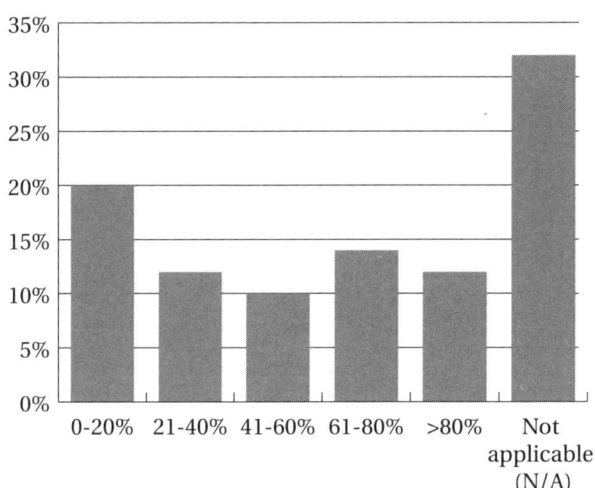

4. Conclusion

This practice-based summary has focused on an important SCM theme—SRM. The facts reveal that firms do find SRM relevant but that they only practice it to some degree (with an average score of 2.80). Moreover, only 20 percent of the companies work with a special SRM model or methodology, indicating a need for a more structured SRM approach among the panel members. An interesting finding is that although SRM plays a major role in companies' competitiveness, the panel members find it difficult to turn the SRM effort into hard, measurable benefits. This also indicates a development area, which in turn could also lead to a higher degree of top management awareness when one can document that SRM does pay off! The data also shows that SRM is not well understood by other functions in the company, which indicates a need for internal marketing efforts to promote SRM. Major SRM practices are listed as differentiated approaches toward suppliers, supplier development, and joint product development. Finally, main barriers for working with SRM are reported as a lack of time, methods, and appropriate performance measures. This practice-based summary can help stimulate discussions on the status of SRM in your company. Are you at the right level, and if not, what should you do about it?

Endnotes

1 Stentoft, J. and Rajkumar, C. (2017), "Supplier relationship management is important for competitiveness but it is difficult to measure its hard benefits," *Dilf Orientering*, Vol. 54 No. 3, pp. 10-17.

2 Kraljic, P. (1983), "Purchasing must become supply management", *Harvard Business Review*, Vol. 61 No. 5, pp. 109-117.

7.
Operations and maintenance

Operations and maintenance (O&M) are becoming increasingly important in the wind power sector. More offshore wind turbines are constantly being put into operation, and in 2017, a new record was set in Europe, where 623 new offshore wind turbines were erected. All of these new turbines, existing turbines, and future turbines will call for maintenance in their 20 to 25 years of expected lifetime. The service sector for wind power is therefore expected to grow in the future and generate a stable revenue, which may support wind turbine manufacturing companies during hard times. The Danish weekly newspaper *Monday Mornings* has, for instance, reported that when Vestas in 2013 was suffering, the company received "artificial respiration" from its service sector.

Even though a dramatic drop in cost of energy has been experienced—e.g., in Denmark from 134 Euro/MWh at the Anholt wind farm in 2010 to 49 Euro/MWh in 2016 at the Kriegers Flak offshore wind farm—O&M still constitute between one-third and one-fourth of the whole life cycle cost for an offshore wind farm. Offshore wind power installations are moving further and further offshore. Therefore, hotel vessels are now used during maintenance campaigns to reduce the cost of transportation of crew and spare parts. Hotel vessels and even an artificial island like the North Sea Wind Power Hub may therefore be expected in future O&M and in that way support access to offshore wind power installations far from the coast.

Data analysis is becoming more in focus, but still the ideas of big data analysis do not seem ready for use. However, when establishing new wind farm systems, the foundations and layout of wind farms are developed through simulation programs, and these simulations seem to bring the O&M sector better estimation and planning of maintenance campaigns.

The leading Original Equipment Manufacturers in the wind turbine industry like MHI Vestas and Siemens Gamesa seems to develop further on their turbines and the 6-7-8 (10) MW platform. However, because major changes in design and the introduction of radical new technology is extremely costly, even the large OEMs may find it challenging to pay back a major change in the platform design because contracts for the individual wind farms are most often made for only around 100 turbines. The future of O&M is therefore expected to meet challenges in maintaining an incremental development of new technology and new turbines, which are more or less based on the same platforms.

Because today's offshore wind turbines constitute a whole power plant in size, fewer man-hours are expected to be spent on O&M per. produced kWh in the future. More talented and well-educated maintenance persons will therefore be needed around the world to carry out maintenance of offshore wind power, and this seems to be an issue. Talented, well-educated O&M persons of the future need to be able to handle complicated technology for many different areas, such as monitoring, interpretation of data, visual inspection, carrying out service jobs, and even tightening bolts.

Some of the above-mentioned O&M aspects will be further discussed in the next chapters.

Improving maintenance of offshore wind farms through modularization[1]

Erik Skov Madsen
SDU Center for Sustainable Supply Chain Engineering
University of Southern Denmark

Kristian R. Petersen
Vattenfall Wind Power

Arne Bilberg
SDU Technology Entrepreneurship and Innovation
University of Southern Denmark

Idea in Brief
The focus of this paper is on how the offshore wind industry can reduce complexity in its operations and maintenance through modularization. We discuss this by addressing

- *Maintenance of offshore wind turbines that calls for rescheduling and re-planning;*

- *The need for modularization of maintenance tasks; and*

- *The need for bundling of resources into different resource packages.*

---

[1] This paper is based on Petersen, K.R., Madsen, E.S. and Bilberg, A. (2016), "First lean, then modularization: Improving the maintenance of offshore wind turbines", *International Journal of Energy Sector Management*, Vol. 10 No. 2, pp. 151-171.

1. Introduction

As offshore wind power installations in, for example, the northern part of Europe are moving further off the coast, operations and maintenance (O&M) is becoming more challenging. The offshore wind power industry has been successful in reducing the cost of energy produced from offshore wind turbine generators (WTGs), e.g., from 134 Euro/MWh at the Anholt wind farm in 2010 to 49 Euro/MWh in 2016 at the Kriegers Flak offshore wind farm, both located in Denmark. However, to reduce costs even further and extend the whole lifetime of offshore wind farms, it is important to focus on all aspects of the life cycle. Consequently, the O&M phase should receive more attention.

O&M of offshore WTGs is a complex process that often requires highly skilled technicians, complex tools, crew boats or helicopters, and expensive spare parts. In cases of exchange and overhaul of main components like gearboxes, generators, blades, or main shafts/bearing, very expensive jack-up vessels need to be hired, too. It is logical that offshore wind farms are at optimal locations for power production at high wind speeds. However, these high wind speeds and heavy weather conditions make maintenance difficult to perform, as these conditions lead to increased wave heights and hinder safe access to turbines from vessels. Because of the harsh weather, it is also difficult to handle spare parts because craning from vessels is normally needed. Several studies have identified that offshore wind farms are accessible between only 50 and 70 percent of the time because of harsh sea, wind, or visibility conditions.[1] Maintenance tasks are therefore subject to constant rescheduling, making maintenance of offshore wind farms difficult to plan and execute. There have been studies of how, e.g., the principles from Lean[2] can be used to make maintenance more efficient in the wind power sector. However, the purpose of this paper is to explore modularization in maintenance—namely, how modularization of O&M resources can reduce the complexity of planning of work. In turn, this can create O&M readiness in ever-changing and rough sea conditions so that when weather conditions allow for certain maintenance jobs, the operator is fully prepared and ready to carry them out.

2. Method

This paper is based on a study in a large energy company located in the northern part of Europe.[2] The company operates more than 1,000 wind turbines both on- and offshore. The case study method has been used in an examination of O&M processes of a large offshore wind farm consisting of 80 WTGs. The wind farm was commissioned in 2002, and since then, innovations have been undertaken to improve the O&M aspect of the value chain. Data for the study has been gathered through surveys, interviews, observations, and participation in maintenance activities.

3. Conceptual framework: Modularizing O&M of WTGs

Traditionally, modularization has been understood as a design concept in product development and manufacturing. In this case, modularized components are merged into modules that are composed into products. Through modularization, companies have been able to create a large variety of products that they then supply to consumers in a mass customized production setup. Some examples are illustrated in the automotive industry and the computer industry, in which the concept of a common platform and modularity is applied, and components are combined into modules that, again, through interfaces can be developed to a large variety of subassemblies and end products.[3]

For more than a decade, the concept of modularization has been extended beyond the field of product development and manufacturing into service.[4] Maintenance is, in this paper, regarded as a service because the purpose of an O&M organization in the wind power sector is to provide maintenance service and constantly ensure that WTGs are ready for full production when the free "fuel" (the wind) is available for the generation of power.

Based on a literature study of modularization and on our field studies, a flexible conceptual framework has been developed. The intention of the conceptual framework is to support management in a maintenance organization to create readiness and thereby prepare for more-flexible planning and execution of maintenance tasks. The conceptual framework is illustrated in Figure 1. The figure illustrates how modularization is used in two main parts of maintenance: (1) modularization of maintenance tasks (row 4 at the bottom) and (2) modularization of resources from resource groups (row 1 at the top).

As illustrated in Figure 1, the individual maintenance tasks (row 4) are bundled and clustered into maintenance task modules. These modules need to be solved by other modules, which are denoted as resource packages (RPs; row 2). The RPs are developed from a base of resources. In Figure 1, these resources are illustrated in four different resource groups (row 1), and by combining different resources into RPs (row 2), preparation for how to solve maintenance task modules can be considered and planned. A stepwise explanation will be made in the next section.

Figure 1. Modularization of a resource process in WTG maintenance

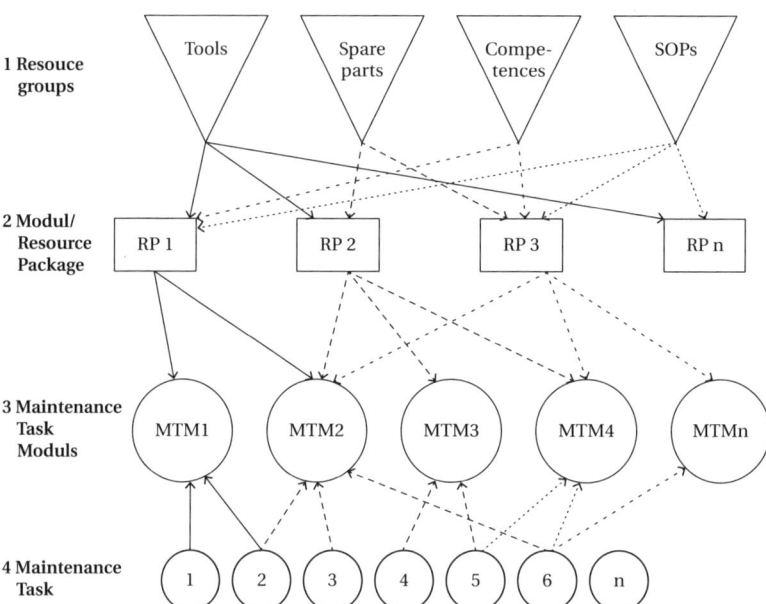

3.1 Maintenance task modules

The maintenance task modules (row 3) are generated and drawn from a large number of maintenance tasks, which are illustrated in the bottom row (row 4). The development of maintenance task modules follows three main steps:

Step 1: Identification of maintenance task modules. Maintenance tasks need to be structured and related to each other in a logical sequence, in which the workflow makes it easy for technicians to carry out these tasks. Through observations in the field, it is suggested to include up to six or seven maintenance tasks (from row 4) and merge these tasks into modules (row 3) to increase flexibility. By this, a maintenance task module represents a group of maintenance tasks.

Step 2: Identification of required competencies. After creating modules of the maintenance tasks, the required human competencies to carry out these modules should be identified. This is done by grouping modules of tasks that require the same kinds of competencies. In this way, maintenance task modules can effectively be divided between typical two technicians with different competencies. Maintenance task modules that require a higher level of training and education can be grouped to take place for, e.g., a whole working day, whereas tasks that require basic training and education can be grouped to be completed on another day.

Step 3: Development of maintenance task modules. After identifying the competencies required for each of the modules created in step 1, it is possible to start building modules of maintenance tasks. This is like a large puzzle with many pieces that must fit together to ensure the lowest waiting times and the highest efficiency. In this puzzle, several alternative combinations are to be developed, and finally, the best solution is chosen. In our study, we identified the importance of developing maintenance task modules that last a whole working day. Alternatively, two or three maintenance task modules that together make up a full day of work can be combined. In this way, planning work is easier, and transporting technicians between individual WTGs is minimized during a work day.

3.2 Modules/RPs

When maintenance tasks have been systemized in maintenance task modules (row 3), considerations of resources and how to bundle needed resources into module/RPs can take place. We have used the term resource packages (RPs) because RPs can be used for multiple maintenance task modules. The development of RPs takes place in three steps.

Step 1: Identification of resources. When identifying resources, a mix of two approaches has been proposed: (1) identify available resources (regarded as competences) among the employees within the company, and (2) look for the required resources (tools, SOPs, and spare parts) to fulfil the maintenance tasks. The groups of resources are illustrated in row 1 in Figure 1. The identified resources, including employees' competences, must be mapped, e.g., through appraisal interviews and development of a skills matrix. All the needed resources may not be available within the company, and special competences required from outside the firm also need to be mapped.

Step 2: Pooling resources into RPs. After all the required resources have been identified, they can be divided into resource groups comprising tools, spare parts, competencies, and SOPs as separate resources (row 1). In this way, it is easier to look for specific resources in the resource groups when required.

Step 3: Developing modules: RPs. The modules, which are defined as RPs, are used to carry out both preventive and corrective maintenance tasks, and they are developed based on the requirements of the various maintenance tasks. These modules must be rather small to be easily combined into larger modules.[5] This allows for more flexibility, ensuring that each module can be used for multiple tasks. The development of RPs is the most challenging part of the modularization process because it requires an overview of all tasks and their required resources.

3.3 Advantages in using the conceptual framework

The proposed conceptual framework (Figure 1) is developed to work as a management tool to prepare maintenance tasks. This is done by (1) structuring the individual maintenance task (row 4) into maintenance task modules (row 3) and (2) solving the maintenance task modules by using RPs (row 2) made up of resources from the different resource groups (row 1).

Maintenance of offshore WTGs is heavily depending on weather conditions, and replanning and rescheduling of maintenance tasks is constantly required in the offshore wind power sector. Through this case study of an O&M company, it was identified how RPs can constitute simple bags in which, e.g., tools, spare parts, SOPs, etc. (from row 1) can be packed and ready for certain maintenance jobs. As illustrated in Figure 1, some maintenance task modules need more than one RP. For instance, maintenance task module 2 (MTM2 in Figure 1) calls for RP1, RP2, and RP3 to be solved, whereas MTM1 only needs resources from RP1. In this study, it is documented that this kind of preparation for maintenance makes the replanning and rescheduling much more efficient in an ever-changing offshore environment that heavily depends on the weather.

So far, this concept is considered as a manual process, in which management and technicians in collaboration can develop structured processes for easier maintenance planning and replanning. However, the concept leaves room for further development of software tools to support this process.

4. Conclusion

This paper has introduced a conceptual framework for modularization of maintenance tasks and RPs. This study recommends that maintenance tasks for offshore WTGs are considered and merged into maintenance task modules that can be carried out by using RPs. By structuring maintenance tasks and resources of offshore WTGs in modules, an O&M service provider can gain more-efficient maintenance processes through less-complex replanning and rescheduling, in which maintenance heavily depends on ever-changing weather conditions.

Endnotes

1 Breton, S.-P. and Moe, G. (2009), "Status, plans and technologies for offshore wind turbines in Europe and North America", *Renewable Energy*, Vol. 34 No. 3, pp. 646–654.

2 Petersen, K.R., Madsen, E.S. and Bilberg, A. (2016), "First Lean, then modularization: Improving the maintenance of offshore wind turbines", *International Journal of Energy Sector Management*, Vol. 10 No. 2, pp. 221-244.

3 Baldwin, C.Y. and Clark, K.B. (2000), *Design Rules – the Power of Modularity*, The MIT Press, Cambridge, Massachusetts.

4 Voss, C.A. and Hsuan, J. (2009), "Service architecture and modularity", *Decision Sciences*, Vol. 40 No 3, pp. 541-569.

5 Hyötyläinen, M. and Möller, K. (2007), "Service packaging: Key to successful provisioning of ICT business solutions", *Journal of Services Marketing*, Vol. 21 No. 5, pp. 304-312.

Operations and maintenance issues in the offshore wind energy sector[1]

Jan Stentoft
Department of Entrepreneurship and Relationship Management
University of Southern Denmark

Victoria Baagøe-Engels
Department of Entrepreneurship and Relationship Management
University of Southern Denmark

Idea in Brief
In this paper we focus on operations and maintenance (O&M) challenges in offshore wind parks. Based on literature studies four themes of challenges are identified. These are supplemented by a Delphi method including data from 16 experts where ten O&M challenges leading to increased O&M costs are added in a ranked order.

1. Introduction

Offshore wind energy parks have increased in number in the last few decades. This also means that the operation and maintenance (O&M) of the parks is now of vital importance. Research has documented that O&M accounts for around 20 to 35 percent of the total energy costs in this sector.[1] The offshore wind industry is experiencing significant development; however, the industry is still in its preliminary stages and therefore incurs several costs.[2] These costs are categorized as CAPEX and OPEX[3], with each category composed of different elements corresponding with the life cycles of offshore wind farms.

CAPEX refers to all the activities—design process, location deci-

---

[1] This paper is based on Baagøe-Engels, V. and Stentoft, J. (2016), "Operations and maintenance issues in the offshore wind energy sector: An explorative study", *International Journal of Energy Sector Management*, Vol. 10 No. 2, pp. 245-265.

sion, logistical processes for components, and project management of the installation process—undertaken prior to the commissioning of the offshore wind farm. CAPEX consists of mainly four elements: wind turbine, foundation, electrical infrastructure, and assembly and installation.

OPEX refers to the daily management, or O&M, of the offshore wind farm. In recent years, interest in CAPEX has increased because the investments in CAPEX are significantly higher than for OPEX. Nevertheless, OPEX is also considered important, since O&M can contribute to significant cost reductions in the offshore wind sector.

The purpose of this paper is to provide an overview of O&M issues in the offshore wind energy sector to propose initiatives to reduce the cost of energy generated from offshore wind farms.

2. Operations and maintenance

O&M can be spread out in different categories, with the maintenance portion of the O&M strategy divided into corrective and preventive maintenance. *Corrective maintenance* is unscheduled maintenance that needs action as soon as possible because of its resulting downtime in energy production. *Preventive maintenance* can be further subdivided into scheduled and condition-based maintenance. Scheduled maintenance is mainly set by legislation and by the turbine manufactures. This can, for example, include topping up oil in the gear box, checking lifts, checking safety systems, or making changes at regular intervals. Condition-based maintenance is calculated maintenance based on estimates from the monitor systems installed in the wind farm or based on observations at regular intervals.

O&M strategy is becoming more important as offshore wind farms move toward large-scale projects.[4] O&M costs refer to the wind farm's daily management costs, which include labor, spare parts, transportation to the wind farms' sites, lease of equipment for repair and maintenance, support from jack-up vessels for replacement of major components, monitor systems, cable repairs, and foundation inspection and repair.[5,6] O&M costs are directly influenced by the design of the wind farm, the environment, and the selected maintenance strategy. Several unknown and unpredictable factors can increase O&M costs, thereby making it difficult to estimate the exact costs for breakdowns or repair. The following is a costs breakdown of a typical offshore wind farm[7]:

- Development and project management counts for 2 percent.

- The wind turbine counts for 26 percent.

- The balance of the plant—i.e., foundations, substations, and cabling—is 19 percent.

- Installation and commissioning are 14 percent.

- Operation, maintenance, and service are 39 percent.

This cost breakdown does not include decommissioning, as large-scale wind farms do not initiate that process until about 20 to 25 years from the start of operation.

3. O&M challenges in the offshore wind energy sector: The literature perspective

A review of academic literature on O&M with respect to the offshore wind energy sector has revealed four groups of challenges:

1. Immature industry
2. Distance and water depth
3. Weather window
4. Policy

3.1 Immature industry

The offshore wind industry can be described as an immature industry still at an early stage.[8] This industrial immaturity could be the reason why there is no optimal solution to current O&M processes and why there is a tendency to "learn by doing." Finally, industrial immaturity explains the lack of standardization in processes and components, which results in greater variations in approaches to O&M issues.

3.2 Distance and water depth

The offshore wind industry faces various challenges related to longer distances between the supply and the facilities, the water depth, and the practicalities involved in actually bringing technicians to the wind farms. Logistic management of O&M process is considered a challenging and important profession that has a direct influence on O&M costs. The logistic setup with proper vessels for crew, components, and tools to accomplish the O&M tasks is, therefore, crucial because an insufficient logistic setup may result in a decrease of generated power and in expensive waiting time. Although the literature focuses on developing an optimal logistic setup, the only existing consensus is that the setup is a crucial part of O&M tasks.

3.3 Weather window

As opposed to the onshore wind industry, the offshore wind industry needs to consider the weather window and the climate changes in managing O&M tasks. Weather conditions can increase costs, and waiting for good weather to enter a turbine often leads to downtime and no power generation.[9] The accessibility of the wind farms depends to a large extent on weather conditions, which therefore indirectly impacts the successful performance of O&M tasks.

3.4 Policy

The offshore wind sector is dependent on the government's political support to create financial conditions that would benefit the offshore wind sector. Policies vary depending on the country where the wind farms are established; for example, safety rules for O&M regarding the work force and equipment are not identical. The lack of uniform rules can in some instances be a challenge for companies who operate across national boundaries. Government policies could also encompass guidelines on performing O&M tasks; however, these policies and/or strategic decisions are left to the operators of the wind farms. Therefore, there are many different approaches to performing O&M tasks. One example is the differences in preventive maintenance, which depends on the installed turbines and the components used.

4. Delphi study results

The empirical part of this paper is based on a conducted Delphi study consisting of 16 experts. The sampling of experts was initiated by contacting offshoreenergy.dk, which is an industry association in the Danish offshore wind sector. The association possesses a significant amount of knowledge about the offshore wind industry—specifically, issues from members and the different types of actors involved in the industry. Thus, offshoreenergy.dk is perceived as a strong source for identifying the key experts in O&M issues in the offshore wind supply chain. Based on information from the association, an initial list of 10 experts was generated, which was further expanded to 16 by involving the first 10 experts. The expert panel consisted of three groups of experts. The first group was operators of wind farms, such as site managers, who were managing O&M in the companies. The second group consisted of experts from knowledge organizations, such as the industry association offshoreenergy.dk, which facilitated the offshore wind sector. The last group included actors and companies that manufacture wind turbines and foundations, help create the wind farm design, and provide vessels and crew to O&M or installations face.

Table 1. Ranked statements about what makes O&M costs increase

1. There is a lack of flexibility in planning O&M. There are too many predefined rules that limit the possibility for development.
2. There is a lack of coordination between the different services in the wind farm. Tasks concerning the same wind turbines are not coordinated; therefore, repeated trips are made to the same wind turbine to perform different tasks.
3. There is no common understanding on how O&M should be managed.
4. Every site manager has his or her unique view on how O&M should be managed.
5. Contracts concerning O&M agreements are too short-term.
6. The wind farms have moved farther from shore.
7. Lack of knowledge about what type of logistics setup (e.g., use of vessels, helicopter, habitation platforms, or hotel vessels) would be most beneficial for the sector.
8. There is too much wear in the blades.
9. The wind farms are becoming larger in size.
10. The wind turbines are becoming larger.

As shown in Table 1, experts agreed that the most important challenge for O&M in the offshore wind energy sector was the inflexibility of planning in O&M. This statement illustrates a need for reviewing predefined rules that hamper further development within the industry. In relation to the extant literature, this issue belongs to the immature dimension. The lack of flexibility on how to manage O&M has only been addressed indirectly by the literature, which is more concerned with the lack of maturity in general in the offshore wind sector.

The second most ranked challenge that tends to increase O&M costs is the lack of coordinated planning for the different O&M services at the wind farms. In relation to the existing literature, this statement can be placed in two dimensions—policy and distance/water depth. The literature prescribes various ways to optimize O&M strategies with respect to distance and water depth. For example, health-monitoring systems are put in place to reduce the number of unplanned trips while simultaneously amassing reparation and inspection.

The third and fourth issues are closely related, as they are both concerned with how O&M is managed in the wind farms. They are both closely related to the policy dimension. The lack of uniform solutions to manage O&M strategies may result in too much variation, as every site manager has his or her own unique viewpoint on how to manage the O&M strategy. There seems to be a lack of understanding on how to optimize O&M activities of wind farms to balance the overall performance on parameters such as costs, time, quality, and flexibility. At least five activities could include (1) the choice of a specific type of transport (e.g., helicopters, service vessels, or crane vessels) for an O&M activity; (2) the utilization of crew for other purposes when the weather window is closed (heavy weather during which turbines and constructions cannot be accessed); (3) the balance of planned versus unplanned O&M; (4) the supply structure for spare parts, which involves required speed and harbor logistics; and (5) signing the most appropriate O&M contracts.

The fifth most important statement on how to reduce O&M costs was described as the focus on O&M contracts, which were too short. The shorter the contract period, the higher percentage of depreciation is allocated to the contract. This statement seems not to have been addressed in the present literature. A future cost-benefit analysis could be required to define the need for an extension of the current O&M contracts, which the expert panel found to be too short.

The sixth and seventh statements concerned the dimension of distance and water depth. Distance and water depth may exert a strong influence on the logistical setup for O&M strategies simply because farther-offshore distances require detailed planning.

Finally, the eighth, ninth, and tenth statements do not fit any of the existing categories and are only briefly addressed in the existing literature. The literature does not directly address the issue of too much wear on the blades (statement eight), even though concerns are being raised that climate conditions (size of rain drops and hail) and very high tip speeds can cause problems in this regard. Currently, there is a lack of available data that can be used to improve forecasts for O&M strategies.

5. Conclusion

The purpose of this paper has been to identify the issues in offshore wind within O&M that two groups—academic researchers and industry experts—identify as important in reducing the cost of energy. Four O&M issues were identified from the literature: (1) the immaturity of the industry, (2) distance and water depth issues, (3) weather window issues, and (4) policy issues. The industry's point of view was based on a Delphi study, in which the expert in the final round of interviews ranked 10 statements according to their perceived importance on increasing O&M costs.

The study identified the top five ranked issues connected to rising O&M costs as (1) inflexibility of planning for O&M, (2) lack of coordinated planned services at the wind farms, (3) lack of common understanding on how O&M should be managed, (4) heterogeneous views on how O&M should be managed at sites, and (5) the short-term nature of O&M contracts.

When comparing the experts' view on O&M challenges with extant literature, there is both consensus and gaps between theory and practice. The inflexibility of O&M processes due to predefined rules that restrict the innovation possibilities could be researched in the future through an analysis of the industry's viewpoint on this lack of flexibility, the definition and actual empirical referent of the concept, and an identification of the said predefined rules with a view to presenting their consequences. It can also be argued that there is a need for more research that identifies specific areas within O&M in the offshore wind energy sector that could be standardized or that could be given greater flexibility.

Endnotes

1 Ortegon, K., Nies, L.F. and Sutherland, J.W. (2013),"Preparing for end of service life of wind turbines", *Journal of Cleaner Production*, Vol. 39, pp. 191-199.

2 MacAskill, A. and Mitchell P. (2013), "Offshore wind – an overview", WIREs *Energy Environ*, Vol. 2, pp. 374-383.

3 Shafiee, M. (2015), "Maintenance logistics organization for offshore wind energy: Current progress and future perspectives", *Renewable Energy*, Vol. 77, pp. 182-193.

4 Karyotakis, A. and Bucknall, R. (2010), "Planned intervention as a maintenance and repair strategy for offshore wind turbines", *Journal of Marine Engineering and Technology*, Vol. 9 No. 1, pp. 27-35.

5 El-Thalji, E. and Liyanage J.P. (2012), "On the operation and maintenance practices of wind power asset – a status review and observations", *Journal of Quality in Maintenance Engineering*, Vol. 18 No. 3, pp. 232-266.

6 Scheu, M., Matha, D., Hofmann, M. and Muskulus, M. (2012), "Maintenance strategies for large offshore wind farms", *Energy Prodecia*, Vol. 24, pp. 281-288.

7 BVG (2014), *UK Offshore Wind Supply Chain: Capabilities and Opportunities*, BVG Associates, https://assets.publishing.service.gov.uk/government/uploads/system/uploads/attachment_data/file/277798/bis-14-578-offshore-wind-supply-chain-capabilities-and-opportunities.pdf (Accessed March 2, 2019).

8 Utne, B.I. (2010), "Maintenance strategies for deep-sea offshore wind turbines", *Journal of Quality in Maintenance Engineering*, Vol. 16 No. 4, pp. 367-381.

9 O`Connor, M., Lewis, T. and Dalton, G. (2013), "Weather window analysis of Irish west coast wave data with relevance to operation and maintenance of marine renewable", *Renewable Energy*, Vol. 52, pp. 57-66.

8. Maturity

This section's articles focus on the development of maturity models. The origin of the maturity model can be traced back to quality improvement through a five-level maturity grid followed by a process maturity model (PMM) and capability maturity model (CMM). After the development of these two models, the maturity model concept became popular among researchers and practitioners.

The first article in this section, by Govindan, investigates "Developing a process map for CSR in supply chain management—A maturity model." The chapter proposes a corporate social responsibility (CSR) maturity model with a particular focus on supply chain management supported by CSR practices. In this chapter, CSR practices are integrated into the proposed maturity model of CSR. This study also tries to reveal and explore the relationship and influence of CSR practices over their maturity levels through two case studies from India focusing on a reverse supply chain. The results of this study also reveal that managers are more focused on the economic values of the firm than on moral ethics and innovation.

The second article of this section, by Govindan and Shankar Kalidoss, evaluates the essential barriers to offshore wind energy farms in an Indian context. The authors propose a framework that focuses on identifying common barriers for implementing offshore wind farms, the most important barrier, and its level of priority, using a multicriteria decision-making tool called analytical hierarchy process (AHP).

Developing a process map for CSR in supply chain management—a maturity model

Kannan Govindan
Center for Sustainable Supply Chain Engineering
University of Southern Denmark

Idea in Brief
This executive proposes a corporate social responsibility (CSR) maturity model with a particular focus on supply chain management (SCM) supported by CSR practices. Further, the implementation of CSR initiatives in Indian firms using the proposed maturity model as an organizing framework has been investigated. Two case studies from India have been discussed by focusing on reverse supply chains. The data explores the maturity level of CSR in the case companies and provides useful recommendations to improve their CSR maturity level in SCM.

1. Introduction

Maturity models are a means of achieving excellence in supply chain operations. Maturity models were first developed in quality management, and because of the significant benefits of maturity models in quality management, they have been adopted in various contexts, including supply chain management (SCM). Much literature has discussed the maturity models with various supply chain perspectives, including lean SCM, green SCM, sustainable SCM, and others. This influences researchers to explore maturity models of sustainability implementation in SCM. Surprisingly, on the other hand, sustainable SCM studies have paid less attention to social considerations when compared to the other two pillars of sustainability—namely, economy and environment. Hence, the time is ripe for researchers to look for a sustainable strategy with concern for societal value. Among such sustainable strategies, corporate social responsibility (CSR) is the only strategy that addresses all the dimensions of sustainability, whereas other strategies—such as triple bottom line; corporate citizenship; corporate social performance; people, planet, and profit; social responsibility; business ethics; cleaner production; and corporate responsible investment—tend to address limited dimensions of sustainability. Implementing CSR in a supply chain results in obvious benefits for firms. Those that integrate CSR practices understand their benefits, and they recognize that CSR allows them to benchmark high standards to improve their supply chain effectiveness. In this paper, initially, CSR practices from the literature are integrated into the proposed maturity model of CSR; then, the proposed maturity model is validated with a case study conducted in the developing context of India. As a nation, India is the second highest in human power and one of the fastest-growing economies.

2. Maturity model for CSR in SCM

From the review of literature, it is evident that existing maturity models are not fit for the integration of CSR into SCM. With the objective in mind of proposing a maturity model for CSR in SCM, we decided to start with an understanding of the core principles of CSR. Knowing the origin of CSR and its theoretical background will help determine what factors are vital to the maturity model. When a close relationship exists between CSR implementation and organizational behavior, firms are more likely to adopt CSR practices voluntarily. CSR practices are the only means by which organizational resources are appropriately used to create profits and ensure stakeholder values. In addition, CSR practices are the only viable way to integrate organizational behaviors for successful implementation of CSR in a firm's activities. Accordingly, this study considers CSR practices as fundamental criteria for measuring the maturity level of CSR in SCM, a view that previous studies lack. Hence, CSR practices under consideration were identified from existing literature through a systematic review; further, these practices were evaluated by experts to gain an objective perspective on their relevance to this study. Table 1 shows the final list of CSR practices identified in this process.

Table 1. CSR practices collected from literature

S. no	Levels of maturity	CSR practices	Explanation
1	Preventive	Disclosure of environmental and social performance (**CSR–P1**)	The firm discloses its performance in environmental and social matters periodically.
2	Proactive	Generous financial donations (**CSR–P2**)	The firm supports the community through continuous financial donations to create and motivate societal value initiatives.
3	Preventive	Support for local community (**CSR–P3**)	The firm aims to provide full support to the local community through all means.
4	Reactive	Environmental audits (**CSR–P4**)	The firm engages in regular environmental audits through external and internal audits.
5	Proactive	Environmental policies, organization, and management (**CSR–P5**)	Tightening governance on environmental policies is combined with fair organizational management.
6	Proactive	Waste management (**CSR–P6**)	The firm manages waste created through production/manufacturing/other operations. The firm has a system design to manage all types of waste.
7	Proactive	Energy conservation (**CSR–P7**)	The firm engages in the conservation of energy by creating optimized energy models.
8	Reactive	Effective emergency response (**CSR–P8**)	The firm is always ready to respond effectively to emergency/uncertainty conditions.
9	Preventive	Value for money (**CSR–P9**)	The firm provides a product worth its value.
10	Proactive	Truthful promotion (**CSR–P10**)	The promotion of the product is correct; the firm does not provide promos that do not suit the product.
11	Preventive	Encourage suppliers to provide innovative suggestions (**CSR–P11**)	The firm encourages innovative suggestions.
12	Preventive	Encourage staff ownership of shares (**CSR–P12**)	The firm supports and encourages company staff to buy a share in ownership of the firm.
13	Proactive	Full product disclosure (**CSR–P13**)	The firm discloses all relevant details of the product.
14	Proactive	Develop and build relationships with shareholders (**CSR–P14**)	The firm maintains a good relationship between shareholders and stakeholders.
15	Preventive	Assist suppliers to improve their environmental/social performance (**CSR–P15**)	The firm assists suppliers to promote their environmental and societal status with its performance through collaborative activities.

It is helpful to classify the CSR practices into three categories[1], namely, "reactive," "preventive," and "proactive." Thus, our research team decided to frame a maturity model based on these practices with various intensities of adaption. The proposed maturity levels of CSR in SCM are shown in Figure 1.

Figure 1. Maturity levels of CSR in the supply chain based on CSR practices

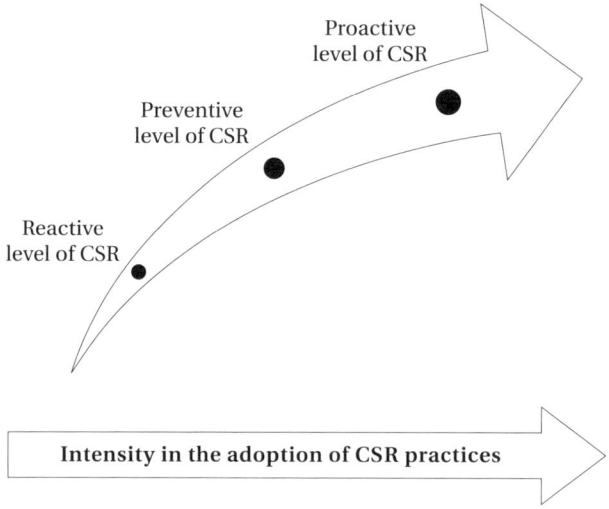

As mentioned earlier, the CSR practices are categorized into three levels. At the initial level (reactive stage), a firm typically adopts CSR practices for mandatory compliance, not for financial profit; ergo, the reactive level is nothing more than a firm reacting to pressures and mandatory factors. When future value and cost-effectiveness are not a firm's primary concern, that firm is considered to have a reactive level of CSR maturity. After a firm has gained some experience, managers begin to think about cost-effectiveness through CSR (economy is one of the pillars/dimensions of CSR) as a long-term strategy to ensure the firm's financial competitiveness in the market. This decision signals firm's move from the reactive level to a preventive level. The second (preventive) level is acquired if the firm practices CSR to improve cost-effectiveness in addition to mandatory factors, hence the second level of maturity. Finally, once the firm attains a strong foothold in the business market, they are likely to focus on improving their reputation and enhancing brand value in the fluctuating business realm, which proves that the firm has reached a proactive level. When the firm practices CSR that focuses on future value generation and value-added benefits, then that firm is considered to have attained a proactive level of CSR maturity. This CSR maturity level gives the firm a competitive advantage, and from this innovation, the firm evolves and transforms risk-based CSR to innovative CSR, which alters their organizational behavior from risk management to value creation.

3. Case studies

The aim of this paper is to propose a maturity model for CSR, especially one that is applied in a developing context such as India by linking CSR practices with a particular focus on SCM. This paper also explores the relationship and influence of CSR practices over their maturity levels through two case studies. For this study, two different application sectors were chosen, but both focus on reverse supply chains—i.e., remanufacturing. Therefore, to explore the CSR maturity model, the case research was completed in two Indian case companies. In both cases, three decision makers are considered for the study because of their authority in their firm and their industrial experience. These respondents were picked from three important areas: the supply chain, human resources department, and top-level technical administration. Mainly, this study focused on CSR practices–based maturity models; hence, the questions and discussions were about key CSR practices and how well they perform under given circumstances. The questionnaire from the study included 15 CSR practices collected from existing literature, as shown in Table 1.

3.1 Case 1: Remanufacturing of earthmoving equipment

This case company is a manufacturer of passenger cars and has many divisions in various locations throughout India. As such, a plant in southern India was set up for earthmoving equipment like dumpers, front-end loaders, crawler tractors, etc. This company already practices many sustainable strategies including remanufacturing, in which products (engines, drive trains, undercarriage, and hydraulics of earthmoving equipment) are remanufactured and offered for sale. This case company collected end-of-life (EOL) products under an exchange scheme and remanufactured them for sale. Because of pressure from international clients, the firm is interested in integrating CSR in their SCM; however, it is difficult in the Indian context to succeed because of, for example, lack of transparency, awareness, training, or policies, among others.

Status of CSR practices—Case 1

Figure 2. Status of CSR practices—Case I

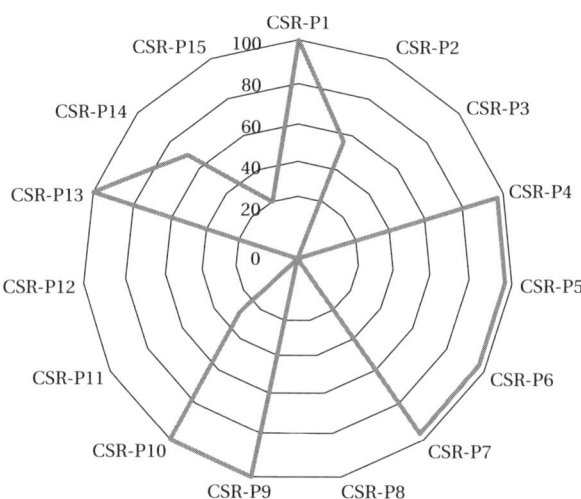

After analyzing the case firm 1, it is clear that the firm is highly focused on practices like disclosure of environmental and social performance, environmental audits, environmental policies, organization and management, waste management, energy conservation, value for money, truthful promotion, and full product disclosure (Figure 2). Most of these practices lie at the reactive and preventive levels. For instance, the firm practices environmental audits, disclosures, and policies that show how the firm reacts to mandatory factors. Likewise, the case firm practices waste management, energy conservation, and full product disclosure policies, which demonstrates that they focus on cost-effectiveness. That attention to cost-effectiveness moves the firm to the preventive level of CSR. Because the firm has a limited focus on practices such as societal activities, innovativeness, and support for suppliers, the case firm is not at the top level (the proactive level) of CSR maturity.

3.2 Case 2: Remanufacturing of printer cartridges

In recent years, cartridge refilling and remanufacturing (CRR) industries have experienced rapid growth in the Indian market, with increases from 30 to 40 percent. Because of these dramatic rises, many players entered the CRR markets as remanufacturing firms. Our case firm is a cartridge and printer toner remanufacturing firm that entered the market three years ago, and it has been tough for them to follow a sustainable strategy within the firm. The firm has 300 employees, including engineers with relevant experience in e-waste management. This company collects EOL cartridges through agents who work as dealers. Because of the volatility and competition in this market, the company needs to enact sustainability strategies to remain viable. Thus, they practice value-added strategies to improve their corporate image, and CSR is one strategy they follow to ensure sustainability. They are highly interested in the effective implementation of CSR, as well as in learning about their level of CSR implementation. But due to their early stage in business, it is tough to determine their CSR level. With such considerations, they accepted our research team's request to investigate their level of CSR maturity.

Status of CSR practice— Case 2

Figure 3. Status of CSR Practices—Case 2

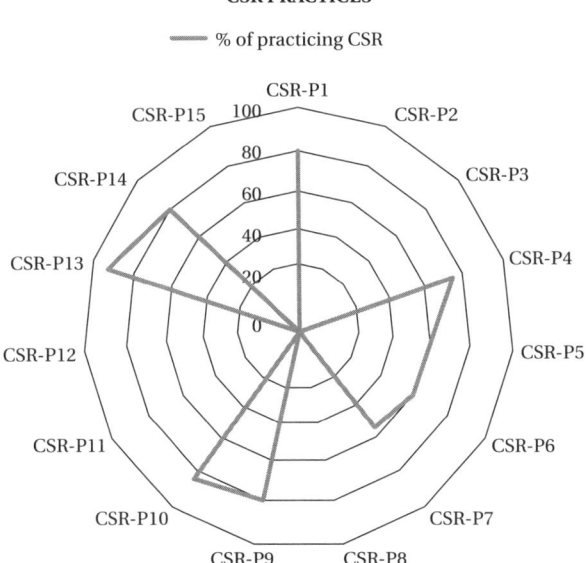

Like case 1, CSR practices are charted in Figure 3 from the replies of case 2 industrial managers. It is clear that the firm focuses on practices like disclosure of environmental and social performance, environmental audits, value for money, truthful promotion, full product disclosure, and developing and building relationships with shareholders. All the above-mentioned practices are likely to be practiced due to the mandatory activities of governance. Other practices like energy conservation and waste management are not very effective in this case firm, which reveals that it is still at a reactive level of CSR maturity. As a young company, it is still growing, with much pressure to capture and stabilize the market. Consequently, they first need to place themselves in a safe position with mandatory CSR practices. The company has not yet started work on societal activities, and their stakeholder relationships are lacking. It is deemed that case firm 2 is currently at a reactive level of CSR maturity, and much work is needed to upgrade this firm's CSR maturity to the next level.

4. Relationship and influence of CSR practices in the maturity level of CSR

From the above two cases, it is clear that the level and degree of CSR practices directly influence CSR maturity level. The results show that case firm 1 is in the preventive level of CSR maturity, and case firm 2 is at a reactive level of CSR maturity. The sensitivity of results between these two cases is highly dependent on the company's origin: case firm 1 has its origin in the United States, and case firm 2 is of Indian origin. This clearly shows that the awareness level of CSR is more advanced in the US firm than in the Indian firm. Otherwise, the two case companies share some similarities; neither company is involved in good stakeholder relationships, societal activities, and communal support. Particularly in terms of stakeholder relationships, the voice of suppliers is neglected in both cases, a weakness that was revealed from our analysis of both firms. If these case companies are able to consider societal issues, make their future value clear to beneficiaries, launch a local awareness campaign, and encourage stakeholder values, each company's maturity level will improve because of their enhanced implementation of CSR. In the Indian scenario, most companies could not fill the societal pillar of sustainability, which results in the ineffective implementation of CSR, leading to a reactive level maturity in CSR. Clearly, apart from the economy, the lack of governmental regulations, poor governance, and limited transparency have considerable influence on CSR implementation.

The companies can use this framework to evaluate their level of CSR maturity; furthermore, they can improve CSR performance through effective practices. As discussed earlier, there are many direct and indirect benefits the company can reap from CSR implementation. To achieve maturity in CSR, the companies should implement effective CSR practices that fall under the proactive level, for which the companies need to assign a CSR manager (who would educate, promote, and train the employees in CSR) to track and analyze CSR maturity performance. With this regular auditing and practicing, the company can achieve higher levels of CSR maturity, which not only improves their social status but also increase the firm's economy with fewer resources.

5. Implications and recommendations

This study clearly states the current position of the two leading Indian companies regarding CSR maturity level; both case companies lag behind "best practices" expectations. Hence, case industrial managers need to think hard about the benefits of CSR for their firm's effectiveness. Both cases in our study lacked moral ethics rather than supporting regulations and financial additives. To improve their status, we offer some preliminary recommendations. These recommendations fall into two categories: voluntary and mandatory recommendations.

Mandatory recommendations:

- The government needs to provide strict legislation to firms to monitor their support to the local community through welfare campaigns and local labor recruitment.

- Firms that practice CSR should be given relief from export and import taxes by the government.

- In the Indian scenario, the government should monitor firms following strict labor codes as a vital issue, because over time new recruitment is reduced.

Voluntary recommendations:

- Industrial managers should bring awareness of CSR to top-level management and other employees by establishing CSR's long-term benefits.

- Apart from mandatory regulations, with moral ethics, top-level management should pay customs, taxes, and rights for workers. In addition, top management should provide jobs and other welfare benefits to local communities.

- An important role in the supply chain is played by suppliers; thus, the focal firm should motivate suppliers for innovative, sustainable ideas and give preference to those suppliers over alternatives.

6. Conclusions

The aim of this paper is to propose a maturity model for CSR, especially one that is applied in a developing context such as India, by linking its CSR practices with a particular focus on SCM. This paper also explores the relationship and influence of CSR practices over their maturity levels through two case studies. For this study, two different Indian case application sectors were chosen, but both focus on reverse supply chains—i.e., remanufacturing. The study results reveal that case 1 is at a preventive level of CSR maturity, and case 2 is at a reactive level. Neither case 1 nor case 2 belongs to a proactive level of CSR. This study also reveals that managers are more focused on the economic values of the firm than on moral ethics and innovation. This attitude of managers is influenced by many factors, including lack of government support, customer willingness to pay more for sustainable products, and poor governance.

Endnote

1 Maialle, G., Jabbour, A.B.L.D.S., Arantes, A.F. and Jabbour, C.J.C. (2016), "Environmental management maturity of local and multinational high-technology corporations located in Brazil: The role of business internationalization in pollution prevention", *Production*, Vol. 26 No. 2, pp.488-499.

Evaluating the essential barrier to offshore wind energy - an Indian perspective

Kannan Govindan
Center for Sustainable Supply Chain Engineering
University of Southern Denmark

Madan Shankar Kalidoss
Center for Sustainable Supply Chain Engineering
University of Southern Denmark

Idea in Brief
The purpose of this paper is to evaluate the essential barriers and to reveal the priority of common barriers of offshore wind energy in an Indian context, with the assistance of the proposed framework.

1. Introduction
Due to its various benefits, energy generation through wind has gained a good reception from practitioners, which has led to the development of onshore wind farms. Owing to these developments, many nations started to install wind farms but soon recognized that these wind farms consumed a major land area of the nation. This limitation became the seed for offshore wind power; in recent decades, offshore wind energy has become popular[1] due to the consequences (less sustainable power) of onshore wind farms. Due to their benefits, the pioneering of offshore wind energy has been launched globally. However, some developing nations are still striving hard to implement and construct offshore wind farms. Compared with onshore wind farms, offshore wind farm installation is more difficult.[2] Therefore, new methodologies are needed to successfully implement offshore wind farms in developing nations. But prior to formulating the methodology, we need

to analyze the hindrances involved in the implementation of offshore wind farms, particularly in developing nations, and based on the hindrances, a robust methodology can be formulated more easily. Hence, this study focused on the common barriers involved in the implementation of offshore wind farms from an Indian perspective; further, the research sought to find the most important barrier and its priority. The essential barrier is being evaluated among a group of common barriers, which makes this study a multicriteria problem. Thus, this study applied a multicriteria decision-making tools, analytical hierarchy process (AHP), to evaluate the essential barrier and to assign priority among common barriers involved in the implementation of offshore wind energy farms in India.

Figure 1. The proposed framework for the study

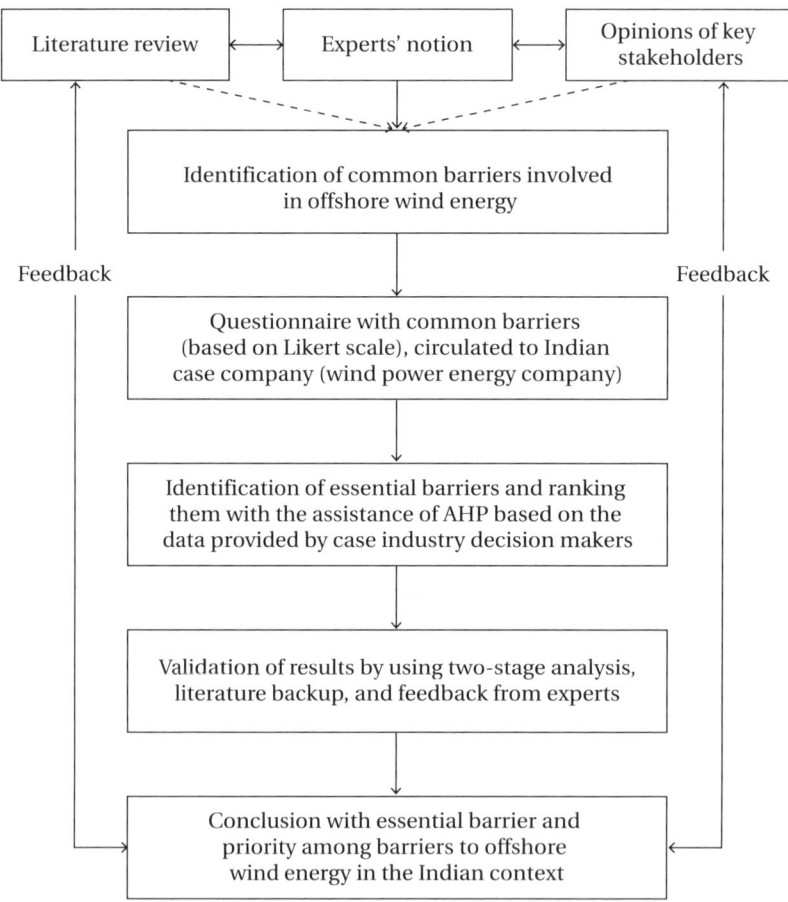

2. Approach

Based on the proposed framework, a five-phase methodology was adapted to explore the essential barrier step-by-step. The common barriers, which were collected from the existing literature through systematic review, were further validated with field experts. The collected common barriers were evaluated with the assistance of case industry field professionals through an AHP, a multicriteria decision-making tool, to evaluate the barriers to Indian offshore wind energy.

2.1 Phase I: Identification of common barriers involved in offshore wind energy

The first phase identified the common challenges involved in the installation of offshore wind energy farms. To complete this phase, a two-step methodology was proposed. The first step was to secure a literature foundation, and the next step was to seek assistance from experts and key stakeholders. Once the basic preliminaries and nomenclature of the study were detailed to the experts, the collected common barriers were shown; after many rounds of discussions, 12 barriers were finalized, as shown in Table 1.

Table 1. Common barriers of offshore wind energy

S. No	Barriers
1	Wind characterization (**B1**)
2	Physical constraints related to seabed usage (**B2**)
3	Ineffective policies (**B3**)
4	Lack of transmission and infrastructure (**B4**)
5	High capital cost (**B5**)
6	Lack of knowledge and experience (**B6**)
7	Lack of involvement from stakeholders (**B7**)
8	Lack of technological learning (**B8**)
9	Unavailability of local expertise (**B9**)
10	Lack of ecosystem R&D (**B10**)
11	Lack of incentives (**B11**)
12	Environmental clearance problems (**B12**)

Source: Adopted from Govindan and Shankar (2016)[3]

2.2 Phase II: Questionnaire with common barriers of offshore wind farms circulated to case industry

Our research team sent an e-mail to 20 leading wind power companies throughout the nation's vast geography but only received a positive reply from five companies. From those five companies, our research team chose a wind power (case company) company that is a well-known wind energy provider in India, located in the southern part of India. It has various sister concerns all over the nation. Our research team asked them to rate the barriers based on the Likert scale, which was further converted into the Saaty scale for processing the data in AHP.

2.3 Phase III: Identification of essential barriers and their priority, with the assistance of decision makers through AHP

To identify the essential barrier and its priority among common barriers of offshore wind farms, the steps of AHP to be followed are detailed below.

- Step 1: Identifying the common attributes
- Step 2: Set up the pairwise comparison matrix
- Step 3: Estimation of global weights
- Step 4: Check for consistency
- Step 5: Prioritization of attributes

2.4 Phase IV: Validation of results by using two-stage analysis, literature support, and feedback from experts

In this phase, the results from the previous phases were examined through existing literature and discussions with the case company decision makers. However, because these results are based on human judgments, there is a chance of a bias, and a gap may arise between practical implementation and state-of-the-art theory. Hence, this validation phase will be detailed in the upcoming sections.

2.5 Phase V: Conclusion with essential barrier and priority among barriers of offshore wind energy in the Indian context

Once the validation was made from the existing literature and feedback from the case industry professionals, the ranking of barriers of offshore wind farms in an Indian context was revealed for dissemination.

3. Findings

Among the 12 common barriers of offshore wind energy, it is clear that "high capital cost" (B5) is the most essential barrier involved in the implementation of offshore wind energy farms in the Indian context. In addition, lack of involvement from stakeholders (B7) and ineffective policies (B3) hold the second and third positions, respectively. The fourth and fifth positions belong to lack of incentives (B11) and lack of knowledge and experience (B6). The remaining barriers claim their place as per their weightage. The overall importance of the barriers are as follows: B5 > B7 > B3 > B11 > B6 > B12 > B2 > B1 > B4 > B8 > B9 > B10. For any developing nation, finance is a major reason for many unsuccessful innovative strategies. Similarly, for offshore wind power installation, cost is a major barrier, as is evident from this study. The decision makers in developing countries are bound by limitations of finance and many governmental policies. These constraints do not allow them to think about the long-term effectiveness of these renewable strategies, so the study's results indicate cost as a major influential barrier to Indian offshore wind power. As in earlier discussions, it is worth mentioning that onshore wind farms are not economically better than offshore wind farms, but the energy generation in offshore wind farms is less compared to onshore wind farms. However, the initial installation and building costs for offshore wind farms are heavier, so many organizations still think about the major capital required.

Next to cost, lack of involvement among stakeholders is recorded as the second most essential barrier, and it is normal that high-cost strategies are always less attractive to stakeholders, including shareholders, government, employees, media, local supporters, NGOs, and so on. Due to the high cost, stakeholders (mainly shareholders) are reluctant to become involved in such strategies. Among stakeholders, apart from shareholders, governments play a major role, because less involvement among government officials in offshore wind power development has become a major roadblock that can cut short other actions to improve renewable strategies. This lack of involvement from government is demonstrated through a lack of policies, which is a major challenge for offshore power developments. Ineffective policies are highly correlated with the unsuccessful implementation of offshore wind energy projects. However, all the stakeholders are not playing the same role in Indian offshore wind power, because the implementation strategies of offshore projects are highly dependent on the shareholders and government. From these discussions, it became clear that the study results are highly consistent and validated with existing literature. It was time to explore the results with the case company decision makers.

The results were shown to the decision makers of the case company to evaluate the soundness of the results and to get their feedback. They confirmed that they were facing a major problem of financial constraints. One of the decision makers said that his top-level management thinks twice about investing money in these new offshore wind power (OWP) strategies where there is no previous experience. He also admitted that it was tough to be involved in such operations without government support and policies. Another decision maker stated that the employees were not ready for such new strategies unless they were engaged in hands-on training rather than theoretical education. However, in general, contrary to the view of the decision makers, the financial constraints are not raised by the lack of experience. Their hesitation may be just a convenient reason; if they were willing to spend, then the shareholders could avail some offshore strategies developed by foreign professionals in the implementation of offshore wind farms in India. Therefore, the major threat is not experience, since it is dependent on capital investments. After several rounds of discussions, each barrier was explored depending on its priority level, and at the end, the decision makers were satisfied with the results. They will likely try to eradicate these barriers for the effective implementation of offshore wind energy systems.

Based on the above discussions, our research team recommends that the case company provide training and knowledge regarding the paybacks of offshore wind power systems especially to investors and to other government officials in related energy departments. The team also advises that an endorsement of wind energy's renewable contributions to society is made. As a private firm, it is difficult for the case company to make big decisions on its own, so decision makers were told to work out a proposal to get government incentives for such projects. In this regard, employers need to know about all technical challenges of offshore wind power. For this, employers need to be trained in pioneering offshore systems such as those found in Denmark and the United Kingdom.

4. Implications and recommendations

This study reveals the importance of offshore wind power as a long-term profitable strategy to the case company within the Indian context. By addressing the essential barriers of offshore wind farms, Indian offshore wind system managers can train their employees to counteract the impediments through benchmarking of pioneering global offshore wind power developers like Denmark and the United Kingdom. Further, this study provides useful suggestions to the Indian government regarding policies for offshore wind energy; it also clearly projects the current status of Indian offshore wind farm implementation. This study assists Indian key stakeholders of offshore wind energy by indicating the essential barrier in an Indian context, from which they can remove the particular barrier instead of focusing on others that previous studies identified. Further, this study highlights the importance of offshore wind power in an Indian context, which can urge stakeholders to invest more in offshore wind farms. For effective implementation of offshore wind farms, the following recommendations are suggested.

- Our study clearly demonstrates that high capital cost is the main barrier to offshore wind energy in India. According to the studies, this barrier can be eliminated by exploring the scale of economics, learning effects, and research and development activities over the long term. Hence, government and private offshore departments need to spend some funds on an annual budget for these kinds of sustainable energy projects.

- Government involvement is a major driver to move forward in offshore wind energy sectors, but according to the current situation, unlike with European nations, the policies are not yet tight. Therefore, the Indian government needs to focus on policies, which are recommended by Kota et al.[4]

- The government needs to fund innovation in offshore wind power systems to study wind characterization and optimization of installation cost.

- In addition to the government, shareholders should also voluntarily come forward to implement such sustainable energy generation strategies by keeping long-term success in mind rather than considering only the capital investments.

5. Conclusion

This study sought to evaluate the essential barriers and their priority levels among the barriers of offshore wind energy in India. The model framework was proposed to address the research question raised earlier. Based on the methodological framework, the barriers are evaluated with the assistance of case industry managers. Common barriers were identified with the combined assistance of a literature review and expert opinions. The identified barriers were compared based on the replies of the case company decision makers, and further data was processed through AHP. The results revealed that high capital cost (B5) is the most essential barrier to offshore wind energy implementation in an Indian context. The obtained results were validated and explored with appropriate literature and experts' backup. By identifying the essential barrier, the stakeholders of offshore wind energy systems can easily eradicate that specific barrier; hence, this study contributed scientifically and socially. By eradicating the barriers, more power production can be developed through sustainability to balance the nation's energy scarcity.

Endnotes

1 Dannenberg, L. (2014), "Offshore Wind Energy", in: Schaffarczyk, A. (Ed.) (2014), *Understanding Wind Power Technology: Theory, Deployment and Optimisation*, Wiley, pp. 406-454.

2 Sun, X., Huang, D. and Wu, G. (2012), "The current state of offshore wind energy technology development", *Energy*, Vol. 41 No. 1, pp.298-312.

3 Govindan, K. and Shankar, M. (2016), "Evaluating the essential barrier to off-shore wind energy–an Indian perspective", *International Journal of Energy Sector Management*, Vol. 10 No. 2, pp. 266-282.

4 Kota, S., Bayne, S.B. and Nimmagadda, S. (2015), "Offshore wind energy: A comparative analysis of UK, USA and India", *Renewable and Sustainable Energy Reviews*, Vol. 41, pp. 685-694.

9.
Emerging issues

In view of the uncertain dynamics of today's global marketplace, it is important to explore emerging future trends that may influence industries. Supply chains are seen as a valuable component of all business planning, and hence, they must be continuously monitored. Notably, supply chain management (SCM) as a concept in the offshore wind industry (OWI) has gained significantly more attention recently because of technological development, digitalization, and globalization. We all realize how digitalization of the retail industry is changing how we do business. However, the evolution of business technology also affects how we store data and how our machinery operates. It is an exciting time to work in the OWI. Technological advancements might be complex initially; however, they will greatly improve speed, efficiency, and overall quality of the OWI and the supply chain. SCM provides enterprises, particularly manufacturers, with enormous competitive as well as business advantages.

Nevertheless, SCM is associated with challenges/issues especially in today's business/market environment. Some of the key emerging issues in SCM in OWI are globalization, fast-changing markets, quality and compliance, challenging functional silos, adapting to the unpredictable environment, more digitalization or "the Internet of Things," big data, etc. This section reflects on the views as well as contributions of various authors concerning these key emerging issues in managing supply chains in the OWI.

The first article in this section addresses big data in a service supply chain. The second article addresses the framework on offshore wind energy circular economy maturity by employing a circular business model approach. The third article discusses the need for vocational education in operations and maintenance of offshore wind power. The fourth article focuses on the degree of knowledge, perceived importance, and current practice of Industry 4.0 among Danish manufacturers. This article presents various Industry 4.0 technologies and practices across different firm sizes and conveys how Industry 4.0 enables the reduced cost of energy (ReCoE).

Overall, the four articles in this section offer practical thoughts on various emerging issues that are crucial to OWI firms.

Value creation mechanisms of big data in supply chain management

Morten Brinch
Department of Entrepreneurship and Relationship Management
University of Southern Denmark

Idea in Brief
The focus of this paper is to explore big data and its value creation mechanisms in supply chain management (SCM) from a business process and focal firm perspective. The paper

- *Provides an SCM conceptualization and understanding of big data;*

- *Highlights firm-level success factors for the value creation of big data in SCM; and*

- *Explains critical alignment practices important to the value creation of big data*

1. Introduction
This article will present the results of an industrial PhD dissertation carried out in an operations and maintenance context in the wind energy industry. The collective PhD dissertation includes four academic articles focusing on areas of terminologies, applications, conceptualization, antecedents, and alignment practices important to the phenomena of big data and its value creation in supply chain management. Two of the four articles are published in international peer-reviewed journals.[1][2]

2. The importance of big data

Big data is a new concept that has entered the business world and has been outlined as the next frontier for innovation, competition, and productivity. Supply chain management (SCM) practices traditionally use data and information to improve supply chain performance, for example, to achieve lower costs, better service, shorter lead times, and increased productivity. Studies have documented that companies implementing data-driven decision-making were, on average, 5 percent more productive and 6 percent more profitable than their competitors[3], and top-performing companies were twice as likely to apply analytics to activities.[4]

A data-driven approach in SCM is an important means to deal with the complexities of the end-to-end process of products and services through sourcing, inventory management, planning, manufacturing, logistics, sales, and R&D that also can span across firm boundaries. Currently, SCM is undergoing significant changes that count numerous disruptive technologies, in which the concept and technology of big data has emerged as a widely used buzzword for insightful data analysis on large datasets. Big data can be used for a wide range of supply chain applications[5] and will to a large extent disrupt existing decision-making practices. The motivation is to improve current decision-making capabilities as an intermediate effect on improving business process outcomes, which include descriptive, predictive, and prescriptive analytic capabilities for making decisions faster, more precisely, and more informedly. Descriptive analytical capabilities are is the summarization and description of data patterns using simple statistical methods to identify problems and opportunities within existing processes and functions. Predictive analytics use mathematical algorithms and programming to discover explanatory and predictive patterns within data to accurately project what will happen in the future. Prescriptive analytics use data and mathematical algorithms to determine and assess cause–effect relationships among analytic results and business process optimization policies to improve business performance.

Although the utilization of big data can increase the performance and competitive advantage of a company, we see that big data and digitalization are weakly presented in company strategies, and profound challenges exist in transforming from a "data" approach to a "big data" approach focused on SCM issues and opportunities. Thus, companies are struggling to realize the potential value of big data. The perception that "the more data gathered, the better the decision-making" is too simplistic a view; additional capabilities are needed. Some companies have successfully created value from big data in certain application areas but have not delivered repeated benefits to the organization. Therefore, there is a need for developing holistic SCM and big data capabilities that span across the organization, processes, and functions.

2.1 Big data in operations and maintenance

The operations and maintenance (O&M) of wind turbines is an industry that particularly benefits from big data analytics. Big data in O&M is typically associated with the wind turbine as a smart-connected product that includes sensor technologies, allowing for remote diagnostics of monitoring, control, optimization, and autonomy to reduce costs and increase yield and turbine availability.[6] But big data in O&M is more than high-frequency turbine data and machine learning hereof to allow for condition-based maintenance. Machine learning is a type of artificial intelligence aimed to design algorithms that allow computers to evolve behaviors—e.g., through the discovery of knowledge—and make intelligent decisions automatically. Big data in O&M encompass the entire database ecosystem that surrounds the wind turbines, wind farms, service providers, manufacturers, utilities, energy storage, transmission, distribution, and trading as well as other actors in the wind energy value chain. Notably, the wind energy value chain is by exemplar a particularly complex end-to-end process that includes a high-tech product and a long, complex value chain with many actors, subcontractors, and stakeholders. The importance of big data to the industry has been recognized, and original equipment manufacturers (OEMs) and energy utilizes are investing in digitalization to turn data into value through the development of analytic capabilities in combination with condition-based maintenance practices. However, the wind industry is rather immature, which limits the degree to which the actors of the wind industry currently are benefitting from big data.

3. Defining big data

The concept of big data represents a new management paradigm, wherein intuition and knowledge-based reasoning have been replaced by a discourse reasoning based on logic, facts, and evidence that disrupts the status quo in the pursuit of higher competitiveness. The typical definition of big data is viewed as "a holistic approach to manage, process and analyze 5 Vs (i.e., volume, variety, velocity, veracity and value) in order to create actionable insights for sustained value delivery, measuring performance and establishing competitive advantages"[7], where:

- **Volume** refers to the rapid exponential growth of data volumes in the business world.

- **Variety** refers to the variety in data formats and the variety in data sources.

- **Velocity** refers to the frequency of data generation, the frequency of data delivery, or both.

- **Veracity** refers to the need to deal with imprecise and uncertain data.

- **Value** refers to how an enterprise can exploit big data to create added value.

4. An SCM understanding of big data

The fact that big data tends to be understood differently can constrain an organization's ability to implement big data and its enabling capabilities. Some refer big data to advanced analytics, others refer big data to comprise the large and growing data and system landscape that has become too difficult to comprehend, and others integrate big data with SCM theories and supply chain analytics. Therefore, a conceptualization of big data in SCM is needed to properly understand its terms and dimensions before big data can be utilized across the organization.

Despite different views toward big data, one characteristic for big data has been emphasized as value; however, a single dimension of value has been found too simplistic, and big data in SCM needs to be understood with more granularities. Figure 1 presents the conceptual understanding of big data in SCM through three value dimensions:

- **Value discovery** represents the ability to generate, locate, collect, store, and govern trustworthy data that relies on a transparent yet complex network of systems, platforms, and databases embedded with multiple data sources, diverse data characteristics, and various technologies enabling the collection, management, processing, and analysis of data.

- **Value creation** represents the use value of big data in domain-specific business processes and the ability to utilize the information generated from the big data ecosystem for strategic and/or operational decision making by using decision (support) systems.

- **Value capture** represents the exchange value of big data and the strategic components enabling big data–derived economic improvements, competitive gains, better performance, or other incentives that are realized through value discovery and value creation activities.

The framework is centered around business processes, which are found to be central to the value creation of big data, where the value of big data is created through business process activities and decisions made herein. On the one hand, business processes adopt strategic innovation through the exploration of data to implement more effective process configurations while, on the other hand, managing efficiency through exploiting existing data and systems in a faster way.

Figure 1. Big data SCM framework

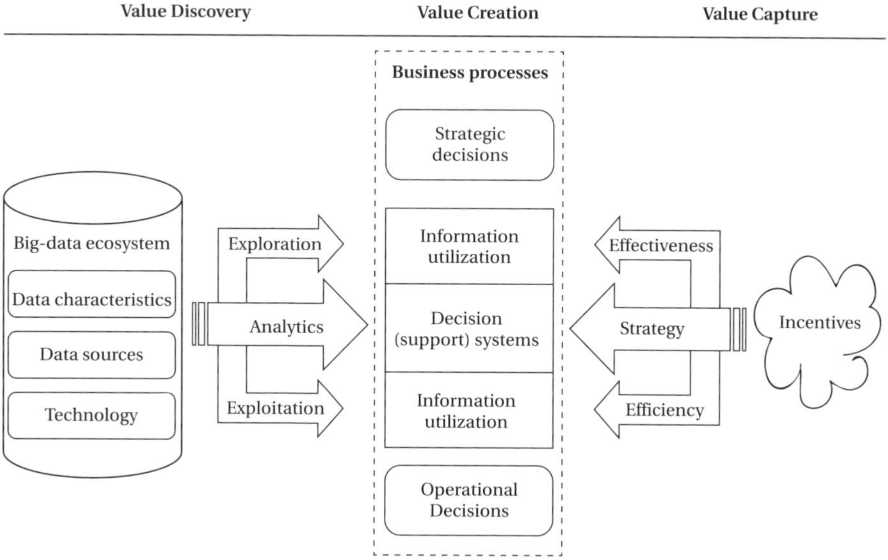

Source: Brinch (2018)[1]

5. Value creation of big data in SCM

The findings of this research have focused on three aspects of how value from big data can be created in SCM, namely through business processes, firm-level success factors, and critical alignment practices.

5.1 The implications of business process maturity on big data

As proclaimed, the value of big data is created through business process activities, in which data and information are a new/enhanced resource and input to a specific process or activity. Business Process Management (BPM) is thus an important concept that should be considered to reap the benefits of big data across the organization. This logic rests on the assumption that a low BPM maturity level will constrain a company's ability to utilize big data, whereas a high BPM maturity level will enhance a company's ability to create value from big data.

Participants interviewed noted that functional areas with a higher process maturity had better data collection, data management, and data utilization capabilities, thus securing a consistent inflow of data and information to inform specific activities as well as securing the alignment of process designs toward IT systems and applications. Additionally, a low degree of trust in data was observed in cases with absent or weak process descriptions and in cases with manual data entry rather than automated data collection through IT.

Obviously, companies have different process maturity levels. Immature companies typically find themselves having, e.g., silo-structured process definitions, lack of process standardizations, stand-alone IT systems, nonaligned performance measures, and poor coordination among functions and without the needed cross-functional expertise in redesign projects. Mature companies are typically process-oriented rather than functional-oriented, in which customer requirements are applied to improve cross-functional processes and the organizational structure assigns formal responsibility for cross-functional process management.

The research concludes that business processes are affected by the entry of big data. Business processes should adapt to the increasingly complex information flows to ensure that activities and processes are fit to the data and system environment. Therefore, whether a company has low or high BPM maturity, it must be willing to innovate on current business process designs to comply with the requirements of big data. Within BPM, innovation can come in two forms. One form of innovation is to make radical process innovations (also known as business process reengineering), which typically apply to cases of low levels of BPM maturity but also comes with certain risks because of its radical nature. Another form of innovation is incremental innovation, which includes the continuous improvement of business processes and typically applies to higher levels of BPM maturity. The type of innovation needed to create value from big data thus depends on the BPM maturity level.

5.2 Firm-level success factors of big data's value creation

Big data is often viewed as predominantly an IT phenomenon. But big data is more than an IT phenomenon—big data intertwines with other organizational practices such as strategy, processes, and organizational structures, thus affecting functional tasks across the organization. This research has identified additional five practices aside from IT practices that are important to the value creation of big data. The view of big data should be an organization-wide view that moves beyond the IT view and the data characteristics of volume, variety, velocity, veracity, and value. In total, 24 types of success factors are identified within IT, process, organizational, human, strategic, and performance practices (see Table 1).

Table 1. Firm-level success factors of big data's value creation

IT-related success factors	Process-related success factors	Organizational-related success factors
IT architecture	Process standardization	Organizational structure
Informatization	Process design	Organizational collaboration
IT governance	Process integration	Change management
Software applications	Process governance	Human resources
IT automation		Culture
Human-related success factors	**Strategic-related success factors**	**Performance-related success factors**
Knowledge	Objectives	Innovation of practices
Usage	IT strategy	Project management
Commitment	Business process strategy	Performance measurements
	Strategic alignment	

5.2.1 IT-related success factors

IT-related success factors comprise the technical capabilities of collecting, managing, and utilizing big data through the exploration and exploitation of data analytics. For example, this includes having an IT architecture that provides transparent data storage services to business functions, preferable through the ideology of providing a single source of truth to the users. Moreover, an effective informatization process (the activities of data collection, data preparation, data analysis, data visualization, and decision-making) is critical to ensure that analytics quality is readily generated and visualized in software applications support with important information on critical business decisions. Additionally, the success factors of governance include attributes of data standardization, policy making, process alignment, data maintenance, data ownership, system ownership, and security. Finally, IT automation allows for automated data collection, consistent data utilization, workflow integrations, and maybe even automated decision-making.

5.2.2 Process-related success factors

Concerning process-related success factors, this research confirmed, consistent with existing knowledge of how IT creates value, that the value of big data is created through business processes. Hence, data, information, and analytics knowledge by themselves do not create value but must be implemented in business processes and as part of decision-making activities. Furthermore, the maturity of BPM practices is found to affect the degree to which value from big data can be created. For example, immature business processes tend to fail in generating, capturing, storing, and governing data that later could bring valuable insights to the same or another process. Moreover, a company with a process-oriented structure and mindset is better capable of readily collecting, accessing, and sharing data across the organization and better capable of utilizing big data across business functions.

5.2.3 Organizational-related success factors

Organizational-related success factors are means to provide the structure and behavior supporting the value creation of big data. This could include reshaping the current organizational structure to reflect the criticality of digitalization, e.g., by deploying a digital transformation program, strengthening the IT function, or by developing analytic competence centers. Some companies organize big data as a centralized function, and others apply a decentralized approach.

Notably, a functional organizational structure is found to constrain the value creation of big data because it constrains process integrations, where roles, responsibilities, and resources may not be clearly distinguished between departments, thus limiting transparency, data access, and information sharing. The results of a functional structure would include data collection being uncoordinated across functions and processes and data being collected and stored to remain within functional boundaries. Therefore, a process-oriented organizational structure should be aspired to, as it hinders silo structuring, and data could be readily shared and used for multiple processes across the functions.

5.2.4 Human-related success factors

Human-related success factors represents the knowledge, usage and commitment of employees and managers. Knowledge about IT, digitalization, business processes, and big data combined with a holistic business understanding are obviously critical to develop effective big data solutions across the organization. Therefore, executives should be developing human resource strategies on how to secure analytics expertise either by training existing personnel or by hiring big data analytics experts. By extension, usage is a success factor that refers to how employees are adopting IT services, using informational insights in their decision-making, and complying with process standardizations. Finally, committing to the digitalization strategy regarding the degree of investments, willingly executing digitalization projects, and making the required change of practices were found to be important in adapting to a big data environment.

5.2.5 Strategic-related success factors

Strategic success factors are important because they help in guiding toward a desired set of practices related to big data and digitalization. In particular, the success factor of business objectives was often observed in the research project because the use of big data must be accompanied by a concrete business objective—e.g., to develop condition-based maintenance capabilities, increase turbine availability, decrease maintenance costs, or increase delivery reliability of turbine spare parts. Thus, the utilization and value creation of big data should be driven by a concrete business objective to make an impact to the organization. Another success factor was observed to include the IT strategy. The research found that the IT strategy should support digitally enabled end-to-end processes as well as define how IT can enable analytics innovation in the different business functions.

5.2.6 Performance-related success factors

Finally, the performance-related success factors represent a strong need to innovate current practices. It is found that certain practices need to change at the intersection of big data because new capabilities are needed—for example, the implementation of an Internet of Things (IoT) platform, the development of analytic competence centers, and the development of digitalization strategies. Additionally, existing practices need a higher level of maturity. Therefore, innovation is needed to unlock the value of big data, whose progress must be monitored through carefully selected performance measurements. Furthermore, project management capabilities are found to be important for ensuring that the developed innovations are fit to become operationalized and thereby create value to the business processes. The attributes of project management are observed to include business case development, portfolio management, cross-functional collaboration, and project execution.

5.3 Critical alignment practices

A company can have successful big data application by developing strong IT and analytics capabilities in a certain functional area. However, as an extension to the success factors, alignment between practices and success factors are needed to create a multiplier effect on the value creation of big data across the organization. Following the alignment logic, an analysis was made through eighteen interviews in a case study, from which alignment between success factors and practices was mapped and analyzed. The results are presented as different degrees of criticality and are based on the total amount of case observations made (see Table 2).

Table 2. Critical alignment practices of big data's value creation

Observed criticality	Alignment practices
High criticality	IT–process alignment, IT–performance alignment, human–IT alignment, and performance–process alignment
Intermediate criticality	human–performance alignment, human–process alignment, IT–strategic alignment, and organizational–process alignment
Low criticality	human–organizational alignment, human–strategic alignment, IT–organizational alignment, organizational–performance alignment, performance–strategic alignment, process–strategic alignment, and organizational–strategic alignment

Figure 2 portrays this need for alignment to differentiate between integral alignment practices and complementary alignment practices. The integral alignment practices of IT–process alignment, IT–performance alignment, and performance–process alignment were found to have the highest criticality toward the value creation of big data. The interplay and fit between the IT, process, and performance variables must be closely aligned in the data-to-information process, thus leading to better informational use and decision-making within business processes.

The complementary alignment practices support the integral alignment practices in being more effective and efficient toward the value creation of big data. These alignment practices include, for example, the alignment between human, organizational, and strategic practices. Further, they include certain IT, process, or performance alignment practices that are not grouped as an integral alignment practice—for example, human–process alignment, IT–human alignment, and IT–strategic alignment.

Figure 2. Big data value-creating alignment framework

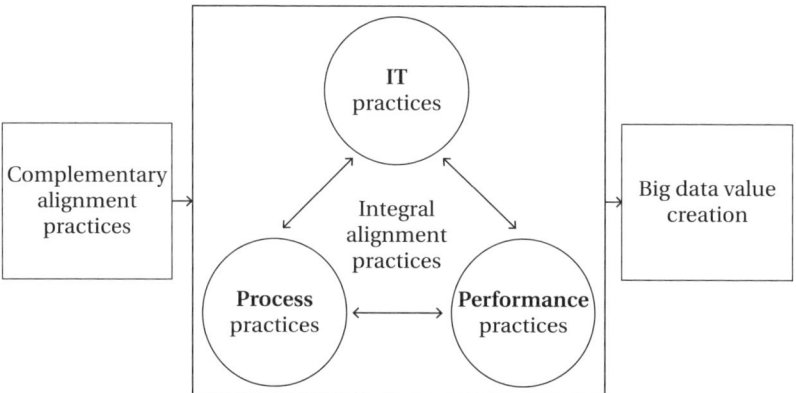

6. Conclusion

Although big data may profoundly change SCM practices and the benefits of being data-driven are well documented, organizations are struggling to create value from big data and have yet to capture the benefits. Consequently, knowledge regarding big data and big data value creation in SCM is in a nascent state. This article has provided valuable insights about how to understand big data in SCM, outlined important value creation mechanisms, and discussed the criticality of alignment between practices and success factors.

Endnotes

1 Brinch, M. (2018), "Understanding the value of big data in supply chain management and its business processes: Towards a conceptual framework", *International Journal of Operations & Production Management*, Vol. 38 No. 7, pp. 1589–1614.

2 Brinch, M., Stentoft, J., Jensen, J.K. and Rajkumar, C. (2018), "Practitioners understanding of big data and its applications in supply chain management", *The International Journal of Logistics Management*, Vol. 29 No. 2, pp. 555–574.

3 McAfee, A. and Brynjolfsson, E. (2012), "Big data: The management revolution", *Harvard Business Review*, Vol. 90 No. 10, pp. 60–68.

4 Lavalle, S., Lesser, E., Shockley, R., Hopkins, M.S. and Kruschwitz, N. (2011), "Big data, analytics and the path from insights to value", *MIT Sloan Management Review*, Vol. 52 No. 2, pp. 21–32.

5 Wang, G., Gunasekaran, A., Ngai, E.W.T. and Papadopoulos, T. (2016), "Big data analytics in logistics and supply chain management: certain investigations for research and applications", *International Journal of Production Economics*, Vol. 176, pp. 98–110.

6 Porter, M.E. and Heppelmann, J.E. (2014), "How smart, connected products are transforming competition", *Harvard Business Review*, Vol. 92 No. 11, pp. 64–88.

7 Fosso Wamba, S., Akter, S., Edwards, A., Chopin, G. and Gnanzou, D. (2015), "How "big data" can make big impact: Findings from a systematic review and a longitudinal case study", *International Journal of Production Economics*, Vol. 165, pp. 234–246.

Framework on offshore wind energy circular economy maturity—a circular business model approach

Kannan Govindan
Center for Sustainable Supply Chain Engineering
University of Southern Denmark

Idea in Brief
This paper aims to propose a framework that connects the maturity level of circular economy (CE) implementation in the offshore wind energy value chain through by implementing proposed circular business models. From the framework, the concern drivers and barriers of CE maturity in the offshore wind sector are explored. Further, the conclusions highlight the research gap concerning a focus on effective implementation and sustainability of CE in offshore wind energy sectors.

1. Introduction

The past few decades have produced several technological advancements in offshore wind power, including use of composites, lightweight materials, effective supply chain operations, and so on. In the line of development, the offshore sector has come under the pressure to address sustainable development goals (SDGs), which were adapted by United Nations members in the "2030 agenda for sustainable development." Recently, it has proven that to sustain the business, economic success alone is not sufficient; in addition, the system needs to satisfy the other two dimensions (environment and society) of sustainable developments. Various strategies have been introduced and developed by researchers and practitioners around the world to encourage sustainable development practices in various fields, including the offshore wind power sector. Among those strategies, in recent years the circular economy (CE) has become an irreplaceable option for achieving sustainable development. After the report from MacArthur Foundation 2012 and 2015, more researchers were engaged to promote the CE practices in their operations. It is due to the momentous impacts of CE on economy, environment, and society. From the earlier reports, it has been estimated that CE can assist in carbon emission reduction and increasing job opportunities. The CE is the concept of transforming a business model from linear to circular, as shown in Figure 1. Figure 1 explains the technical and biological nutrients of the CE business model. However, offshore wind farms are new to the field; hence, more focus has been given to installation and operation, concerning large costs, difficulties in logistics, and environmental impacts without concerning the end-of-life activities through the circular loop. Furthermore, the offshore sectors are in a position to achieve sustainable development through their closed loop operations, and similar benefits can be obtained from the implementation of CE. Hence, this study considers implementing CE in offshore wind energy. CE is defined by several loops, which can indicate level of maturity; accordingly, to achieve a higher level of maturity across the offshore value chain, several circular business models (CBMs) are needed. This study has collected some of the CBMs and combined the offshore value chain and CE maturity to identify the drivers and barriers of CE implementation in the offshore wind sector.

Figure 1. Loops of circular economy[1]

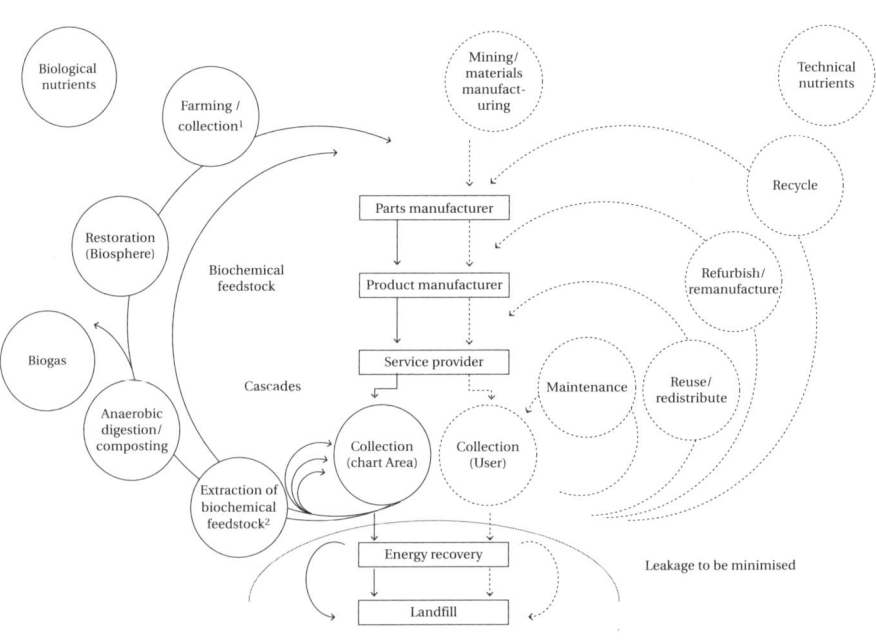

1 Hunting and fishing
2 Can take both post-harvest and post consumer waste as an input

2. Offshore wind energy value chain—a CE perspective

In the offshore sector, 83 percent by weight, excluding foundation, were recycled whereas only 8 percent were reused, which clearly shows that the offshore wind sector is in the preliminary level of the CE. Also, there is a clear urge to propose new CE perspectives on the offshore wind sector to achieve the inner loops of CE. Offshore wind turbine farms having five different value chains (shown in Figure 2)—namely, design phase, sourcing and manufacturing, siting and installations, operational phase, and decommissioning. With this concern, the potential of CE across the offshore value chain is discussed in Table 1.

Figure 2. Offshore wind energy value chain

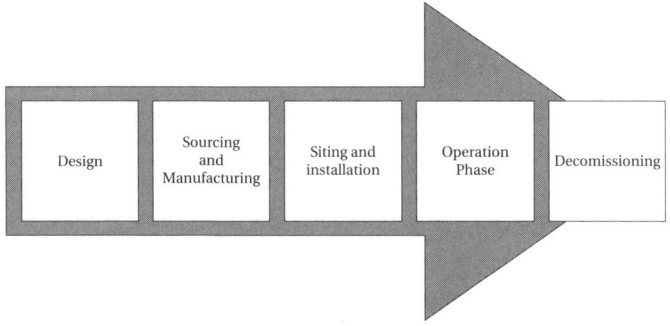

Table 1. Offshore value chain with CE perspective

Value chain	CE perspectives
Design	Designing the components involved in offshore wind farms needs to consider the circular design principles, which can help form a structured approach for various standards, including eco-design and sustainable design. In this stage, the designers need to include modern technologies in the form of modularized design to make dismantling easy. The design of offshore wind should maintain product performance targets through an extended lifetime (over 25 years) and less carbon footprint while encouraging renewable energy use and waste reductions. In addition, the designer perspective on offshore wind farms should consider minimum usage of nonrecyclable/reusable materials and toxic materials. New material selection methodology should be engaged with the selection of circular materials.

Sourcing and Manufacturing	Due to the presence of more than 25,000 parts, sourcing plays a major role in the offshore wind sector. However, suppliers need to be assessed with circular criteria and considered based on their respective weights on circular performance. Also, the offshore wind sector involves transportation of big vessels, extra size turbine blades, and so on; hence, the supplier has an optimized transportation plan that can reduce the carbon footprint of the transportation and reduce the moving cost. Next, for sourcing, manufacturing of parts involved in the offshore wind sectors is frequent. Most of the turbines and blades are manufactured by the company itself. During manufacturing, the company needs to apply various CE principles, including industrial symbiosis, which means one business's waste is another's raw material. This can promote waste minimization in offshore wind sectors, especially during the production of wind turbines and blades. The secondary materials can be also used in manufacturing, which promotes repurposing or reuse in the offshore value chain. If possible, tracking the materials can improve the reliability of the material, which encourages process transparency. This tracking can be done through modern technologies like blockchain.
Siting and installation	Siting and installation involve more transportation and allocations. Hence, circular supply chain strategies can be adopted to avoid unnecessary movements. Moreover, circular thinking helps supply chain engineers to fully utilize the transport equipment. In these stages, there is a possibility of using recycled materials, including transport frames.
Operational phase	This phase has a huge potential to deploy CE to close the loop by minimizing the cost of transportation, recovery, storage, and remanufacturing. Effective utilization of reverse logistics and smart maintenance can assist the operation in running smoothly. The operating line can be upgraded with recycled or remanufactured components during maintenance. In addition, several measures need to be taken to extend the lifetime of the components. Effective technologies can be used to replace the rotten parts with new parts, which can reduce downtime and improve operations.
Decommissioning	This is the final phase, at which the CE reaches its full potential. Making the decommissioning as effective as possible depends on the best operation and maintenance strategies being used along with life-extension business models. Hence, decommissioned parts can be used for various purposes (repurposing) or can be reused. All possibilities in decommissioning should be explored, including take-back policies and reuse of end-of-life materials. New business models for the remanufacturing and reusing the turbine blades, instead of recycling them, should be developed.

3. CBMs in the offshore wind sector

The business model concepts are not new to the research realm, dating back in the 1940s. They have been used to visualize and capture the value mechanisms involved in the companies. There have been numerous definitions for a business model but one of the most cited definitions, from Osterwalder and Pigneur (2010)[2], is, "A business model is a rationale of how an organization creates, delivers and captures value." With the success of the business model, more researchers started to explore a various business model approach to achieve sustainable development, including sustainable business models, CBMs, lean models, and so on. Among such business models, CBMs are designed to implement the CE successfully. As per the literature perspective, CBMs are not yet defined well. However, the two most cited CBMs come from the Ellen Macarthur Foundation[3] (ReSOLVE) and Bocken et al.[4] ("Resource cycles: Slowing, closing and narrowing loops"). CBM mostly aims to function under certain principles such as closing the material cycle as quickly as possible, utilizing the full potential of the materials and energy, and reducing material and energy use within the cycle. Though the CBM has many advantages, there are very few case studies working with CBMs in which the offshore wind energy sector is one of the applications, as the CBM has not yet been considered in the offshore wind energy sector. This study considers CBMs as tools to achieve higher maturity levels in CE among the offshore value chain. Some key CBMs are discussed below.

3.1 Circular design

This business model helps offshore wind farms get closer to the inner loops of CE. The main principle of circular design is to select the materials and design the part to provide higher residual value and last longer. Hence, there is no need to change the entire part; instead, it is easy to upgrade, repair, and maintain with respective conditions. In terms of materials, new materials can be developed to prioritize long-lasting life without diminishing the technical targets. Design engineers need to work with operational managers of the offshore wind farm to explore the full potential of reuse and recovery.

3.2 Circular supplies

This model aims to give the input as circular supplies, which means all materials and energy used as input for offshore wind farms are fully renewables, reusable, remanufactured, and repaired. This business model supports circular production and consumption throughout the value chain. The material supplies within the offshore wind power system should be maintained with less environmental footprint and minimal use of rare and toxic resources. This model tries to eliminate virgin products completely with high-quality secondary products. Further, the supply chain and suppliers are monitored and optimized with relevant strategies, including circular supplier selection, circular transportation, and so on.

3.3 Resources recovery

This business model is proposed to avoid the material and energy leakage throughout the value chain. Usually, existing systems fail to capture the economic value of reverse supply chain at the time of decommissioning or maintenance. Hence, it is necessary to focus on reverse waste streams to reclaim the potential. Furthermore, the reclaim should be cost-effective, as in an application like offshore wind power the turbine blades are recycled through various ways at their end of life; therefore, this business model can assist such processes for reclaiming the original product as well as the by-products.

3.4 Product life extension

This model can help offshore companies maintain the value of their assets over time by extending the life cycle of the products. This business model greatly relies on the power inner circles of the CE that extend the product life through maintenance, repair, refurbish, and sometimes even upgrade. In offshore wind farms, products can be taken back and refurbished and even sold in new markets. For instance, the grids installed in the offshore wind farms can be removed at decommissioning and sold to an underdeveloped nation for conceding minimum output power.

3.5 Sharing economy

The sharing economy business model is more popular in recent days with cab and taxi applications, but it can also serve a beneficial impact in offshore wind sectors. This model promotes the full utilization of resources by collaboration with shared use. Exchanging knowledge and resources among and between companies can improve the whole system in regard to circular principles. This model also helps during times of more and less demand; that is, the companies with more and less capacity can adapt the shared model to beat the demand fluctuations.

3.6 Servitization

The servitization business model, which is more popular recently, treats the product as performance and service. The service providers are the owners of the product, and they are paid based on their performance but not on their product. The life of the product is extended because of the servitization business model, which helps to achieve the inner loops of the CE. Operational managers need to pay per use; thus, the cost of the business is adjusted with the level of demand. This business model could be adopted by the offshore wind energy sectors because this model works best with products that involve high cost, and the offshore wind sectors are fully equipped with such high-cost products. Hence, the high-cost offshore products are serviced, upgraded, and maintained regularly with this servitization business model.

3.7 Tracking facility

This business model assists managers in tracking materials and other components involved in the system so that they can assess the material quality as virgin or secondary material. This tracking system records the product installed, and once the product reaches its end of life, the system assists in take-back. Furthermore, the data is stored in the cloud, which might be used in secondary market sales. In addition, this business model allows multiple stakeholders to see the data so that end-of-life waste management becomes easier. This tracking facility with the assistance of modern technology like blockchain can improve performance and efficiency with the combined knowledge of technology, processes, and people.

4. Proposed framework

By combining all views, a framework has been proposed (Figure 3). The triangle indicates the levels of maturity in CE implementation, starting from disposal and leading to prevention/maintenance. On the left, the value chain of offshore wind energy farms is listed. To achieve CE maturity in offshore value chains, CBMs are used. However, in this process, there may be several drivers and barriers that promote and hinder the implementation of CE in the offshore wind sector value chain through CBMs. Hence, the drivers and barriers are extensively collected from the existing literature with the assistance of a theoretical background in implementation of CE in the offshore wind energy sector. Table 2 shows the common drivers and barriers involved in the process; however, this is not an entire list. There are several other drivers and barriers involved, but as a pioneering work, this study includes the major common drivers and barriers.

Figure 3. Proposed framework on achieving CE maturity in the offshore wind sector value chain through CBM

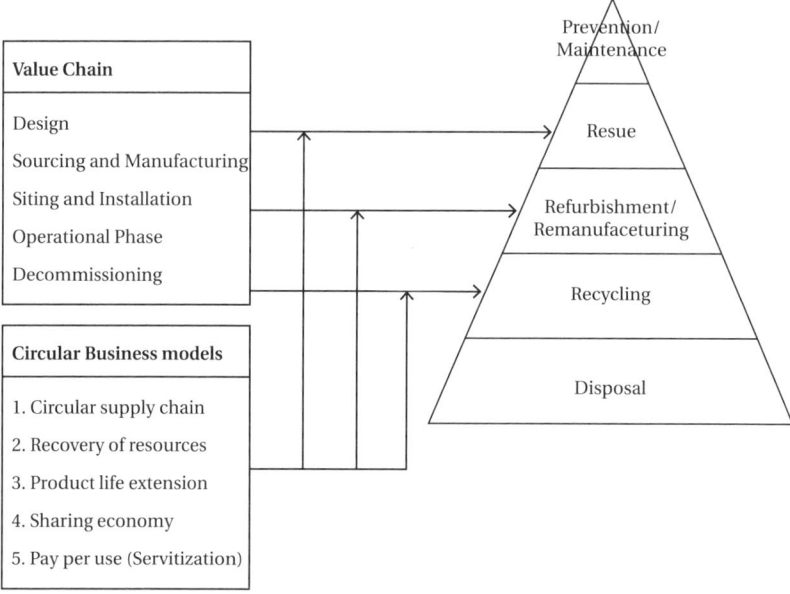

Table 2. Drivers and barriers of implementing CE in the offshore wind sector value chain

S. No	Drivers	Barriers
1	Economic losses	High initial cost
2	Price and supply risk	Lack of circular design expertise
3	Natural system degradation	Industry perception of decommissioning purely as "cost"
4	Technology advancements	Limited experience in offshore CBMs
5	Stakeholder pressure	Limited reprocessing facilities
6	Acceptance of CBMs	Offshore market relatively young
7	Regulatory pressures	Few incentives for manufacturers
8	Waste generation	Difficulties in recertification of used equipment
9	More decommissioning yet to come	No steady secondary market
10	The arrival of new materials	International policy barriers
11	Existing offshore wind farms lack sustainable perspective	Handling, including dismantling, involves more time and labor
12	Capacity set to double in upcoming years	The unclear vision of CE in the offshore wind sector value chain

5. Conclusion

Offshore wind energy has become a highly successful alternative to nonrenewable energy sources, with less negative impact on the environment. However, this relatively young industry has yet to achieve sustainable development because of a lack of sustainable development business models. With this concern, this study has focused on the offshore wind energy sector with a CE, which is one of the best strategies to achieve sustainable development. To reach the maturity level of the CE in the offshore wind value chain, new business models are needed. Hence, this study has suggested some well-known CBMs from an offshore wind energy perspective. During implementation of CE through CBMs, several drivers and barriers that elevate or hinder CE implementation may be involved. With this combined framework, the common drivers and barriers are identified and tabulated (but not limited to this list). This study pioneers a new field by integrating CE maturity with offshore wind energy sectors. In addition, this study recommends utilizing recent technologies like Industry 4.0, additive manufacturing, smart manufacturing, blockchain, and so on to capture the full potential of resources. However, 85 percent (by weight excluding foundation) of products from offshore wind farms are recycled, which shows the sector is still in the preliminary stages of CE. More CE practices should be integrated over the offshore value chain to increase the maturity level of CE implementation through maintenance, repair, and refurbishing.

Endnotes

1 https://www.ellenmacarthurfoundation.org/assets/downloads/publications/Ellen-MacArthur-Foundation-Towards-the-Circular-Economy-vol.1.pdf

2 Osterwalder, A. and Pigneur, Y. (2010), *Business Model Generation: A Handbook for Visionaries, Game Changers, and Challengers*, Wiley, New York.

3 https://www.ellenmacarthurfoundation.org/assets/downloads/publications/EllenMacArthurFoundation_PolicymakerToolkit.pdf

4 https://www.ellenmacarthurfoundation.org/assets/downloads/publications/EllenMacArthurFoundation_PolicymakerToolkit.pdf

The need for vocational education in operations and maintenance of offshore wind power

Erik Skov Madsen
SDU Center for Sustainable Supply Chain Engineering
University of Southern Denmark

Idea in Brief

This paper focuses on the need for vocational education and training (VET) of skilled workers who carry out operation and maintenance of large offshore wind farms. This is discussed by addressing

- *Typical tasks in operations and maintenance*

- *Low-skill vs. high-skill labor*

- *Future agendas for VET in relation to offshore wind power*

The discussion of VET is mainly from a Danish perspective.

1. Introduction

The purpose of this paper is to discuss how vocational education and training (VET) among technicians can support operations and maintenance of large offshore wind farms. A short introduction will first be made on modern offshore wind turbines, then typical maintenance tasks will be introduced, and finally the need for vocationally well-educated and trained technicians will be discussed in relation to maintenance of offshore wind turbines.

2. Maintenance of large offshore wind turbines and the issues of availability

Offshore wind turbines are becoming much larger and more efficient, and wind farms in northern Europe are moving further and further off the coast. For instance, an artificial island, the North Sea Wind Power Hub, is planned at Dogger Bank in the middle of the North Sea, partly for service of far-offshore wind power installations and partly for flexible distribution of renewable electrical power for 100 million people in the northern Europe.

Production from offshore wind turbines is often doubled compared to onshore installations. However, operations and maintenance of offshore wind turbines are far more expensive and challenging because turbines are only accessible for 50–70 percent of the year because of rough weather and sea conditions. These circumstances lead to more and much longer stops in offshore installation compared to onshore installation. Some studies report very low availability for production, i.e., between 60 and 70 percent for offshore wind farms.[1]

Maintenance of offshore wind turbines can be divided into preventive and corrective maintenance, under which both scheduled and unscheduled maintenance can take place. Preventive maintenance includes proactive inspections and repair or exchange of components and systems. Scheduled and preventive maintenance is most often made in cycles and planned according to requirements from legislation and maintenance programs developed by the Original Equipment Manufacturer (OEM). Scheduled and preventive maintenance includes, for instance, yearly inspection and check of high-voltage switch gears; inspection and test of installed lift, crane, and safety equipment; and checks and measurements of installed mechanical, hydraulic, electrical, and electronic equipment.

Corrective maintenance is carried out when a turbine sends an alarm or when systems or components have failed. Most often, this includes the involvement of technicians who need to analyze alarm logs, systems, or components before maintenance actions can be made. Some corrective maintenance can be carried out remotely, but corrective maintenance usually must be carried out by technicians at the individual wind turbine.

Because today's offshore wind turbines are more complicated, encompass a whole power plant of 10+ MW, and are located far from the coast, their maintenance technicians need to be well educated, trained, and in a position of knowledge, skills, and competences within many different fields to meet requirements for effective maintenance at a low frequency.

3. Need for VET in offshore wind power

The market for maintenance of offshore wind power installations has developed dramatically since the first offshore wind farm in the world was the established in Denmark in 1991 as the Vindeby Offshore Wind Farm. This wind farm consisted of 11 modified 450 kW wind turbines and was decommissioned in 2017. However, many more offshore wind turbines have been erected; a new record was set in 2017 when 623 new offshore wind turbines were erected in Europe.[2] These new turbines were up to 20 times larger than the 11 decommissioned wind turbines from the Vindeby Offshore Wind Farm. The need for well-educated and well-skilled technicians to carry out maintenance has therefore developed dramatically in little over two decades. Someone may claim that new offshore wind turbines have become more reliable and therefore call for less maintenance. But in general, this seems not to be the case, because wind turbine manufactures have focused on the development of larger and more efficient turbines and have launched new types or a new generation of wind turbines each year or each second year. Some studies illustrate that reliability and availability have been less of a focus, as newer turbines cannot meet availability at the very high 97.7 percent[3], which was achieved at the Danish Horns Rev 1 wind farm established in 2002.

According to the Danish Wind Industry Association[4], 51.6 percent of all 35,000 employees in the Danish wind power sector in 2018 were skilled labor, having a vocational education background. However, the same report found that the Danish wind industry's access to well-qualified employees is within the top three future challenges. Because the wind power industry is still a young industry, this sector has drawn labor forces with very different backgrounds, for example, as an electrician, smith, or engineer fitter. Or, as a motorcycle mechanic explains in an interview, *"The technology is more or less the same as for a motorcycle but the sizes of components of a wind turbine is just much bigger."* Experienced and vocationally educated technicians are well paid in the offshore wind power sector. According to the metal workers' union in Esbjerg (the main harbor for offshore wind power in Denmark), an experienced offshore wind power technician earned around 5,500 Euro/month in 2018, whereas a typical car mechanic earned around 3,500 Euro/month in the Esbjerg area.

3.1 A German/Danish or a UK perspective on VET

Different traditions for VET systems can be found in Europe. In Germany, Switzerland, Austria, South Tyrol, and Denmark, there is a long-standing tradition of focusing on vocational education and skills through a "dual system," in which qualifications are based on the combination of theoretical educating in vocational schools and highly structured practical work and education as an apprentice in the workplace. In addition, the content of the education in Denmark is based on negotiations involving both trade unions and employers to secure high employability. Therefore, the VET system in the above-mentioned countries traditionally focuses on education for occupation. Switzerland seems to be very successful in their vocational education, as VET is the mainstream upper secondary program, serving 70 percent of Swiss young people.[5] The Swiss VET system enjoys very strong support from Swiss employers, who credit it as a major contributor to the continuing vitality and strength of the Swiss economy and to a youth unemployment rate that is the lowest among developed countries.

The United Kingdom has taken a different approach. Their vocational system has proven to be strongly employer-led, an output-based approach in which focus is on direct employability for specific jobs. However, for many years, UK policy makers have highlighted the need for a greater focus on vocational education and skills training. Michael Gove, MP, the Secretary of State for Education, stated in a report about the United Kingdom's VET programs that the "*UK's vocational education and training remains weaker than most other developed nations,*" and "*our capacity to generate growth by making things remains weaker*".[6]

One may wonder why it takes 4.5 years of education as an apprentice to become, for instance, an electrician in the Danish system. However, several studies have identified that it takes a long time to gain knowledge and practice various skills to achieve the required competences. According to studies by Malcolm Gladwell, it takes roughly 10,000 hours of practice to achieve mastery in a field, often referred to as the 10,000-hour rule.

Several studies have found that more advanced technologies in the future and the "Internet of Things" of the workplace will lead to more complicated work tasks and a need for more focus on VET to perform these complicated work tasks. Similar studies have been conducted in the European Union and Cedefop in 2018.[7] These studies explain how a shift toward more skill-intensive jobs will require a demand for highly qualified people. A dual study program (in German, *Duales Studium*) has therefore been developed in Germany. In this program, students with a high school degree attend a 5-year study program and achieve both a vocational education and a BA degree. This program combines a college education with a practical apprentice experience (for example, in engineering), and the program is heavily supported by German industry. In Denmark, a similar but shorter EUX program has been established in which students can obtain both a vocational education and a high school degree via a combination of 5 years of apprenticeship and high school study. This kind of dual study program that focuses on both hand and mind in the development of both skills and knowledge could be important for technicians to optimize operations and maintenance of advanced wind power technology.

3.2 Well-skilled technicians for operation and maintenance

The main focus has for many years been on the development, manufacturing, and erection of wind turbines both on- and offshore. Even though operations and maintenance counts for up to one-third of all life cycle costs of an offshore wind farm, less focus has been given to employees for this phase. In a Danish context, this is evident in the VET programs that are offered in the wind power sector. Two VET programs are offered in Denmark, both programs are relatively short (2.5 years), and the purpose of both programs is to become educated as an operator either in (1) the manufacturing of wind turbine blades or (2) the assembly and erection of wind turbines. In Denmark, no special VET programs target the operations and maintenance phases. However, many standard courses targeting the offshore wind power sector have been developed through the Global Wind Organization (GWO). These courses cover, for instance, mechanical work, electrical work, hydraulic work, working in heights, fire awareness, or first aid. The courses are typically provided by private course activities and may target specific companies.

But what can a well-skilled, well-experienced, and well-paid technician do, and how does that technician work? This will be illustrated through the presentation of two interviews and then discussed.

A project manager from a large northern European leading operator of more than 1,000 on- and offshore wind turbines explains:

> *"In relation to corrective maintenance a good technician is one who can use the computer for the analysis of a particular problem related to a wind turbine and use his mind and hands to solve a problem. In case of a problem he will*

first spend some time at the computer where he will study alarm-logs and read through the history of earlier jobs. Then he will thoughtfully go through earlier adjustments of systems and exchange of components. He may then discuss the instance with his colleagues to have more perspectives on the analysis of the problem. Finally, he will conclude on the diagnosis and gather together spare parts, tools and instructions needed, get on a boat or helicopter and go out there together with his colleague. They will fix the problem and finally they will store their experiences in the job report and in addition share their experiences e.g. at lunch hours or at meetings and in that way make their experiences available for others within the firm."

The head of operations of a large northern European operator of wind power adds and explains the companies; experience:

"A malfunction may for instance originate from component no 3 of an offshore wind turbine. A technician will then sail to the turbine by boat but when investigating components at the turbine, he finds out that component no 3 does not fail but instead the problem is identified to originate from component no 1. A well-skilled and well-educated technician will be able to solve this problem. However, in countries like the UK where the tradition for profound vocational education is rather low we can observe a different pattern. In this case the technician will go back home because his instructions for component no 3 does not fit to component no 1. Instructions are normally developed by an engineer, but the engineer cannot foresee and develop instructions for any kind of malfunction from an office desk. Therefore, we appreciate well-skilled and well-educated technicians who have a broad vocational background and have a broad understanding of the technology and at the same time can collaborate with others. In this way stops of our turbines can be minimized and we can ensure high availability for production."

3.3 Discussion—VET and operation and maintenance of wind power

Much larger offshore wind turbines have been developed and put into operation during the last two decades. These offshore wind turbines have become more efficient and include high-end, complicated technology. In practice, these turbines act as individual power plants. Several studies illustrate that it is still difficult to maintain a high availability of production in these advanced wind turbines. Several attempts, from simple questions and answers (Q&As) and up to machine learning, have been made. However, well-skilled, well-educated technicians are reported to be even more essential to operate and carry out preventive and corrective maintenance in the offshore wind power sector. Because offshore wind power is seen as a main driver to phase out fossil fuels, the consequent extensive development of new offshore wind farms will cause an even higher demand for well-qualified technicians in the future.

Technicians are well paid within this field if they are well skilled, well educated, and well experienced. This goes particularly for the Danish offshore wind power sector, in which these technicians are paid around 60 percent more than a normal car mechanic.

Broad skills and self-dependence are needed among technicians to carry out efficient operations and maintenance of offshore wind turbines. This was particularly clear in the two interviews described earlier in this paper. If only narrow skills are present among technicians, the individual technician will require much more instruction from an engineer. However, as described through the interviews, these instructions are difficult to develop at the engineer's desk because malfunctions may show up differently in each instance, and well-performed preventive and scheduled maintenance requires qualified and careful work and good skills.

The VET system seems to create job opportunities for young people. This is particular true in relation to the Swiss VET systems, where young people are trained in a real work setting, whereas international studies and statistics from the EU, United Kingdom, and even China show young people with a BA from a university having trouble getting a job.

Even though Denmark leads in offshore wind power, no VET targets operation and maintenance of offshore wind power in the Danish context. Therefore, particularly the Danish wind power sector draws on many other VET programs, as 51.6 percent of all 35,000 employees in the Danish wind power sector are skilled labor.

An improvement in the status for VET seems necessary worldwide, as studies from very different countries like Denmark, Germany, the United Kingdom, and even China explain that too much focus is given to achieving an academic degree and less focus is on VET. Moreover, some of the same studies have also identified that VET creates good job opportunities to secure high employment rates among young people; for examples, Chinese studies have illustrated how people who have both a BA and a vocational education have doubled their income.

4. Conclusion

This paper has discussed how VET among technicians can support operations and maintenance of large offshore wind farms. The paper has illustrated how offshore wind turbines have become much larger and more complicated during the last two decades. Unfortunately, the focus on larger and more efficient turbines has also resulted in relatively low availability for production in offshore wind turbines. However, this paper emphasizes that well-educated, well-experienced technicians can support and ensure higher availability for production through flexible maintenance actions. This paper demonstrates a need for VET educational programs that target the offshore wind power sector. These jobs are well paid and present many opportunities. However, to attract more people into VET programs, a higher status compared to university degrees is necessary. A dual study program like Germany's, where students can achieve both a BA and a vocational education after high school, or the Danish EUX dual study, where students achieve both a VET degree and a high school degree, may be a future model of education that can attract more and better-qualified students who will develop profound knowledge and skills that allow them to handle complex technology today and in the future.

5. Implications

The big question is who should take the initiative in the development of a new VET program targeting operation and maintenance of large offshore wind farms and in that way supply well-skilled technicians for the future.

All over the world (from China to Germany, the United Kingdom, and Denmark), companies and policy makers are discussing how to attract more young people to apprentice and to receive a VET diploma. A higher status among VET programs seems necessary, as high schools, colleges, and universities still attract more students. However, Switzerland seems to have been successful in their VET programs, resulting in almost no unemployment among young people[5]. In a Danish context, the joint committee between specific trade unions and specific employers' associations is responsible for the development of new VET programs through the governmental organization Industriens Uddannelse (in English, Industrial Educations). In the development of a new technician VET targeting operations and maintenance of wind power, these three organizations need to work closely together. However, to uncover how to handle future advanced, sophisticated, and high-end technology of wind power installations, a research program may be needed to facilitate this process.

Endnotes

1 Shafiee, M. (2015), "Maintenance logistics organization for offshore wind energy: Current progress and future perspectives", *Renewable Energy*, Vol. 77, pp. 182-193.

2 Wind Europe (2019), *Offshore Wind in Europe: Key Trends and Statistics 2017*, www.windeurope.org

3 Petersen, K.R., Madsen, E. S. and Bilberg, A. (2016), "First Lean, then modularization: Improving the maintenance of offshore wind turbines", *International Journal of Energy Sector Management*, Vol. 10 No. 2, pp. 221-244.

4 Danish Wind Power Association, (2018), *Analysis of suppliers 2018*, (in Danish), www.windpower.org.

5 Hoffmann, N. and Szhwartz, R. (2015), *Gold Standards: The Swiss Vocational and Training System*, National Center of Education and Economy, Washington DC.

6 Wolf, A. (2011), *Review of Vocational Education: The Wolf Report*, Secretary of State for Education, UK.

7 Cedefop, Eurofound (2018), *Skills Forecast: Trends and Challenges to 2030*. Luxembourg: Publications Office. Cedefop reference series; No 108. http://data.europa.eu/doi/10.2801/4492

Industry 4.0[1]

Jan Stentoft
Department of Entrepreneurship and Relationship Management
University of Southern Denmark

Christopher Rajkumar
Department of Entrepreneurship and Relationship Management
University of Southern Denmark

Erik Skov Madsen
SDU Center for Sustainable Supply Chain Engineering
University of Southern Denmark

Idea in Brief

In this paper, we focus on the degree of knowledge, perceived importance, and current practice of Industry 4.0 among Danish manufacturers. We discuss this by addressing

- *Industry 4.0 technologies;*

- *Industry 4.0 knowledge, relevance, and current practices; and*

- *Practices across different firm sizes.*

We discuss how Industry 4.0 has enabled reduced cost of energy (ReCoE).

---

[1] This paper is based on Stentoft, J., Rajkumar, C. and Madsen, E.S. (2017), *Industry 4.0 in Danish Industry: An Empirical Investigation of the degree of Knowledge, Perceived Relevance and Current Practice*, Department of Entrepreneurship and Relationship Management, University of Southern Denmark.

1. Introduction

Technological development continues to develop rapidly. Recently, especially gray literature in terms of various consulting reports promotes new technologies under the umbrella term Industry 4.0.[1] There is no doubt that digitalization processes for some companies already play an important role in their manufacturing setup, and they will play an important role in more companies in the future. In the meantime, the question is, How fast? More critical literature in academic outlets has emerged that includes empirical data about this phenomenon Industry 4.0 and that also relates the degree of application of Industry 4.0 to different levels of firm size.[2] To date, much Industry 4.0 literature is focused on large enterprises that compared with small and medium-sized enterprises (SME) have more resources to experiment and implement such technologies. That is not to say that Industry 4.0 is not relevant for SME. Instead, research is needed to look at specific characteristics of SMEs and, with this, to develop new knowledge on how to approach such new technologies, given their contingencies.[3] In a Danish perspective, the business landscape is dominated by SMEs that, if measured in number of enterprises, include almost 99 percent of all companies. In Europe, an SME is defined as a firm employing fewer than 250 persons, with a total turnover that does not exceed EUR 50 million and that has an annual balance sheet total not exceeding EUR 43 million. Compared with large companies, SMEs share some different characteristics that are important to consider when analyzing and evaluating Industry 4.0 relevance and practice for SMEs. As mentioned, SMEs typically have fewer resources available and less experience in managing new technologies.[4] Other differences are CEOs being involved in daily operations in SMEs and exerting a dominant influence on operations at the expense of strategic and development-oriented activities.[5] SMEs are usually also less bureaucratic and generally have greater incentives to be successful than large firms. Thus, this article is focused on the degree of knowledge, perceived importance, and current practice of Industry 4.0 technologies among Danish manufacturers.

Data was collected through a questionnaire-survey completed in late 2016 and early 2017. In all, 270 complete and useable respondents have been received from 33 large companies and 237 SMEs. Respondents were people with the highest level of responsibility for manufacturing. Such knowledge is deemed important in order to respond to headlines such as "digitalize or die within ten years".[6] The article makes comparisons of the empirical data with respect to different firm sizes. The topic is also relevant to the offshore wind energy sector, as these new technologies can help to both bring the cost of energy further down and develop new business models.

2. Terminology

The concept of Industry 4.0 was originally developed as a German Federal Government initiative to strengthen the competitiveness of the German manufacturing industry.[7] Adjacent terminologies have been developed in other parts of the world like "Industrial Internet," "Integrated Industry," and "Smart Industry or Smart Manufacturing." Industry 4.0 is an umbrella term for several technologies involving the technical integration of cyber-physical systems into manufacturing and logistics and the use of the Internet of Things (IoT) and Services in industrial processes. A cyber-physical system is the integration of computation with physical processes. These new technologies open up new possibilities for effectiveness, efficient processes, and the development of new business models.

2.1 Application pull and technology push

In the literature, two development directions behind Industry 4.0 are described: application-pull and a technology push.[8] The application pull is:

- A need for shorter product development periods (time to market)

- Increased individualization of products (batch size one)

- Need for higher flexibility in manufacturing

- Need for decentralization in order to obtain faster decision-making processes

- Need for improved resource efficiency

The technology push is related to:

- Further increasing mechanization and automation (using more technical aids in work processes)

- Digitalization and networking (increased amount of actor and sensor data supporting functions of control an analysis)

- Miniaturization (electronic devices become smaller and smaller, which create new fields of application in production and logistics)

2.2 Industry 4.0 technologies

In the literature, there is a wide variety in developing a gross of Industry 4.0 technologies. In Table 1, the technologies used in this survey have been divided into three groups: (1) materials and manufacturing smart technologies, (2) connectivity smart technologies, and (3) computing and big data.

Table 1. Industry 4.0 technologies[9][10]

Materials and manufacturing smart technologies	Connectivity smart technologies	Computing and big data
- 3D printing	- Mobile internet	- Simulation
- 3D scanning	- Advanced sensors	- Big data
- Robotics	- Remote control	- Digital documentation
- iBin	- Enterprise resource planning	- Automatic analysis and visualization of data
- Advanced materials		- Cloud computing
- Augmented reality		- Internet of Things

2.2.1 Materials and manufacturing smart technologies

3D printing is a technology that prints an object in layers. 3D printing is an additive technology often used in prototyping and manufacturing of individual components. For this reason, it is also named additive manufacturing.

3D scanning is a device that enables one to analyze real objects by capturing their shapes, colors, and their look in digital information.

Robots are programmable manufacturing equipment with manipulators such as a gripper arms and sensors that controls the robots' behavior.

iBin, or intelligent Bin systems, is a material management system that automatically orders items when they are needed (when the amount reaches the reorder point).

Advanced materials (also termed "lightweight materials") are generally divided into three categories: metals, composites and polymers, and new materials such as ceramics, carbon nanotubes, and other nano-materials.

Augmented reality is a technology that extends real-world elements with 2D or 3D computer-generated components, enabling the users to interact with them.

2.2.2 Connectivity smart technologies

Mobile internet is a technology that allows one to access the internet through a mobile smartphone.

Advanced sensors are devices that take input from the physical environment and use integral computing resources to make predefined functions upon detection of specific input and then process data before passing it on.

Remote control is the establishment of individual communication solutions between the machine supplier and the user. The technician can connect to machines directly via a modem. The objective is to remotely diagnose and control the machine in order to reduce the duration of unscheduled stoppages and downtime.

Enterprise resource planning (ERP) is computer software that integrates all the company's main functions (e.g., customer, orders, inventory management, manufacturing planning, purchasing, and finance) into one database. ERP as such is not a new technology, but some new applications to the ERP platform have this status.

2.2.3 Computing and big data

Simulation is the process of creating a model of an ongoing or a new proposed system with the purpose of identifying and understanding the factors that control the system as well as predicting the future behavior of the system.

Big data is related to business intelligence and business analytics and has emerged as a separate concept. Big data can be perceived as a holistic approach to obtain actionable insights to create competitive advantages, which differs from business analytics in terms of the 5 Vs: volume, variety, velocity, veracity, and value.

Digital documentation covers areas such as digital production orders (e.g., on tablets) and other foundations for production such as a bill of materials, production routings, and technical drawings. Furthermore, it covers digital product and service manuals.

Automatic analysis and visualization of data is a process that helps in handling data as well as in gaining knowledge from data. Nowadays, data is produced at an unbelievable rate, and the capability to collect and store the data is increasing more rapidly than the capability to analyze the data. This technique combines automated analysis practices with interactive visualizations for effective understanding, reasoning, and decision-making based on very large and complex data sets.

Cloud computing is a concept denoting the distribution of software and services through the internet. When data is available in the "cloud," it can be more easily and ubiquitously accessed, which increases its potential value with enhanced integration, collaboration, and data analysis enabled by a shared platform.

Internet of Things
IoT refers to a network of internet-connected devices that can collect and exchange data using embedded sensors.

3. Degree of knowledge, perceived relevance, and current practice
3.1 Materials and manufacturing smart technologies
With respect to the degree of knowledge, not taking company size into account, it is clear from Figure 1 that the companies have some good knowledge about robots (an average of 3.41 on a 5-point Likert-scale, where 1 = to a very low degree and 5 = to a very high degree). Additionally, they also have some knowledge about 3D printing (an average 2.83) and 3D scanning (an average of 2.41). In contrast, it seems clear that the companies do not have enough knowledge about iBin, advanced materials, and augmented reality.

Figure 1. Materials and smart production technologies: Degree of knowledge, perceived relevance, and current practice

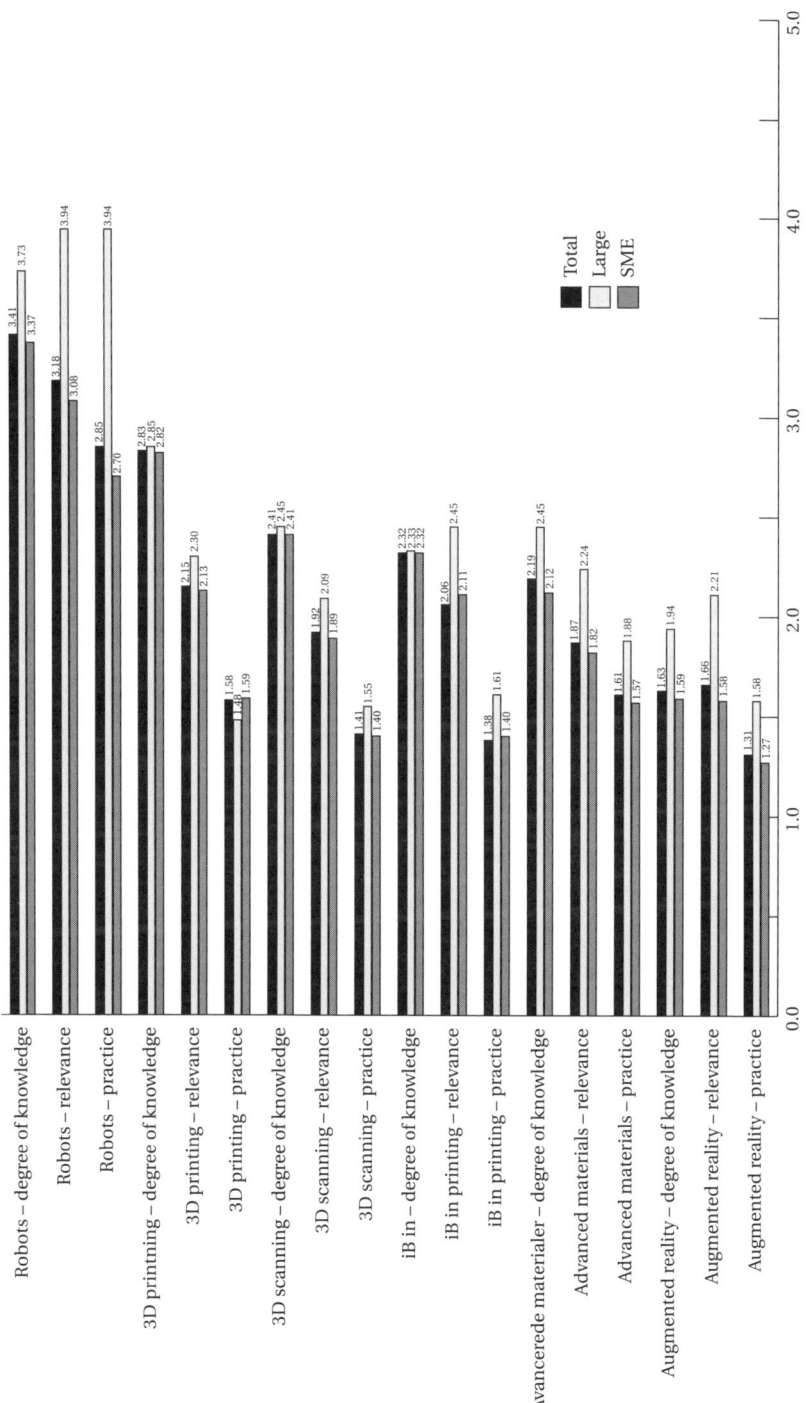

Considering company size, it is evident from Figure 1 that the large companies in general have more advanced knowledge about materials and manufacturing smart technologies than the SMEs. Regarding robotics, the large firms have more knowledge; they find it more relevant, and they also apply robotics to a higher degree than SMEs. Following robots, it is clear from Figure 1 that to some extent, practice of 3D printing (an average of 2.41) scores higher than its perceived relevance and perceived knowledge about it. The same picture is evident for 3D scanning. There are no significant differences between large and SMEs here.

3.2 Smart IT connecting technologies

This section reviews the degree of knowledge, relevance, and current practice of the various smart IT connecting technologies (Industry 4.0) like mobile internet, remote control, advanced censors, and ERP. It is clear from Figure 2 that companies generally have some knowledge about mobile internet (an average of 3.01) and rate its practice at 3.55 on average.

There also seems to be some knowledge about remote control (average score of 2.50), advanced censors (average of 2.33), and ERP (average of 2.25). The large companies do obtain higher averages here on knowledge, relevance, and practice than the SMEs.

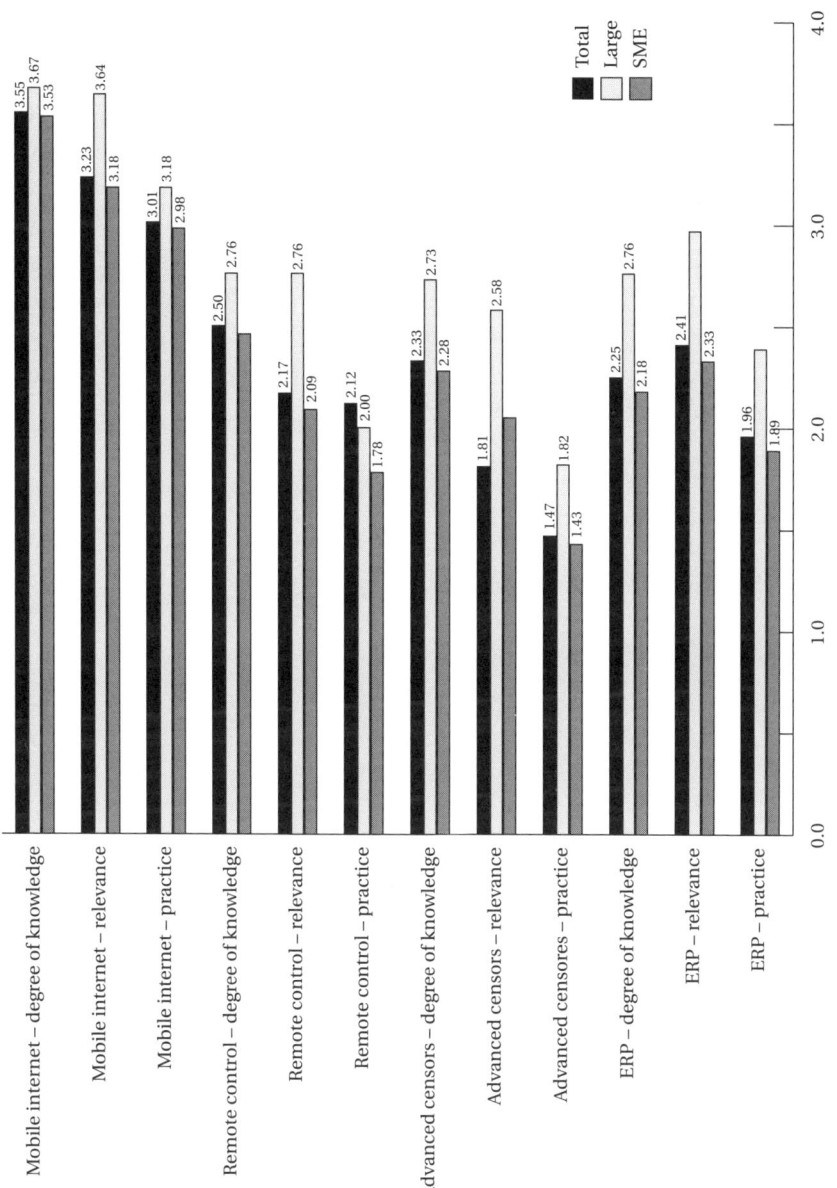

Figure 2. Smart IT connecting technologies: Degree of knowledge, perceived relevance, and current practice

3.3 Computing and big data

This section reviews companies' degree of knowledge, relevance, and current practice regarding data processing and big data (Industry 4.0), which includes digital communication, automatic analysis and visualization of data, simulation, cloud, big data, and IoT. As can be seen in Figure 3, digital communication has obtained the highest average knowledge level, with a score of 3.31. It is followed by automatic analysis and visualization of data, with an average of 2.84. Simulation is the third highest scoring, with an average of 2.51, followed by cloud with an average on 2.10. Surprisingly, big data only obtains an average of 1.99 and IoT an average of 1.69. There is also a clear difference between large companies and SMEs, in which the large firms generally have more knowledge, find it more relevant, and practice the technologies at a higher level than the SMEs.

Figure 3. Data processing and big data: Degree of knowledge, perceived relevance, and current practice

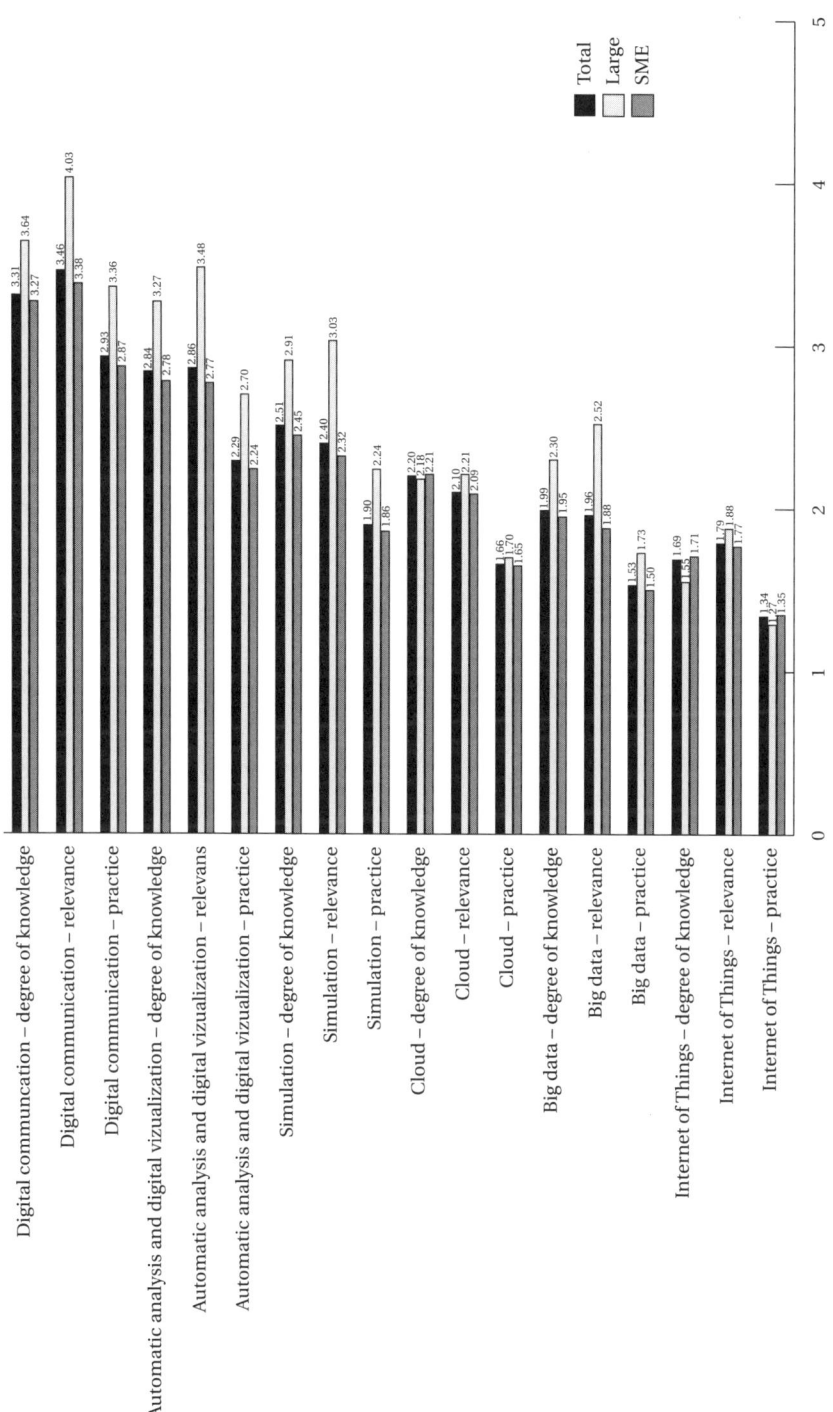

4. Conclusion

The survey reported in this article reveals that the participating manufacturing companies have some knowledge about Industry 4.0, including materials and smart production technologies, smart IT connecting technologies, data processing, and big data. In general, the large companies are more advanced in knowledge about Industry 4.0 than SMEs. Companies do understand the importance and relevance of Industry 4.0; however, there is no evidence of effective practice. There seems to be a gap between perceived importance and relevance and current or actual practice. The results indicate a need to increase the knowledge level about Industry 4.0 technologies to develop more effective and efficient processes and to offer the market new opportunities with changed or new business models. Most importantly, this article discloses that:

a. Industry 4.0 plays a role in reducing the cost of energy (ReCoE)

b. Industry 4.0 initiates opportunities for new business models

Therefore, it is necessary to understand Industry 4.0's terminology and investigate which technologies are relevant.

Endnotes

1 Liao, Y., Deschamps, F., Loures, E.D.R. and Ramos, L.F.P. (2017), "Past, present and future of Industry 4.0 - a systematic literature review and research agenda proposal", *International Journal of Production Research*, Vol. 55 No. 12, pp. 3609-3629.

2 Mittal, S., Khana, M.A., Romero, D. and Wuest, T. (2018), "A critical review of smart manufacturing & Industry 4.0 maturity models: Implications for small and medium-sized enterprises (SMEs)", *Journal of Manufacturing Systems*, Vol. 49, pp. 194-214.

3 Moeuf, A., Pellerin, R., Lamouri, S., Tamayo-Giraldo, S. and Barbaray, R. (2018), "The industrial management of SMEs in the era of Industry 4.0", *International Journal of Production Research*, Vol. 56 No. 3, pp. 1118-1136.

4 Zach, O., Munkvold, B.E. and Olsen, D.H. (2014), "ERP system implementation in SMEs: Exploring the influences of the SME context", *Enterprise Information Systems*, Vol. 8 No. 2, pp. 309-335.

5 Buonanno, G., Faverio, P., Pigni, F., Ravarini, A., Sciuto, D. and Tagliavini, M. (2005), "Factors affecting ERP system adoption: A comparative analysis between SMEs and large companies", *Journal of Enterprise Information Management*, Vol. 18 No. 4, pp. 384-426.

6 Jørgensen, E., Knudsen, P.T. and Pietras, P. (2017), *Ledelse i d-land – om ledelse på tærsklen til et digitalt samfund*, Saxo Publish, e-book.

7 Kagermann, H., Wahlster, W. and Helbig, J. (2013), *Recommendations for Implementing the Strategic Initiative INDUSTRIE 4.0*, Linda Treugut, M.A. and acatech – National Academy of Science and Engineering.

8 Lasi, H., Kemper, H.-G., Fettke, P., Feld., T. and Hoffmann, M. (2014), "Industry 4.0", *Business & Information Systems Engineering*, Vol. 6 No. 4, pp. 239-242.

9 Deloitte (2015), *Industry 4.0: An introduction*, Deloitte The Netherlands.

10 Dujin, A., Geissler, C. and Horstkötter, D. (2014), *Think Act: Industry 4.0*, Ronald Berger Strategy Consultants, Munich, Germany.

SECTION III

10. The offshore wind energy sector: Past, present and future

The aim of this final chapter is threefold. First, it aims to summarize some of the major developments in the offshore wind energy sector over the last five years and thus during the time of the ReCoE project. The subsequent section looks ahead by providing perspectives of what will be the major developments and challenges for the sector in the upcoming five to ten years. The final subsection contains a reflection from the ReCoE research team about the nature of the team's contribution in terms of theory and practice. The first two subsections draw on valuable interviews that have been conducted with influential industry people within the offshore wind energy sector in March 2019. The following persons were interviewed:

- Glenda Napier, CEO, Energy Innovation Cluster

- Jan Hylleberg, CEO, The Danish Wind Industry Association

- Michael Glavind, CEO, A2Sea (part of DEME Offshore)

- Henrik Stiesdal, CEO, Stiesdal Offshore Technologies

- Christina Aabo, Head of R&D, Ørsted

- Leif Winther, Head of Cross Portfolio Development, Ørsted

- Henrik Bæk Jørgensen, Chief Project Manager, Head of Product Management, MHI Vestas Offshore Wind

All interviews lasted from 30 minutes to one hour and were concerned with two main questions: (1) How has the offshore wind energy sector and supply chain developed over the last five years? And (2) how will the offshore wind energy sector and supply chain develop during the next five to ten years, including drivers and barriers? We would like to thank all those interviewed for your interesting, important, and insightful knowledge about the past, present, and future of the sector.

10.1 Main developments in the offshore wind energy during the past five years

Based on the completed interviews with the aforementioned seven persons, the main developments in the offshore wind energy sector have been summarized into five main sections: (1) reducing cost of energy, (2) industrialization, (3) consolidation, (4) industry maturity, and (5) a green/sustainable political clime. In the following sections, each of these headlines are briefly addressed. The order of the headlines is not prioritized, and in some places, there might be overlap between them. There are, of course, more developments than this section can outline, but what is presented here covers the developments most important to the ReCoE project.

Reducing Cost of Energy
The overall purpose with the ReCoE project has been to focus on various means to reduce the cost of gaining energy through offshore wind turbines by focusing on supply chain innovation. All respondents provided examples of how the industry has succeeded with this mission:

> *"The sector has been through a dramatic development with high costs reductions of 50 to 60 percent within the last few years across the supply chain. And offshore wind will in the coming years be free from public subsidiaries. The speed of this development has surprised most players in the industry."* Jan Hylleberg, CEO at The Danish Wind Industry Foundation

According to Henrik Stiesdal, five points especially have led to this cost reduction. First, immense competition has forced the industry to drive down costs by all means. Second, the implementation of serial production has reduced unit prices (economics of scale and better capacity utilization; improved productivity). Third, steel prices have been at a favorable level, which has reduced much of the material cost. Fourth, there has been and still is a low interest rate that makes financing assets cheaper. Fifth, a change in mindset among the big players in the industry has emerged and pushed the players to move beyond their own company silos into the supply network to include them in innovation processes, which has led to further cost reductions. However, the success should not lull the industry into a false security:

> *"Cost as an issue does not disappear, it is a basic term. The industry has become commercialized and subsidiaries will disappear."* Michael Glavind, CEO, A2Sea (part of DEME Offshore)

Industrialization (serial production)
Industrialization of the sector concerns improving productivity and driving down costs by building strong processes. Such processes are related to both the physical production and movement of the goods as well as in administrative processes. Again, serial production is mentioned as the main lever. However, standardization is also an important element, in which the industry has worked together to develop common guidelines. Industrialization has taken place especially in the construction and manufacturing of the turbines, whereas there still seem seems to be room for improvements concerning the balance of plants (BoP). For example, the modus operandi for installation is still basically the same as it was years ago. It is still a one-off project working mode for suppliers to BoP.

> *"… the individual actors are much more professional now than five years ago, so actors are more mature. However, we lack economies of scale, which is hard to achieve, as we lack more strategic collaboration to deal with the current business model [for the industry]."* Michael Glavind, CEO, A2Sea (part of DEME Offshore)

Consolidation
A major development in the industry has been a consolidation of firms within the industry.[1] Some of the drivers have included small and medium-sized enterprises during the recent period being faced with increased requirements for documentation, which increases their indirect cost levels; likewise, they have faced higher cost reduction requirements from their customers. These enterprises have also encountered bigger projects and therefore have become a higher financial risk partner for the big players to enter into a business relationship with.

> *"In relation to cables, substations etc. we will still see companies as ABB; Siemens and GE. The projects are large and very few companies have got the capacity and muscles to become sub suppliers for these large offshore wind power project".* Christina Aabo, Head of R&D, Ørsted

Industry Maturity

There was a general agreement among the respondents that the industry has become more mature in terms of professional business relationships between the parties. The industry has moved from a predominantly "Excel spreadsheet behavior" to select, manage, and control suppliers in the sector to also include elements other than costs, such as innovation. Furthermore, the sector also contains several subsectors in which some of the latest within service and operations and maintenance are relative newcomers and still have some tasks to do before they become more mature. Likewise, the whole decommissioning phase, has yet to "take off," will create a subindustry that needs to go through learning curves and with this become more mature. Thus, an evaluation of maturity depends on perspective. Overall, the industry in Denmark has become more mature, even becoming the world's foremost producer of offshore wind energy. Technology-wise, the industry has also become more mature. A dominant design has been established to explain why a larger share of the industry's further innovation may be found in the processes (i.e., the supply chain) carried out by the actors. The manufacturing of the turbines has become mature with the introduction of serial production.

> *"The next step is to include other activities in the BoP in the serial production paradigm such as foundations which could drive the cost even further down."* Henrik Stiesdal, CEO, Stiesdal Offshore Technologies

Green/sustainable political climate

During the last five years, the political climate has changed much in favor toward offshore wind energy. With an increased demand for energy and with a greener and more sustainable mindset among citizens not only in Denmark but also in other parts of Europe, North America, and Asia, this attitude seems to increase. Even countries like Poland, Japan, and the United States have begun discussing offshore wind energy as an alternative energy source to oil, coal, and nuclear.

"The political climate has changed so dramatically as the costs has decreased. Today it is not a question about the cost to build offshore wind parks but more a question about access to grids and sites …and international collaboration about this energy resource and how it has to be deployed in the coming years." Jan Hylleberg, CEO, The Danish Wind Industry Association

"There is a good economy in offshore wind; the parks are being located far from shore and the first subsidy free projects have been approved and this is a trend that will continue. Furthermore, it creates jobs. All these points are like candy for politicians." Henrik Bæk Jørgensen, Chief Project Manager, Head of Product Management, MHI Vestas Offshore Wind

"The political environment for offshore wind in Germany, UK and Denmark is very positive". Even though Denmark is a stable marked for Ørsted, the Danish marked is small when comparing to Germany and the UK." Christina Aabo, Head of R&D, Ørsted

10.2 Outlook: Possible developments in the offshore wind energy sector during the next ten years

This subsection looks toward possible developments in the offshore wind energy sector. Again, this list should be viewed not as exhaustive but rather as a synthesis of what the answers experts have provided regarding this topic. Furthermore, the topics are not prioritized, and there might be overlap between them in some places. In all, nine future development areas have received special attention from experts: (1) storage of energy, (2) further technology development and innovation, (3) energy islands, (4) market outlook, (5) increased requirements for local content, (6) a shift from cost to value system, (7) decommissioning, (8) new competences, and (9) new forms of collaboration. Below, these nine topics are briefly addressed.

Storage of energy

"The industry still needs to crack the code to store production of energy in a market-based system, so energy demands always can be met." Jan Hylleberg, CEO, The Danish Wind Industry Association

One of the major challenges that must be addressed in the near future is how to store wind power energy. Offshore wind energy parks are able to deliver much energy when the wind is blowing. The more wind, the more energy is produced. Thus, the amount of energy produced is unstable and depends on wind speed. The turbines do also produce energy for 24 hours, 7 days a week, and 52 weeks in a year. However, the price of energy depends on demand and supply. If energy can be stored, energy can better influence the market price of wind energy production.

> *"One of the biggest challenges is to develop new [offshore wind] storage technologies."* Glenda Napier, CEO, Energy Innovation Cluster

Further technology development and innovation
This theme concerns the technologies of the turbines, BoP, and other equipment used in the supply chain such as land transportation and vessels. It seems that turbines continue to be made bigger. This imposes requirements on other parts such as foundations and towers. Likewise, it imposes requirements on the supply chain partners, e.g., in terms of transportation and installation. Hence, it has been of special interest to question the size of offshore wind turbines. How big can the turbines be? Will their size continue to increase? Is there a tipping point? There might be challenges with the physical size that impose some limits, but on the other hand, new materials that are both strong enough and lighter can be utilized.

> *"The prediction of the size of offshore wind turbines has in the relatively short history always been wrong. We have consistently underestimated the growth rate. However, there might be a tipping point where the costs on increasing the size might offset the benefits it generates. But, again, past predictions about size have always been wrong!"* Henrik Stiesdal, Stiesdal Offshore Technologies

> *"The turbines become larger and larger. The challenge is that the turbines can become so large that it become costlier on the balance of plant. We need to look at it from a total cost perspective. The infrastructure should also be able to keep up with this pace like the platform that also should have as long life-cycle as possible to make it economic attractive."* Michael Glavind, CEO, A2Sea (part of DEME Offshore)

> *"We may still observe an incremental development in the size of turbines and we expect that the offshore turbines still are built on today's existing 6 - 7 - 8 MW platforms. It is very expensive to develop a new turbine platform because when*

> *only around 100 turbines are ordered for each windfarm the development costs are very difficult to pay back."* Christina Aabo, Head of R&D

Another form of innovation is concerned with the foundations:

> *"There is also a need to look at floating fundaments and to move the building of fundaments from shipyards to factories in order to reduce the costs by new designs and by serial production."* Henrik Stiesdal, Stiesdal Offshore Technologies

As the turbines become larger and are installed farther from shore, there will be increased requirements for logistics, service, and maintenance:

> *"We will see new technology and drones and unmanned vessels in O&M. However, we will still need well-educated technicians in O&M."* Christina Aabo, Head of R&D, Ørsted

> *"[Increased size and distance to shore] puts increased demands on logistics, service and maintenance. We will in the future see new technology such as drones that will solve some of those tasks."* Glenda Napier, CEO, Energy Innovation Cluster

Furthermore, we will see developments with more digitalized O&M, in which sensors send performance data back to operators and sensors with advanced analytics can monitor offshore wind parks more intelligently. And there will be a continued need for what can be called "low-prestige development"…

> *"…that is concerned with improving all the things that have led to unscheduled maintenance and stops."* Henrik Stiesdal, Stiesdal Offshore Technologies

Finally, from a decommissioning perspective, technical innovation is also needed for cutting and scrapping turbines and lifting them to integrate them better in a circular economy.

Energy Islands

This theme is about how through collaboration, countries can develop energy islands that further reduce the costs of offshore wind parks moving farther offshore. Right now, governments of the Netherlands,

Germany, and Denmark are collaboration in investigating the possibilities for an energy island at Dogger Bank in the North Sea. Such an island could be like a mini-city with own airport and facilities for living.

> *"We will probably see new types of collaborations that establish hubs in the North Sea where offshore parks connect with an island/infrastructure in the North Sea and from this bring electricity to shore through a number of transmission lines."* Jan Hylleberg, CEO, The Danish Wind Industry Association

> *"Energy islands for wind, gas and so on … it is going to happen within a short horizon."* Glenda Napier, CEO, Energy Innovation Cluster

Market outlook
The market for offshore wind energy is expected to increase dramatically. The climate agenda seems to have only an upward direction. The population of the world is growing, as is energy consumption. There is increased awareness of using fossil-free energy resources, and the political climate is also maturing for further wind farm installations. The costs of building offshore wind farms have been reduced significantly during the last 5 years, which is why we now see the first parks in tender-processes without public subsidiaries.

> *"Over the last eight years, we have moved from public subsidies at a reasonable level to nothing at some parks."* Leif Winther, Head of Cross Portfolio Development, Ørsted

The market growth perspective also looks good:

> *"Moving from being merely a North European market it has developed into a global market, which for the value chain brings new challenges and changes in the coming years."* Jan Hylleberg, CEO, The Danish Wind Industry Association

There will be a further commoditization of the installation processes. More actors are expected to penetrate the market (e.g., in design, installation, and project management) who will increase the supply and decrease the price further. Another new actor will be hotel boats, which will be used in connection with O&M activities to reduce the use of crew boats.

There is also an increased demand for green energy in other parts of the world:

"… and these markets may bypass some of the stages that we have been through to and come cheaper into the production of offshore wind." Jan Hylleberg, CEO, The Danish Wind Industry Association

The competition is tough, and other consortia than Ørsted, Siemens Gamesa, etc. are now in the game:

"… building an offshore wind energy park has become a commodity and to own it is also a commodity. Financial institutions such as pension funds and investment funds are part of the game now and this interest is closely related to the maturity of the industry. Even oil and gas has now been involved in the industry." Michael Glavind, CEO, A2Sea (part of DEME Offshore)

"Competition in every part of the offshore wind supply chain is important, and we believe that this competition will be a catalyst for further cost reduction." Henrik Bæk Jørgensen, Chief Project Manager, Head of Product Management, MHI Vestas Offshore Wind

There are also some barriers related to this apparent growth market for green energy. The infrastructure especially requires some attention:

"We need the right investments to move the electricity-power from North to South in Europe. This is a major challenge. Also, the infrastructure in the North Sea that needs also to fit in with national plans for fishing, birds, ferries, and so on." Jan Hylleberg, CEO, The Danish Wind Industry Association

Increased requirements for local content
As the offshore wind energy market becomes more global and the public subsidiaries are reducing or even totally disappearing, there is also an increased demand for local content when new offshore wind energy parks are commissioned. Thus, there are requirements for a certain level of value-added created in the country, and this creates jobs and wealth instead of importing final components, systems, and services. This development has set up new requirements for designing and setting up supply chains—i.e., harbors, infrastructure, and a supply network. However, the requirement for local content might also be

challenged by new requirements for sustainability and CO_2 footprint that may outweigh requirements of local content.

> *"In tact with an increasing demand from the large markets around the world, it makes sense to manufacture closer to the market where the projects are located – also to fulfil a political demand to create local jobs. Whiteout public subsidies this may change in years to come."* Jan Hylleberg, CEO, The Danish Wind Industry Association

From a cost to value system
A new perspective on the future development of the energy sector is a paradigm shift from a predominantly cost perspective to a value system perspective. The future requires a solution for an entire energy system that brings together different energy sources into a common value system:

> *"There is an increasing need to look at hybrid solutions where different energy sources [e.g. wind, solar and biomass] are suppliers to a common energy system."* Glenda Napier, CEO, Energy Innovation Cluster

Decommissioning
The first Danish offshore wind park was installed in 1991 and was decommissioned in 2017. The turbines' estimated life cycle was 20 years, but they achieved a life cycle of 26 years because of maintenance activities. New turbines have a design life cycle of 25 years, and in the future, the operators will to an increasing extent look toward extending the parks' life cycles. In considering such extended life cycles, the operators can make at least three decisions:

> *"Firstly, they can decide to make a main restoration of the turbines. Secondly, they can decide to install new turbines (repowering), and thirdly, the operators can decide to continue with maintenance activities."* Leif Winther, Head of Cross Portfolio Development, Ørsted

Furthermore, there is a need for more regulation in connection with decommissioning. At the same time operations obtain permission to build offshore wind parks, they also commit to dismantle and take down the parks. Governments require plans for the decommissioning part to issue permissions to take down the parks. But there seem to be some challenges in this process:

> *"In order to make a plan, one needs to know how do it [the method]. And here we need to go to the market with a tender to get a fixed price. But we can, however, not be sure that the method offered the market will be approved. When we apply for the permission we need to know how to do it. So, it seems that the process goes rounds in circles. There is a need for regulation where permissions are given with a wider span, so we can obtain learning that can drive the process further."*
> Leif Winther, Head of Cross Portfolio Development, Ørsted

When offshore wind parks are decommissioned and taken down, it is not only a question of simple reverse installations. Thinking in new logistical flows is required, in which the different parts of the park are sorted and may be transported on, e.g., new forms of ships. Electronic parts must be divided from metal parts and so on. This is a question of circular economy. There is a need for developing new harbors that have the capacity, perhaps for a period of time, to set up reverse supply chains that can handle different vessels and transport solutions with the required tact time.

New forms of collaboration
There will also be an increased need for a change of mindset in the industry. Instead of performing as usual, the industry will be forced to collaborate more and to innovate together. This might take s as new types of collaborations termed co-opetition, in which partners both collaborate and compete.

> *"There is a need to move from a conservative project form with stacked contingencies in each part of the project to a more flexible approach where each part is optimized."* Henrik Stiesdal, Stiesdal Offshore Technologies

New competences
The development in the sector also calls for new competencies:

> *"A barrier will be access to well-educated and competent people". The employees who have to work in the field may be hard to find and an effort to educate; this is not an office job. Earlier, a person would start as floor sweeper; then he or she became a smith or an electrician and then develop his knowledge and become a good technician in the wind power sector. This is not sufficient talent supply chain for the future in some of the new offshore wind power markets. There will be a need for more education."* Christina Aabo, Head of R&D, Ørsted

Another need for further competence development is to understand better collaboration between both vertical (suppliers and customers) and horizontal (competitive) partners.

10.3 ReCoE reflections

Throughout the project's duration, the ReCoE research team has reflected on what the contributions of the project have been in terms of theory and practice. Tables 10.1 and 10.2 list such perceptions. These tables close the dissemination of part of the overall ReCoE project.

Table 10.1 Contribution from the ReCoE project to theory

Supply chain management
- Delineating the role of SCM practices in a complex project environment

Innovation
- Contributed to enhanced theoretical understanding of supply chain innovation as a concept and as a lever for competitive advantages
- Conceptual model of innovation practices in a complex project environment
- Explicating the role of supply chain innovation in knowledge acquisition and deployment for innovation
- Explicating the role of "open" innovation
- Explicating the role of ambidexterity in supply chain innovation
- Explicating the role of governance and flexible control of supply base for innovation

Supply network
- Develop theory of interfirm relationship formation for the case of developing new suppliers in offshore wind industry
- Reveal major factors that make the offshore wind supply network complex
- Explain sources of complexity in offshore wind supply network
- Reveal different governance mechanisms used to control or influence offshore wind supply network

O&M
- Conceptual model of modularization of maintenance task and maintenance resources

Others
- Knowledge management in complex project environment
- Explicating new vocational education for O&M in the OWI
- Empirical research on big data and other Industry 4.0 technologies (how it can reduce costs and develop new business models)

Table 10.2 Contribution from the ReCoE project to practice

Supply chain management
- Explicating the valuable role of SCM practices in managing OWI projects
- Promoting the concept of "industrialization" in the OWI context
- Identifying common barriers for potential implementation in OWI
- Identifying best practices from the manufacturing context for potential implementation in OWI
- A framework for strategic transformation to system integrator within OWI context

Innovation
- Innovation fostering practices and their role in OWI context
- Explicating the role of governance in complex projects
- Importance of network-based learning in complex projects
- Need for creating knowledge cells in the EPC firm to promote innovation
- Strategies to promote innovation culture in EPC organization

Supply network
- Inform offshore wind industry of effective methods for searching for new suppliers
- Inform offshore wind industry of reasons for failing to develop new suppliers, from a supplier perspective
- Explain and help managers in the offshore wind industry understand how complexity in their supply network is created by the ways they manage contracts
- Explain and help managers in the offshore wind industry control or influence supply networks

O&M
- A framework for modularization of planning and execution of maintenance task
- Identifying practices in O&M of OWI installations offshore wind
- Identifying how lean can streamline maintenance processes of OWI

Maturity
- Identifying the role of "maturity models" and process benchmarking in industrialization in the OWI context

Others
- Uncovering need for vocational education in O&M of OWI

Dissemination
- Facilitate knowledge sharing and social networking among leaders in the offshore wind industry
- Facilitate discussion on methods to reduce the levelized cost of energy in the offshore wind industry
- Dissemination of work in practice-oriented journal (DILF/SCM)
- Participating in industry speeches in Denmark and the UK

Endnotes

1 The Danish Wind Industry Foundation (2018), *Leverandøranalysen 2018 – analyse af leverandører til vindmølleindustrien* [Supplier analysis 2018 – an analysis of suppliers to the wind turbine industry], The Danish Wind Industry Foundation, Copenhagen.

ReCoE publications during the project

Academic publications

Baagoe-Engels, V. and Stentoft, J. (2016), "Operations and maintenance issues in the offshore wind energy sector: an explorative study", *International Journal of Energy Sector Management*, Vol. 10 No. 2, pp. 245-265.

Brinch, M. (2018), "Understanding the value of big data in supply chain management and its business processes: Towards a conceptual framework", *International Journal of Operations and Production Management*, Vol. 38 No. 7, pp. 1589-1614.

Brinch, M., Stentoft, J., Jensen, J.K. and Rajkumar, C. (2018), "Practitioners understanding of big data and its applications in supply chain management", *The International Journal of Logistics Management*, Vol. 29 No. 2, pp. 555-574.

Brinch, M. and Fosso Wamba, S. (2018), "Big data and its value in business processes: a study of antecedents", in: Stentoft, J. (2018) (Ed.), *Proceedings of the 30th Annual NOFOMA Conference: Relevant Logistics and Supply Chain Management Research*, Department of Entrepreneurship and Relationship Management, University of Southern Denmark, pp. 651-666.

Brinch, M., Stentoft, J. and Jensen, J.K. (2017), "Big data and its applications in supply chain management: Findings from a Delphi study", *Proceedings of the 50th Hawaii International Conference on System Sciences*, HICSS, Hawaii, pp. 1351-1360.

Govindan, K. and Shankar, M. (2016), "Evaluating the essential barrier to offshore wind energy - an Indian perspective", *International Journal of Energy Sector Management*, Vol. 10 No. 2, pp. 266-282.

Govindan, K. (2019), "Framework on offshore wind energy circular economy maturity – A circular business model approach", (working paper).

Hennelly, P. and Wong, C.Y. (2016), "The formation of new inter-firm relationships: A UK offshore wind sector analysis", *International Journal of Energy Sector Management*, Vol. 10 No. 2, pp. 172-190.

Jensen, J.K. and Thoms, L. (2015), "Industry life cycle theory - a literature review", *The 15th Annual EURAM Conference*, Warsaw, Poland, June 17-20.

Johnsen, T. E., Mikkelsen, O. S. and Wong, C. Y. (2018), "Supply network strategies: Findings from the offshore wind power industry", In: Stentoft, J. (ed.), Proceedings of the 30th Annual NOFOMA 2018: Relevant Logistics and Supply Chain Management Research, Department of Entrepreneurship & Relationship Management, University of Southern Denmark, pp. 177-192.

Kavin, L. and Narasimhan, R. (2018), "An investigation of contextual influences on innovation in complex projects", In: Moreira A., Ferreira L. and Zimmermann R. (eds) *Innovation and Supply Chain Management*. Contributions to Management Science. Springer, Cham, pp. 51-77.

Kavin, L. and Narasimhan, R. (2017), "An investigation of innovation process: The role of clock speed", *Supply Chain Forum: An International Journal*, Vol. 18 No. 3, pp. 189-200.

Kavin, L. and Stentoft, J. (2017), "Fostering of innovation within green growth industries: How the Danish national innovation systems affect supply-network enabled innovation", *International Journal of Energy Sector Management*, Vol. 11 No. 4, pp. 574-594.

Kavin, L. (2015), "How to design an appropriate supply network structure to reduce the cost of energy in the Danish offshore wind power industry", In: Stentoft, J., Paulraj, A. and Vastag, G. (eds.) (2015) *Research in the Decision Sciences for Global Supply Chain Network Innovations*, Pearson Education, Old Tappan, New Jersey, pp. 189-212.

Krægpøth, T.S., Stentoft, J. and Jensen, J.K. (2017), "Dynamic supply chain design: A Delphi study of drivers and barriers", *International Journal of Production Research*, Vol. 55 No. 22, pp. 6846-6856.

Martinez-Neri, I.F. (2016), "Supply chain integration opportunities for the offshore wind industry: A literature review", *International Journal of Energy Sector Management*, Vol. 10 No. 2, pp. 191-220.

Martinez-Neri, I., Mikkelsen, O.S. and Stentoft, J. (2015), "Supply chain integration in engineering, procurement, and construction projects: An explorative study in the offshore wind power industry", In: Stentoft, J., Paulraj, A. & Vastag, G. (eds.) (2015) *Research in the Decision Sciences for Global Supply Chain Network Innovations*, Pearson Education, Old Tappan, New Jersey, pp. 213-232.

Martinez-Neri, I., Mikkelsen, O.S. and Stentoft, J. (2014), "Assessing the level of integration in the offshore wind industry value chain", *23rd IPSERA Conference*, Pretoria, South Africa, April 13-16.

Mikkelsen, O.S., Johnsen, T.E. and Wong, C.Y. (2017). Strategies for managing complex supply networks: initial case study findings from the offshore wind power industry. *Proceedings of the 26th Annual IPSERA conference, Budapest/Balatonfured, Hungary.*

Rajkumar, C. and Stentoft, J. (2018), "The relationship between supply chain strategy and supply chain innovation along with the mediator ambidexterity", In Stentoft, J. (Ed.), *Proceedings of the 30th Annual NOFOMA Conference: Relevant Logistics and Supply Chain Management Research*, Department of Entrepreneurship and Relationship Management, University of Southern Denmark, pp. 1001-1016.

Rajkumar, C. and Stentoft, J. (2017), "Harnessing capabilities and practices for sourcing innovation: An exploratory study", *Logistics Research*, Vol. 10 No. 1, pp. 1-21.

Petersen, K.R., Madsen, E.S. and Bilberg, A. (2016), "First Lean, then modularization: improving the maintenance of offshore wind turbines", *International Journal of Energy Sector Management*, Vol. 10 No. 2, pp. 221-244.

Stentoft, J. and Rajkumar, C. (2018), "Does supply chain innovation pay off?", In: Moreira, A.C., Ferreira, L.M.D.F. and Zimmermann, R.A. (Eds.). (2018*), Innovation and Supply Chain Management*, Cham, Switzerland, Springer, pp. 237-256.

Stentoft, J., Rajkumar, C. and Madsen, E.S. (2017), *Industry 4.0 in Danish Industry*, Department of Entrepreneurship and Relationship Management, University of Southern Denmark.

Stentoft, J. and Mikkelsen, O.S. (2016), Guest editorial: Supply chain innovation in the offshore wind energy sector", *International Journal of Energy Sector Management*, Vol. 10 No. 2, pp. 146-150

Stentoft, J., Narasimhan, R. and Poulsen, T. (2016), "Reducing cost of energy in the offshore wind energy industry: The promise and potential of supply chain management", *International Journal of Energy Sector Management*, Vol. 10 No. 2, pp. 151-171.

Tian, Y., Govindan, K. and Zhu, Q. (2014), "A system dynamics model based on evolutionary game theory for green supply chain management diffusion among Chinese manufactures", *Journal of Cleaner Production*, Vol. 80, pp. 96-105.

Narasimhan, R. (2018), "The fallacy of impact without relevance - reclaiming relevance and rigor". *European Business Review*, Vol. 30 No 2, pp. 157-168.

Practice-oriented publications

Brinch, M. and Stentoft, J. (2017), "Digital supply chains: Still more "wannabe" than practice", *DILF Orientering*, Vol. 54 No. 2, pp. 22-28.

Brinch, M. (2016), "Big data i supply chain management: Værdiskabelse og praktiske anbefalinger", *DILF Orientering*, Vol. 53 No. 3, pp. 50-52.

Kavin, L. and Narasimhan, R. (2016), "Innovation aktiveret af forsyningsnetværket", *DILF Orientering*, Vol. 53 No. 2, pp. 46-49.

Krægpøth, T.S., Stentoft, J. and Paulraj, A. (2018), " Supply chain design is perceived important but more can be done in practice", *DILF Orientering*, Vol. 55 No. 4, pp. 1-9.

Martinez-Neri, I.F. (2015), "Offshore wind industry supply chain integration: Learnings from other industries", *DILF Orientering*, Vol. 52 No. 2, pp. 32-34.

Rajkumar, C. (2016), "Sourcing innovation - making innovations happen through strategic collaboration", *DILF Orientering*, Vol. 53 No. 1, pp. 46-48.

Stentoft, J. (2017), "Process orientation and cross functional collaboration are still in short supply", *DILF Orientering*, Vol. 54 No. 4, pp. 12-17.

Stentoft, J. and Mikkelsen, O.S. (2017), "Supply chain innovation is perceived important for competitiveness", *DILF Orientering*, Vol. 54 No. 1, pp. 48-59.

Stentoft, J. and Rajkumar, C. (2017), "Supplier Relationship Management is important for competitiveness but it is difficult to measure its hard benefits", *DILF Orientering*, Vol. 54 No. 3, pp. 10-17.

Stentoft, J. and Mikkelsen, O.S. (2016), "Do you have the right supply chain talent on board?", *DILF Orientering*, Vol. 53 No. 2, pp. 32-36.

Stentoft, J., Mikkelsen, O.S. and Brinch, M. (2016), "Big data applications in sourcing processes", *DILF Orientering*, Vol. 53 No. 4, pp. 38-42.

PhDs from the project

Towards a theory of sourcing innovation: Conceptualization, antecedents and performance implications

By Christopher Rajkumar

Sourcing innovation highlights how the sourcing function could help organizations be innovative by actively involving their suppliers as well as creating innovative, next-generation products. Sourcing innovation is crucial for firms to endorse intense strategic relationships among supply chain partners to achieve greater firm performance and sustainable competitive advantage. This evolution in the sourcing function's role in developing innovation is timely given the fact that innovations are no longer the result of the efforts put forth by a single organization; alternatively, collaboration with innovative suppliers is necessary to achieve this. It has also become increasingly important for organizations to gain continuous growth that focuses beyond cost reductions alone. Accordingly, it is not just about finding good suppliers; instead, there should be an organized process to identify, select, and effectively collaborate with suppliers to advance or generate new innovations within organizations. Firms do practice sourcing innovation; however, it is not effectively pursued.

This dissertation adopts a definition of sourcing innovation as an "affair between two firms" and broadens it in accordance with today's supply chain relationship perspective. An exploratory study using an in-depth survey method is employed to conceptualize and operationalize sourcing innovation, understand and substantiate the different firm-specific antecedents as well as relation-specific antecedents of sourcing innovation, observe the use of information technology in driving sourcing innovation, and in turn explore the performance implications of sourcing innovation. Thereupon, the study formulates four research questions (RQs) acknowledging these objectives.

RQ 1: What is the theoretical conceptualization and operationalization of sourcing innovation?

RQ 2: What are key firm-specific and relation-specific antecedents that drive sourcing innovation?

RQ 3: What is the role of information technology in driving sourcing innovation?

RQ 4: What are the performance implications of sourcing innovation? The four RQs are answered through five academic papers.

This dissertation contributes to both theory and practice by increasing the understanding of sourcing innovation. It is an initial step in building up constructive knowledge to practice sourcing innovation by applying the proposed research framework to achieve superior performance. This dissertation, by empirically evaluating the performance impacts of sourcing innovation, provides understanding of the various success and failure formulas within sourcing innovation.

Supply network enabled innovation within a non-repetitive manufacturing context

By Lone Kavin

This dissertation starts from the notion that innovation is an important aspect of persistence and success in a competitive, global environment and from the discovery that supply network–enabled innovation does not always concern products intended for repetitive manufacturing developed through a dyadic relationship.

The fact that innovation increasingly is enabled directly or indirectly through the supply network in a nonrepetitive manufacturing context or is politically initiated in a nonrepetitive manufacturing context calls for new perspectives on fostering supply network–enabled innovation. In the wake of this, the study takes a supply network approach that focuses on delineating the factors affecting supply network–enabled innovation and explicating possible innovation fostering practices in nonmanufacturing contexts. Indeed, the literature on supply network–enabled innovation has argued that innovation-fostering practices are crucial elements in improving the potential and competitiveness of supply networks in nonmanufacturing contexts and in influencing innovation performance.

To explore the current state of supply chain management literature and to explain and expand the literature by exposing the concepts of supply network–enabled innovation to different theoretical and empirical contexts, the dissertation is structured around the following main research question: How is supply network–enabled innovation fostered within a nonrepetitive manufacturing context?

New models for maintenance of offshore wind farms

By Kristian R. Petersen

The dissertation revolves around the fact that the offshore wind industry is on a continuous journey to reduce costs to make the renewable source of energy able to compete with other energy sources. The study investigates how lean can contribute to the reduction of time spent on scheduled maintenance, and seven types of operations and maintenance (O&M) waste streams were identified. Furthermore, the study identified how availability could be raised from 96% to 97.7%, which is remarkable and rare for an offshore wind farm.

Furthermore, the study identified how modularization involving maintenance resources and tasks can be used to streamline O&M processes.

Three operational perspectives were identified: a short-term operational, a mid-term tactical, and a long-term strategic perspective. For these perspectives, the study identified how lean, modularization, reliability-centered maintenance, and asset life cycle management, respectively, could be used to achieve both short-, mid-, and long-term improvements in O&M.

Conceptualization and value creation of big data in supply chain management: A business process perspective

By Morten Brinch

This industrial PhD dissertation examines the topic of big data in supply chain management (SCM) through a business-process and focal-firm perspective. Big data is an emergent topic that is expected to disrupt existing SCM practices and has received increased awareness in recent years, as additional value from big data can be created to improve SCM performance.

The PhD has developed four academic articles as a theory-building effort focused on two overall objectives: First, although big data has become a known word, little consensus exists regarding the nature of big data in SCM, and little is known about the concept of big data in SCM. This PhD contributes in clarifying the concept of big data in SCM by addressing terminologies, application areas, and development of a big data SCM conceptual framework. Second, companies are experiencing profound challenges in creating value from big data, and there is a need for developing holistic SCM and big data capabilities that span across the organization. This PhD contributes by identifying value-creation mechanisms expressed as antecedents and by identifying the critical alignment practices important for the value creation of big data in SCM.

The managerial implications of this research could guide practitioners on how to create value from big data in SCM, where important practices, success factors, and alignment practices are identified. The findings can hopefully help companies generate additional value from big data that is not constrained to certain functional areas but is instead utilized across functions and SCM processes.

About the authors

Jan Stentoft, PhD, is a Professor in Supply Chain Management at the Department of Entrepreneurship and Relationship Management, University of Southern Denmark. His research is applied research within supply chain innovation, supply chain strategy, sales and operations planning, business process optimizations, information technology including Industry 4.0, and the movement of manufacturing and business processes abroad and back from home destinations. He has published a large number of academic and practitioner articles in journals such as *Journal of Supply Chain Management*, *Journal of Operations Management*, *International Journal of Production Research*, *International Journal of Production Economics*, *Journal of Cleaner Production*, *International Journal of Physical Distribution & Logistics Management*, *The International Journal of Logistics Management*, *Journal of Purchasing & Supply Management*, *Supply Chain Management: An International Journal*, and *Supply Chain Forum: An International Journal*. He is the head of the research project ReCoE. Jan has practical industry experience from a number of Danish manufacturers and from more than 100 private and public organizations as a management consultant. He is Strategic Advisor at PwC.

Ram Narasimhan, PhD, is a University Distinguished Professor Emeritus and the John H. McConnell Endowed Professor Emeritus in the Department of Supply Chain Management at Michigan State University, USA. His research focuses on strategic issues in supply chain management. He has authored over 150 refereed journal articles appearing in *Management Science*, *Journal of Operations Management*, *Journal of Supply Chain Management*, and other leading academic journals. He is a co-author of three books and several research monographs and one of the most widely cited researchers in supply chain management. He is the recipient of the Distinguished Scholar Award from the Academy of Management for lifetime contribution to operations management research. He is a Fellow of the Decision Sciences Institute and a Fellow of the Pan Pacific Business Association. He has been active as a consultant and executive trainer for Fortune 100 firms.

Chee Yew Wong, PhD, is a professor of supply chain management and director for the Centre for Operations and Supply Chain at Leeds University Business School, United Kingdom. He has work and consultancy experience in operations, purchasing, production, inventory, and distribution management and supply chain design at SMEs and multinational companies in sectors such as beverage, retail, fashion, toys, engineering, metal production, recycling, and polymer distribution. His research interests lie in the areas of supply chain information sharing, integration, digitalization, analytics, and sustainability. He has been a principle investigator for several knowledge transfer partnership (KTP) projects, Newton fund (researcher links workshop), and an ESRC/RGC bilateral grant. He is a frequently invited speaker for supply chain conferences held in the United Kingdom, Belgium, the Netherlands, Thailand, and Turkey. He has held visiting professorial roles in Manheim Business School, Chongqing Jiaotong University (China), and Thammasat University (Thailand). He is a scientific advisor for the Reducing the Cost of Energy Project (ReCoE) at Southern Denmark University.

Thomas Johnsen (B.Sc., M.Sc., PhD, HDR) is a Professor of Purchasing and Supply Management at Audencia Business School (Nantes, France), where he is also Director of the M.Sc. program in Supply Chain and Purchasing Management. Prior to this, he was Gianluca Spina Professor of Supply Chain Management at Politecnico di Milano School of Management in Italy, and he has also held full-time and part-time positions at Rennes Business School (France), University of Bath (United Kingdom), Jönköping International Business School (Sweden), and the University of Southern Denmark. He is currently Associate Editor of the *Journal of Purchasing & Supply Management* and Associate Partner of Aperitas, a Danish start-up company offering a sustainable supply chain management platform. He has been an executive board member of the International Purchasing & Supply Education & Research Association (IPSERA). His research has been cited over 2,850 times; recent publications have appeared in leading international journals, and his book (with M. Howard and J. Miemczyk) *Purchasing and Supply Chain Management: A Sustainability Perspective* was published by Routledge in April 2014 and awarded the ACA-Bruel coup de coeur prize. Thomas currently focuses on two areas of research: purchasing involvement in discontinuous innovation and sustainable purchasing and supply chain management. He has worked with a large number of companies for research and training or consulting projects.

Kannan Govindan is a Full Professor and Head of the Center for Sustainable Supply Chain Engineering, University of Southern Denmark, Odense, Denmark. He received the 2018 Highly cited Researcher Award from Thomson-Reuters/Clarivate Analytics ("one of only 204 researchers to be listed in the engineering category"). His research interests include reverse logistics, closed-loop supply chain, sustainable circular economy, green supply chain management, and sustainable supply chain management. He has published more than 250 international journal articles (with 14,500 + citations and H-index of 65) in leading journals such as *Nature*, *Omega*, *Journal of the Operational Research Society*, *Journal of Environmental Management*, *Renewable & Sustainable Energy Reviews*, *European Journal of Operational Research*, *Journal of Cleaner Production*, *Ecological Indicators*, *Transportation Research Part E: Logistics and Transportation Review*, and *Transportation Research Part D: Transport and Environment*. Many of his papers were selected as the ESI top 1% highly cited papers or 0.1% hot papers or identified and highlighted as the Key Scientific Article contributing to the excellence in Engineering and Environmental research (Source: Web of Science). He was rated as second among top-ten contributing authors in green supply chain management over last 22 years (Source: Sustainable Production and Consumption Journal, 2017).

Ole Stegmann Mikkelsen, PhD, is an Associated Professor in supply chain management at the Department of Entrepreneurship and Relationship Management, University of Southern Denmark, Kolding. He holds a PhD in business administration. His research and teaching areas are in supply chain management, operations management, global sourcing, and strategic sourcing. He has published research articles in both national and international journals such as *Journal of Purchasing and Supply Management*, *Supply Chain Forum: An International Journal*, *Journal of Energy Sector Management*, *International Journal of Procurement Management*, *Journal of Business and Industrial Marketing*, *International Journal of Public Administration*, *Operations Management Research*, and *International Journal of Production Economics*. He also has practical industrial experience as a purchaser/planner from Milliken Denmark A/S and as a Strategic Purchasing Consultant and Director (Group Procurement Development and Support/finance) at Danfoss A/S.

Erik Skov Madsen, PhD, is Associate Professor at the SDU Center for

Sustainable Supply Chain Engineering at the Department of Technology and Innovation at the University of Southern Denmark. When researching, Erik Skov Madsen mainly focuses on maintenance, particularly in the offshore wind power sector, on knowledge management and knowledge transfer in global production, and on sustainability. Erik Skov Madsen in his research draws on several years of experience from the industry by being responsible for maintenance in manufacturing, as well as from a very diverse educational background. Madsen holds four education diplomas: education as a skilled engineer fitter, education as a maritime engineer, a master's degree in adult learning and human resource development, and a PhD in knowledge transfer. Madsen has published in different international research journals, book chapters, newspapers, and journals targeting practitioners.

Christopher Rajkumar, PhD, is Assistant Professor at the Department of Entrepreneurship and Relationship Management (IER) (www.sdu.dk/ier), University of Southern Denmark. His PhD thesis explored the strategic role of the sourcing function in creating innovative products, processes, and/or services (Sourcing Innovation). His research and teaching interests are primarily within the area of supply chain management, which includes sourcing, outsourcing, innovation, supply chain innovation, and supplier relationship management. He is affiliated with the Reduced Cost of Energy (ReCoE) research program at the Department of Entrepreneurship and Relationship Management, University of Southern Denmark. Christopher has published research articles in journals such as *International Journal of Physical Distribution & Logistics Management*, *Logistics Research*, and *International Journal of Production Economics*. Before starting his PhD, Christopher worked for several years in the Indian business process outsourcing (BPO) industry.

Morten Brinch, PhD, is a management consultant at PwC and affiliated with the Department of Entrepreneurship and Relationship Management at the University of Southern Denmark. His industrial PhD was a collaboration with Siemens Gamesa Renewable Energy. His PhD research comprises the conceptualizing of big data and its value in supply chain management and explores how business processes can enable and gain value from big data. His research is affiliated with the research program on reducing the cost of energy in the offshore wind energy sector through supply chain innovation (ReCoE). Morten has published in international, peer-reviewed journals and written practitioner articles published in *Børsens Ledelseshåndbøger* and *Dilf Orientering*.